COMPANION CD

DATE DUE

Demco, Inc. 38-293

PARSEME.1ST

The Charles F. Goldfarb Series on Open Information Management

"Open Information Management" (OIM) means managing information so that it is open to processing by any program, not just the program that created it. That extends even to application programs not conceived of at the time the information was created.

OIM is based on the principle of data independence: data should be stored in computers in nonproprietary, genuinely standardized representations. And that applies even when the data is the content of a document. Its representation should distinguish the innate information from the proprietary codes of document processing programs and the artifacts of particular presentation styles.

Business data bases—which rigorously separate the real data from the input forms and output reports—achieved data independence decades ago. But documents, unlike business data, have historically been created in the context of a particular output presentation style. So for document data, independence was largely unachievable until recently.

That is doubly unfortunate. It is unfortunate because documents are a far more significant repository of humanity's information. And documents can contain significantly richer information structures than data bases.

It is also unfortunate because the need for OIM of documents is greater now than ever. The demands of "repurposing" require that information be deliverable in multiple formats (paper-based, online, multimedia, hypermedia). And information must now be delivered through multiple channels (traditional bookstores and libraries, online services, the Internet).

Fortunately, in the past ten years a technology has emerged that extends to documents the data base's capacity for data independence. And it does so without the data base's restrictions on structural freedom. That technology is the Standard Generalized Markup Language (SGML), an official International Standard (ISO 8879) that has been adopted by the world's largest producers of documents.

With SGML, organizations in government, aerospace, airlines, automotive, electronics, computers, and publishing (to name a few) have freed their documents from hostage relationships to processing software. SGML coexists with other data standards needed for OIM and acts as the framework that relates objects in the other formats to one another and to SGML documents.

As the enabling standard for OIM of documents, SGML necessarily plays a leading role in this series. We provide tutorials on SGML and other key standards and the techniques for applying them. Our books are not addressed solely to technical readers; we cover topics like the business justification for OIM and the business aspects of commerce in electronic information. We share the practical experience of organizations and individuals who have applied the techniques of OIM in environments ranging from immense industrial publishing projects to self-publishing on the World Wide Web.

Our authors are expert practitioners in their subject matter, not writers hired to cover a "hot" topic. They bring insight and understanding that can only come from real-world experience. Moreover, they practice what they preach about standardization. Their books share a common

Moreover, they practice what they preach about standardization. Their books share a common standards-based vocabulary. In this way, knowledge gained from one book in the series is directly applicable when reading another, or the standards themselves. This is just one of the ways in which we strive for the utmost technical accuracy and consistency with the OIM standards.

And we also strive for a sense of excitement and fun. After all, the challenge of OIM—preserving information from the ravages of technology while exploiting its benefits—is one of the great intellectual adventures of our age. I'm sure you'll find this series to be a knowledgable and reliable guide on that adventure.

About the Series Editor

Dr. Charles F. Goldfarb is the inventor of SGML and HyTime, and he is technical leader of the committees that developed them into International Standards. He is an information management consultant based in Saratoga, CA.

About the Series Logo

The rebus is an ancient literary tradition, dating from 16th-century Picardy, and is especially appropriate to a series involving fine distinctions between things and the words that describe them. For the logo, Andrew Goldfarb, who also designed the series' "Intelligent Icons," incorporated a rebus of the series name within a stylized SGML comment declaration.

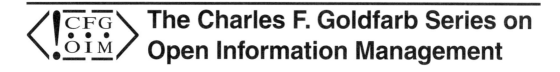

The Charles F. Goldfarb Series on Open Information Management

Donovan	*Industrial-Strength SGML: An Introduction to Enterprise Publishing*
Ducharme	*SGML CD*
Ensign	*$GML: The Billion Dollar Secret*
McGrath	*PARSEME.1ST: SGML for Software Developers*
Rubinsky and Maloney	*SGML on the Web: Small Steps Beyond HTML*
Turner, Douglass, and Turner	*README.1ST: SGML for Writers and Editors*

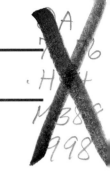

PARSEME.1ST
SGML for Software
Developers

Sean McGrath

To join a Prentice Hall PTR
mailing list, point to:
http://www.prenhall.com/mail_lists/

Prentice Hall PTR
Upper Saddle River, NJ 07458
http://www.prenhall.com

McGrath, Sean.
    ParseMe.1st : SGML for software developers / Sean McGrath.
       p.   cm. — (The Charles F. Goldfarb series on open information management)
    Includes bibliographical references and index.
    ISBN 0-13-488967-3 (hardcover)
    1. SGML (Document markup language)   2. Computer software–
Development. I. Title. II. Series.
QA76.76.H94M388 1998
005.7'2—dc21   97-20192
                                         CIP

Editorial/production supervision: *BooksCraft, Inc., Indianapolis*
Cover design director: *Jerry Votta*
Cover design: *Andrew Goldfarb*
Manufacturing manager: *Alexis R. Heydt*
Acquisitions editor: *Mark L. Taub*
Marketing manager: *Stephen Solomon*

© 1998 by Prentice Hall PTR
Prentice-Hall, Inc.
A Simon & Schuster Company
Upper Saddle River, New Jersey 07458

Prentice Hall books are widely used by corporate and government agencies for training, marketing, and resale.

The publisher offers discounts on this book when ordered in bulk quantities.
For more information, contact: Corporate Sales Department
                               Phone: 800-382-3419
                               Fax: 201- 236-7141
                               E-mail: corpsales@prenhall.com
Or write: Prentice Hall PTR
          Corp. Sales Dept.
          One Lake Street
          Upper Saddle River, NJ 07458

Printed in the United States of America
10 9 8 7 6 5 4 3 2 1

ISBN 0-13-488967-3

Prentice-Hall International (UK) Limited, *London*
Prentice-Hall of Australia Pty. Limited, *Sydney*
Prentice-Hall Canada Inc., *Toronto*
Prentice-Hall Hispanoamericana, S.A., *Mexico*
Prentice-Hall of India Private Limited, *New Delhi*
Prentice-Hall of Japan, Inc., *Tokyo*
Simon & Schuster Asia Pte. Ltd., *Singapore*
Editora Prentice-Hall do Brasil, Ltda., *Rio de Janeiro*

For My Father

CONTENTS

FOREWORD

© 1997 CHARLES F. GOLDFARB

Almost every piece of software comes with a file called **ReadMe.1st** The concept is that the user should do what the file name is asking, in order to install and use the software effectively.

There is a corresponding concept for programmers: That is, every document must be parsed before it can be processed. You're parsing this one as you read it, breaking up the sentences into their constituent parts.

In many ways, parsing is the Achilles heel of document processing software. Every application seems to have its own document representation, each marked up with a different syntax, so programmers need to create a separate parser for each one. And those notations rarely capture the information content of the document in the most useful and effective way. They are geared to the specific needs of their applications—such as page layout—and can't be used for other purposes.

Sean McGrath has found a better way to do it, and in this book he shows you how. Using SGML—the International Standard markup language that is the basis for the World Wide Web's HTML—Sean introduces an approach to document processing software development that is friendly to both users and programmers.

Like a database, SGML lets users identify the information elements they care about in their documents. The users get to choose and name those elements. But because the syntax is standardized and unambiguous, the programmers get the rigor and precision that they need to create robust and powerful programs.

Now you can replace a multitude of ad hoc and proprietary notations and parsing code with a single International Standard and a world-class parser—James Clark's SP, which is included on the CD-ROM and documented in this book.

And Sean is definitely the right expert to show you. He is Chief Technical Officer of Digitome Electronic Publishing and the founder of the Irish SGML Users' Group. He has developed SGML systems for electronic publishing, credit card processing, financial trading, and on-line banking, for companies such as Coopers & Lybrand, Price Waterhouse, and Deloitte & Touche. With Sean's expertise, captured in this book, you can finally do what your document is asking you to do: ParseMe.1st!

PREFACE

SGML (Standard Generalized Markup Language—ISO 8879) is an international standard for the electronic representation of the structure and content of documents.

This one-line definition, like most one-line definitions, may be sufficient to get the points in a quiz show but falls far short of a pragmatic explanation. It is on a par in terms of utility with such statements as "UNIX is a multi-user operating system" or "An object-oriented programming language is a language that supports inheritance, polymorphism, and encapsulation."

SGML simply does not lend itself to succinct definition, and any such definition would fail to do it justice. SGML has many facets ranging from the purely pragmatic through to the philosophical. It affects the working lives (and even the world view) of professionals ranging from authors to typesetters to software engineers to information theorists.

The purpose of this book is to concentrate on fleshing out this one-line definition of SGML for one particular group of people in the vast spectrum of those involved with it, namely software developers. Even having restricted the target audience to the software development community, it is still a gargantuan task to know where to begin, what to include, and what to exclude. The principle reason for this is that SGML, like UNIX or object-oriented programming, is not so much a single idea as a *collection* of interconnected ideas. Moreover, many of the individual ideas are deceptively easy to state yet subtle and far-reaching in their implications.

Reading this book will take a finite amount of time. A well-rounded understanding of SGML, with all its subtleties and far-reaching implications, will follow some indeterminate amount of time later. It will involve reading other books on the subject.[1] It will certainly involve using it, *playing* with it, and thinking about how you can use it. Like most software tools, an ounce of practice with SGML is worth a ton of theory.

To draw an analogy with object-oriented programming, understanding what the terms *inheritance, polymorphism,* and *encapsulation* mean is one thing. It is quite another thing to begin to "think OO." So it is with SGML. Although ostensibly concerned exclusively with documents, SGML has implications for the way we think about computerized information of *all* forms. If you

---

1. At the very least, it will involve regular reference to Charles F. Goldfarb's seminal work *The SGML Handbook* (ISBN 0-19-853737-9).

currently understand the terminology of SGML but have not used it in practice, be warned—the penny (indeed pennies) have yet to drop. When they do—when you begin to "think SGML"—your world view as a software developer will have changed, and the word *document* will take on a whole new meaning.

SGML is blessed with a comprehensive range of software tools ranging from public domain to shareware to commercial applications. The tools used in this book are all readily and freely available on the Internet and from various other sources (see Appendix D—SGML Resources for Developers). The primary workhorse in this book is a utility known as an SGML Parser, called NSGMLS. It was developed and made freely available by James Clark to whom the SGML world owes a great debt of gratitude. NSGMLS is not the only freely available SGML parser but it is the most widely used and discussed. It also has the largest collection of freely available support tools.[2]

Apart from NSGMLS, you will find examples of the use of text-processing applications such as sed and grep along with the Perl, Python, and C++ programming languages. The examples have been kept as simple as possible to avoid any reliance on particular flavors of any of these tools. Moreover, the most important thing about the examples is the *ideas* they illustrate, not the tool they were developed in. One of the great attractions of SGML is the ease with which a developer can pick and choose development tools to work with SGML-encoded information. If your favorite tools do not match the ones used in this book, you should be able to translate the ideas illustrated to your own tools.

Finally, as anyone in the SGML world will tell you, there is a strong sense of community among SGML practitioners. The SGML world probably does not have a higher percentage of "gurus" than any other field of endeavor but the ones we *do* have are very approachable people. They regularly give their time to answer queries posed by those new to SGML. You will find the various Internet newsgroups, mailing lists, etc., where these people communicate (see Appendix D—SGML Resources for Developers), invaluable sources of insight, help, and information.

Acknowledgments

Many thanks to Dr. Charles F. Goldfarb for all his help in the writing of this book. Charles has taught me many things I did not know about SGML and corrected many misunderstandings of things I *thought* I knew about SGML. His formidable knowledge is everywhere to be seen in this book.

Thanks to Neville Bagnall, Noel Duffy, and Dave Croydon for reading the drafts and making many excellent comments, criticisms, and suggestions. Their help was invaluable.

---

2. Strictly speaking, NSGMLS just provides an interface to the core SGML parser—a C++ class library known as SP— also developed and freely distributed by James Clark.

Despite the best efforts of the aforementioned, errors and inaccuracies may yet lurk in these pages. These are all my own work.

Finally, thanks to my wife Johanna who had just cause to wonder if this book would ever be finished so that she could have her husband back.

Sean McGrath
Enniscrone, County Sligo
Ireland

HOW TO USE THE CD

The CD contains complete source code for the three SGML application frameworks developed and demonstrated in Chapters 11 and 12. These are implemented in the C++, Python, and Perl programming languages.

You will also find DOS/Windows executables and complete source code for Python (version 1.4) and Perl (version 4.036). Consult the readme files in both archives for specific installation and usage information.

The CD also contains the DOS/Windows executables and complete source code for the SP parser along with SP-based applications, including NSGMLS—the parser application used extensively in this book.

Finally, you will also find WIN32 executables and complete source code of the Jade DSSSL engine, which is discussed in Chapter 16.

Have fun!

## CHAPTER 1

WHAT IS SGML?

1.1   Introduction

SGML is a standard primarily concerned with documents—their structure, content, and representation as electronic data. A document is a collection of information that is intended for human perception. However the word *document* carries with it a whole range of possible interpretations meaning different things to different people. A popular use of the term is as a catch all to cover computerized information that contains text but is *not* in a database.

SGML has a lot to say about the (apparent) distinction between documents and databases. We will get to this later. In the mean time, it is a useful prelude to the current topic to consider exactly what we mean by the word *document*, specifically the things that differentiate documents from databases.

1.2   What Is a Document?

In computing, the distinction between a document and a database is regularly made but rarely defined. From the vantage point of the casual computer user, the distinction can be difficult to grasp. Users regularly exacerbate software developers by saying such things as "Can I generate reports from these documents the way I can with my product database?" or "Can you build me a new document containing components from some other documents?" or "Can you write a program to add an extra digit to all of the part numbers that occur the maintenance manuals?"

Viewed through the eyes of a software developer, the distinction between a document and a database typically reduces to a distinction between *unstructured* and *structured* data. We think of relational databases, for example, as *structured* information resources. We can look at the database *schema* or *model* and learn a lot about how the data are organized, without looking at the data itself. A one page schema can allow us to build a mental model of a multigigabyte database. The schema acts as our launching pad in understanding the structure and content of the data and thus as the launching pad for developing software to process that data. A relational database schema definition might contain a section something like this:

```
RECORD ComponentPart
# Other field definitions here...
BEGIN FIELD
   Name = "Part_No"
   Type = ALPHANUMERIC
   Length = 20
END FIELD
# Other field definitions here...
END RECORD
```

If the task is to add a digit to all the part numbers occurring in the database, the first port of call is to see if part numbers are an *explicit* component of the database (i.e., if part number is a distinct element in the database schema, normally known as a *field*). If it is, the solution is trivially easy. It is easy because the object of our attention is *addressable* within the database.

If it is not an explicit component of the database, the problem is more complex because we must somehow arrive at an explicit means of addressing part numbers via *implicit* cues as to where they occur within database records. For example, we might conclude by analyzing the data in the database that part numbers always occur at offset 10 into the product name field. Such a situation is a chance encounter with an implicit structural cue that is not an explicit part of the database schema. Clearly however, relying on this fact is less than satisfactory from an engineering point of view and is to be avoided if possible.

When it comes to updating part numbers in *documents*, we typically go *straight* into searching for implicit structural cues. Traditional documents do not have schemas analogous to those found in databases. There is no software model we can consult to ascertain where part numbers can occur in the documents. Furthermore, we have no way of *addressing* part numbers within documents. The data simply is not structured along those lines.

Documents—especially WYSIWYG documents—do not make their structure and content explicit. The structures that are present in such files are concerned with how the content should *look* on the (typically) *printed* page as opposed to what the content *actually is*. In short, the structural cues available to us in processing traditional documents revolve around *visualizations* or *renderings* of the content rather than the nature of the content itself. Furthermore, the structural cues are *procedural* in nature (e.g., "Move to position X on an A4 page. Set the font to Y. Emit the text X.").

If luck is on our side (and the procedural coding used to represent the visualization of the content is known to us) we might be able to write a macro or a C program to process the data looking for part numbers. We might, for example, discover by inspection that part numbers are invariably Times Roman 10 point centered. If we are really lucky we might find that they are the *only* things rendered in that style. This would give us the ability to unambiguously address them. However, there is clearly a strong element of luck involved, and it is a far from satisfactory solution in general.

Imagine for the moment that a search for sufficient implicit structure to allow the unambiguous addressing of all the part numbers in the documentation has failed. Your unenviable task now is to tell your boss that software cannot be written to solve this little problem cost effectively (i.e., it would be cheaper to get the authors to change the documents *manually*). You tell your boss the crux of the problem is that you cannot locate part numbers in the maintenance manuals with 100% accuracy. Your boss retorts, "Why not? They only occur on the first line of *overview paragraphs* within *installation instruction sequences*. Is that not unambiguous enough?"

As the software developer faced with such a scenario, you would be right that the part numbers have not been made explicit. However your boss would also right in saying they are explicitly locatable. The essence of the problem is that the troublesome part numbers are *visually* explicit. They are easily spotted with the amazing acuity of human perception, but this is not so from the computer's perspective. The procedural encoding of the document says nothing about *part numbers* or *overview paragraphs* or *installation instruction sequences* or even *maintenance manual* for that matter. These concepts are simply not captured in the data. All the documents say are things like "move here, set the rendering format to such and such, emit the following text...".

This gets us to the essence of the distinction between traditional documents and databases. Documents are structured—from the computer's point of view—based on how they should *look*. Databases, on the other hand, are structured based on what they *contain* and how the various part of the content are interrelated. Databases have *information content*–oriented models; documents do not. Looking at it another way, a database is a collection of discrete information components with well-defined types and sizes. Documents are collections of words interspersed with "rendering commands" that control how the words should look on the printed page. These rendering commands represent the only information we have, over and above the words themselves, to try and infer what pieces of information *actually are*.

1.3　The Problems with Documents

It may seem to be a trivial change of emphasis to move from representing documents visually—as renditions of their content—to representing them more like databases. However, once made, documents become infinitely more useful forms of data. This change of emphasis is a cornerstone of the SGML philosophy. In one sentence,

> *Documents are much more useful when they can be modeled, created, and processed like databases.*

In some sense, information content–oriented documents have a higher information purity quotient than their format-oriented brethren. They make useful information available to us and to processing software. They are closer to capturing the intellectual models that went through the minds of their creators. In the mind of an author, the process of creating a part number in our example, probably goes something like this:

> *I am starting the overview paragraph for this installation procedure. Therefore I need a part number. So, set the formatting to Times Roman 10 point and insert the part number text.*

In other words, the content of the document—the real-world object that the text is going to speak about—*drives* the formatting process. Cannot the computer do that automatically? Yes it can. This is another core idea of SGML and a number of profound things follow from it. If software can add the presentation formatting to information content–oriented documents automatically, it follows that we can separate the storage of that information from its formatting. We can maintain "pure meaning" for documents and add different presentation formatting codes depending on how we wish to publish the content.

This is a big idea. Look around you at the various documents on your desk or stored on your computer. How many of them have been format encoded in such a way that they are only directly usable for one purpose? How many times have you had problems moving documents from one WYSIWYG system to another? How difficult would it be to turn your format-encoded documents into Web page format? Groupware database format? On-line help format? Imagine the possibilities that would open up for your documents if all this format encoding was controlled by software that generated it?

If you analyze a typical document file format, you will find that the structural elements present have a strong presentational slant. There will most likely be the notions of page boundary, font size, hanging indent, and so on. For example, here are two different file formats (both partial) for this chapter's part number example.

Microsoft RTF (Rich Text Format):

```
\pard\plain \s1\sb240\sa60\keepn
\b\f5\fs28\lang2057\kerning28 Installation Instructions
\par \pard\plain \s2\sb240\sa60\keepn \b\i\f5\lang2057 Overview
\par \pard\plain \f4\fs20\lang2057
This installation instruction relates to Part Number {\b B566-4345}
\par
```

PostScript:

```
/Helvetica-Bold FindFont 13 ScaleFont SetFont
105 184 MoveTo
(Installation Instructions) Show
/Helvetica-Bold FindFont 14 ScaleFont SetFont
316 223 MoveTo
(Overview) Show
/Times-Roman FindFont 10 ScaleFont SetFont
389 873 MoveTo
(This installation instruction relates to Part Number ) Show
/Times-Bold FindFont 10 ScaleFont SetFont
978 388 MoveTo
(B566-4345) Show
```

In both cases, processing these documents presents us with the problem of having to "reverse-engineer" true structural information from the visual cues provided in the coding in order to unambiguously address the part number B566-4345.

This leads to the nontrivial issue of having to *understand* these file formats in considerable detail in order to be able to write parsers to capture the relevant visual cues. If and when we get our application to work, we live in fear of an upgrade to the application that generated the files in the first place. Will the file format have changed? Will anyone tell us if it does? There are numerous other ways in which the application could break (or be broken for us). What would happen if we relied on the fact that part numbers are the only things in Times Roman 10 point and the authors start using that font for something else as well? What happens if the authors decided to move part numbers out of the installation procedures into some other section?

Many of the problems developers face today relating to general document processing, document reuse, and multiformat publishing can be traced back to the lack of information content addressability. When that structure is made explicit, a vista of possibilities present themselves for what we can get software to do with documents. Figures suggest that about 80% of corporate information is stored in documents—not databases. Thus up to 80% of corporate information is unstructured and potentially underutilized. That is a lot of information!

Earlier in this chapter, an example was given of the thought process an author might go through in formatting a part number. Figures from various sources indicate that authors spend a significant amount of time formatting the intellectual content they create. It could be argued that the explosion in WYSIWYG authoring systems has had a detrimental effect on author productivity in this regard. However, this reduction in productivity is probably redressed by the increase in productivity brought about by "one-stop" publishing, at least in low-volume environments. The more serious effect is a subtle one. Traditional WYSIWYG systems make it difficult to reuse, reformat, or repurpose the intellectual content they contain.

1.4 Some Terminology

The discussion so far has been by way of setting the scene for the discussion of how SGML takes a different database-like approach to documents to deal with the problems we have mentioned (and many more besides). In order to discuss the SGML approach, we must first tie down some terminology.

Markup is the general term used to distinguish the actual data content of a document from the processing information that surrounds it (i.e., "\par" is an example of RTF markup). Alternatively phrased, markup refers to *meta-data* that adds information, over and above content, to the document.

Procedural markup is the term used to describe the visually oriented meta-data used in WYSIWYG systems (i.e., markup that effectively lists a set of actions to be performed in order to render the content). For example, setting the font to Times Roman 12 point might be expressed in PostScript as

```
/Times-Roman FindFont
12 ScaleFont
SetFont
```

These markup codes would make no sense to RTF, which would express the same semantics with a coding something like this:

```
\f0\fs24
```

A variation on procedural markup is to make the markup independent of any one output device. For example,

```
.SetFont (Times Roman,12)
```

The difference here is that the document is encoded in a form intended for another level of processing to translate the general-purpose markup into the specific markup for PostScript, RTF, or whatever. Common examples of this technique include UNIX troff and Knuth's TeX typesetting system.

Generalized markup[1] is the term used to describe markup intended to describe a document's structure and content, thence the acronym SGML.

1.5   SGML in Seven Nutshells

SGML, as previously noted, is not so much one idea but a collection of interrelated and over-lapping ideas. For the purposes of structuring a discussion about SGML's various facets, we will break it down into seven areas as shown in Figure 1.1.

1.5.1   Modeling

In the database world and the world of programming language design, modeling is a well-established and powerful technique. In relational databases, models are known as *schemas.* Much work has been done in establishing standards and mathematical methods to put relational database modeling on a firm scientific footing. Ever since the days of the Algol programming language, modeling techniques have also been used to great effect in the field of high-level language design, compiler construction, and so on.

Models contribute greatly to the processing possibilities of the data that conforms to them. The model acts as a "blueprint" upon which we can quickly build our understanding of how the data are structured. We can use software to analyze models, to compare data sets against the models they supposedly conform to, thus proving their correctness. We can build systems that know about the models in order to guide the information creation process and guarantee correct data. We can even use software that processes models to produce new models.

---

1. C.F. Goldfarb, E.J. Mosher, and T.I. Peterson, "An Online System for Integrated Text Processing," *Proceedings of the American Society for Information Science,* 7, 147–150 (1970).

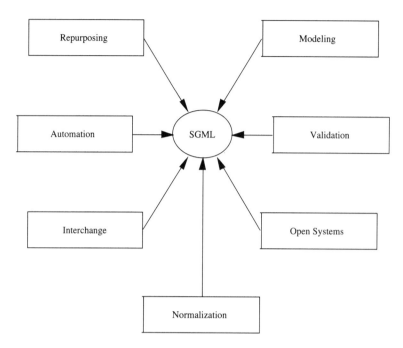

Figure 1.1 SGML in Seven Nutshells

Modeling is another one of the big ideas in SGML. Simply put, the most important thing about a part number, trivially enough, is that it *really is* a part number and that this fact be made known in its digital representation and made available to processing software. The second most important thing about a part number is where it can occur within an overall structure to conform to the desired structural model.

It is readily apparent that the sort of models used to formalize relational databases are insufficient for the purposes of modeling the structures found in documents. The most obvious difference is that document structures are typically variable in size and can sensibly occur in many different permutations and combinations. Moreover, document structures can be *deep* with elements nested within other elements. They can also be *recursive* with elements capable of containing instances of themselves as subelements.

In many respects, the constructs found when documents are analyzed in terms of their content are very similar to those found in high level programming languages. You may be familiar with syntax descriptions such as this one (loosely based on the if construct of the C programming language):

```
statement : if '(' <expression> ')' <statement>
          | if '(' <expression> ')' <statement> else <statement>
```

This is a snippet of a *production rule* that defines the various forms that if statements can take and be syntactically valid in the language. Notice that there are two major forms of if statement and that both are recursive (i.e., if can occur within another if statement).

The formal nature of such models makes them readily convertible into executable programs that will take a program of a given programming language and parse it. The result of executing such a program can range from a simple Yes/No answer as to the validity of the program against the model (the model in this case meaning the model for a valid C program) right through to a translation of the C statements into native machine code.

SGML uses an analogous syntax to capture the details of document models. These models are known as *Document Type Definitions* or DTDs for short.

1.5.2   Validation

The analogy with programming languages goes further in that programs known as SGML parsers have been developed that can compare SGML documents against the SGML models they are supposed to conform to. In other words, SGML parser applications are capable of *validating* documents against their models, just as C parsers validate C programs.

At this point however, the direct analogy with the way traditional compilers are constructed breaks down because there is no single SGML document model per se. A parser for the C programming language, for example, *hard-codes* its knowledge of the syntactic structures that make up the language. It has built-in knowledge of 'if' as a reserved word in the language. Moreover, it knows how to validate the overall structure of an 'if' statement because that capability is built into the parser. This is so commonplace in programming languages that it is rarely given any thought. Unlike programming languages, SGML *soft-codes* a significant proportion of its overall syntactic and semantic structure.

An SGML parser is probably best compared to something like YACC[2] (i.e., a tool that takes a formal description of a model and produces a parser conforming to that model). YACC typically generates C code for subsequent compilation as part of a larger program. An SGML parser is like a variation on YACC that not only generates the parser for the model but also parses instances of the model (programs or, in SGML's case, documents). We look at SGML parsers in detail in Chapter 9—Anatomy of an SGML Parser.

1.5.3   Open Systems

SGML is essentially a text-based data storage format. This makes it seem an unusual "native" format for some developers, especially desktop application developers because we are accustomed

---

2. Yet Another Compiler Compiler—a UNIX utility developed by Steve Johnson. See *The UNIX Programming Environment* by Brian W. Kernighan and Rob Pike (ISBN 0-13-937681-X).

to *real* desktop application file formats being based on binary information with text formats relegated to use for interchange purposes only.[3]

As a result, binary data formats can take on an unwarranted aura of expressive power when compared to text formats. In reality, anything that can be encoded in binary can also be encoded in straight text format. Such textual representations are often less efficient in terms of storage space, processing speeds, and so on, but there is no difference in terms of expressive power.

The downside of binary encodings is that they are often *proprietary* and have a "lock-in" effect on the data they contain. In other words, content created for an application with a binary format can often be difficult to get out of that application completely intact. If the application has bugs, you may need to wait for the company that developed the application to fix it (and possibly pay for the privilege). If the company decides to cease development of the product, you may be faced with a costly and time-consuming "upgrade" requirement not of your own making.

Applications that do support a text-based interchange format for their binary encodings can also suffer from lossy conversions (i.e., added value features that make application A more useful than application B can be lost in the transfer of data from A to B).

Also, it is more difficult to process binary data with common data processing tools such as Perl, sed, grep, etc., which tend to thrive in text-only environments. In some respects, information encoded in binary-based file format is *application owned*. In other words, the data are "owned" by the software that captured them rather than being the exclusive property of the author who originated the data in the first place. That is not to say that binary file formats are intrinsically bad. Indeed, many SGML applications use binary file formats internally for reasons of efficiency. However, no SGML-conforming application can call itself that without having a completely lossless export to native SGML.

SGML's native text format gives you the freedom to choose applications for a range of purposes from a range of vendors, safe in the knowledge that they will interoperate via the "Esperanto" of SGML. It gives you the freedom to innovate in the processing of your own data. If SGML application A is better than application B at a specific task, move your SGML data over to it, perform the task, and move it back to B again. Write little applications yourself with your favorite tools to process the SGML. If an SGML-processing task is best done with a little Perl program then do it with a little Perl program!

As long as your applications do not "break" conformance with the DTD, you will not do any structural harm. SGML files cannot be irretrievably "corrupted" the way many binary formats can. Even when you are unsure if a modification has yielded a valid SGML file, the parser is always there to point out any structural errors made.

This Open Systems philosophy has long been a feature of the database world. We have long

---

3. Of course, all electronic data are ultimately binary. Text is just numbers in disguise as far as a computer is concerned. Text, however, typically uses a subset of the available binary numbers (e.g., numbers 32 to 127 out of the range 0 to 255 are commonly known as "text" characters in the ASCII character set).

expected that data from database program X can be imported to database program Y without any loss of content. This contrasts markedly with the situation in the DTP/WP applications world where incompatabilities between data formats are a common problem for users and developers alike.

The Open Systems approach of SGML not only protects against the vagaries of proprietary technologies extant today. It also *future-proofs* documents against changes in publishing technology in the future. By capturing the structure and content of what the information really is, SGML prepares documents for roles perhaps never envisaged at the time of their creation.

1.5.4   Normalization

By this stage, you may be thinking that SGML effectively allows, what we traditionally describe as documents, to be treated as databases.[4] This is indeed the case. One of the powerful aspects of the programmability of databases is that it becomes possible to get the software to "generate" rather than store information in situations where the content of the information can be harvested from existing information. The terms *base* data and *derived* data are often used to differentiate the two. The phrase *data normalization* is used to describe the process whereby redundancies in the data are removed in favor of generating rather than storing derivable data.

SGML documents can employ data normalization in a variety of ways. SGML's ability to support the removal of redundancy and the reuse of document information is a compelling plus factor for SGML in a lot of organizations. As a result of SGML's content addressing capability, one can locate individual *chunks* of a document such as a table, a paragraph, or a part number. Once located, reuse becomes possible, which leads to reduced redundancy and thus higher data normalization. This chunk-level access to information is commonly known as *granularity*. The more specific the chunks can be, the higher the granularity. Traditional documents on the other hand have very low granularity, typically limited to the file level.

Another aspect of the normalization capabilities provided by SGML is the concept of a self-generating document (i.e., a document that consists entirely of components that have been harvested from existing SGML components). This idea has many applications and allows organizations to leverage the investment in originating content by reusing it repeatedly. We will see some examples of this in Chapter 4—Publishing SGML Documents.

1.5.5   Interchange

In many fields of endeavor, document information must be shared either among different divisions of an organization or among different organizations. Such document interchange can be a costly business with traditional WYSIWYG systems owing to the plethora of systems available and

---

4. In fact, most databases can be modeled with simple SGML DTDs!

the difficulties encountered in moving data from one format-centric application to another. SGML addresses this problem in a number of ways. First, SGML documents can be moved from one SGML application to another without loss. Second, parties wishing to share document information can elect to co-design a DTD or DTDs for that purpose. This capability has lead to the development of so-called industry standard DTDs.

The idea was pioneered in the United States with organizations such as the AAP[5] and the Department of Defense (DOD) designing and adopting standard DTDs. The DOD in particular has mandated the use of these DTDs by their suppliers. From the DOD's point of view, knowing in advance what DTD the SGML coming from the suppliers will conform to allows them to fold new documents into their document-processing/publishing systems without fuss. SGML's ability to validate documents against models allows them to automate part of what used to be a manual Quality Assurance process.

Over the years, initiatives for the development of industry-standard DTDs have sprung up in areas such as Aerospace, Pharmaceuticals, Finance, Publishing, and Electronics to name but a few (see Appendix D—SGML Resources for Developers).

1.5.6   Automation

Many everyday activities involving databases, the sort of activities carried on by database administrators, are difficult to classify—a quick once-off report here, a batch modification there, and so on. The use of SGML allows this sort of once-off data-processing activity to be cost effectively applied to documents. Tasks that in the past would have involved manual intervention can now be automated. Requests for the part number modification described earlier in this chapter can now become as trivial as the also mentioned database modification.

1.5.7   Repurposing

The origins of the SGML standard date back to a 1969 project headed by Dr. Charles F. Goldfarb to allow the encoding of legal texts in a way that would be independent of any one application or output device. In those days the output device was principally paper, and thus the problem was to avoid dependencies on any one typesetting format.

Today, the variety of potential output devices has grown to include an exploding array of purely electronic formats such as CD-ROM, Groupware, and World Wide Web.[6] This has resulted in a situation in which any single document can probably be gainfully employed in numerous formats, both paper and electronic, over its lifetime. Many of these delivery formats require the docu-

---

5. Association of American Publishers. The DTD is now known as ISO 12083.
6. The World Wide Web is in fact an SGML application. See Chapter 4—Publishing SGML Documents.

ment to be reformatted to suit their specific markup codes. SGML's ability to generate arbitrary sets of specific markup codes from a single copy of the source document makes a compelling case for SGML in modern multimedia publishing.

Prior to SGML, many documents were authored once, used for a single purpose and stored, rarely to be used again. The combination of features of SGML we have talked about in this chapter (e.g., normalization, automation) allows documents to be repurposed repeatedly. Their content can be reused in other documents, re-arranged into different orders, formatting can be automatically added to turn them into various publishing formats, and so on.

## CHAPTER 2

STRUCTURE OF AN *SGML* DOCUMENT

In this chapter, we take a simple SGML document from an equally simply SGML application and discuss its contents line by line. The task is to produce an application of SGML aimed at the creation of office memoranda. An English description of the overall structure of a memo might go something like this:

> *A memo consists of the name of who it is coming from, along with the name or names of who it is going to. It must have at least one intended recipient. It will have a date and a subject. Thereafter it will have one or more paragraphs of text.*

Turning this into an SGML application requires the creation of a formal model for this information description. Such a model defines a *class* of documents all sharing the same overall structure. Such a class is known as a document type, and the models are known in SGML as Document Type Definitions. When the model is in place, we can proceed to create documents that conform to the model and are members of the class. In SGML terms, we create *document instances*. By analogy with object-oriented design, DTDs are *classes* and document instances are *objects* of particular classes.

A full SGML document can be partitioned and stored in many separate files, or it can all be stored in a single file. The typical storage arrangement for an SGML document involves at least two files—one for the DTD and one for the document instance itself. A third (often implicit) component is known as the *SGML declaration*. The purpose of the SGML declaration is to define the character set used, what optional SGML features the SGML document uses and various other parameters. We will defer the examination of the SGML declaration and concentrate on the document instance and the DTD for the moment.

Here is an example of an SGML document meeting the description of a memo.

```
C>type memo.sgm

<!DOCTYPE memo SYSTEM "memo.dtd">
<memo>
<FROM>
<fname>Sean
<sname>&mac; Grath
</from>
<to>
```

```
<fname>Mark
<sname>Uplang
</to>
<date YEAR = 1965 MONTH = 4 DAY = 27>
<subject>Greeting
<body>
<para>Hello World!
</body>
</memo>
```

We will discuss the contents of this document line by line:

```
<!DOCTYPE memo SYSTEM "memo.dtd">
```

The first line of an SGML document typically takes this form and is referred to as the Document Type Declaration. It establishes a link between this document (memo.sgm) and the DTD model to which it conforms (memo.dtd).

The syntax used to delineate SGML constructs (markup) from the actual text of a document (content) generally consists of less than (<) and greater than (>) delimiters. Although these are the most commonly used delimiters, there are some exceptions. The delimiters used can be changed if required by modifying the SGML declaration. Informally, this line says, "The document instance that follows conforms to the memo DTD. The DTD for this file can be found elsewhere in the file memo.dtd."

```
<memo>
<FROM>
```

Individual elements of SGML documents are of arbitrary length and granularity in terms of the subelements they can include. A notation is thus required to allow the signaling of the beginning of an element and the end of that element. The former is known in SGML as a start-tag, and the latter, an end-tag. Start-tags typically consist of the element type name in angle brackets.

The preceding two lines denote the opening of the **memo** element and the **from** element inside it. The **from** element has been entered in uppercase simply to illustrate that in this application, case is not significant in element type names.[1]

```
<fname>Sean
```

Here, a third element **fname** (first name) is opened, and the data content of the element—Sean—is supplied. We could have written this as

```
<fname>
Sean
```

which would have exactly the same effect. As a rule of thumb, SGML applications ignore end-of-line characters immediately following a start-tag or immediately preceding an end-tag because they

---

1. This can be changed in the SGML declaration if desired.

do not form part of the real document data content. This is not always the case however (see Section 13.14—Mixed-Content Models).

```
<sname>&mac; Grath
```

Here we open the **sname** (surname) element. Notice that we have not explicitly closed the **fname** element. SGML will *infer* that it has been closed by analyzing the DTD and concluding that opening an **sname** element implicitly closes the **fname** element before it. This is an example of an SGML feature known as *tag omission,* which we will discuss later when we get on to the DTD itself.

The first part of the **sname** element is an SGML construct known as an *entity reference.* It indicates a reference to information stored elsewhere in a variable identified by the name mac. Entities come in many shapes and sizes, which we will encounter as we go along. The particular form of entity referred to here—known as a *general entity*—is usually referenced by means of an ampersand (&) before the entity name and a semicolon afterward.[2] We'll see more on the meaning/usage of this construct when we get to the DTD and also when we look at applications of SGML (see Chapter 5—101 Things To Do with an SGML Document).

```
</from>
```

This is our first encounter with an SGML end-tag. Typically, end-tags are formulated identically to their corresponding start-tag with the addition of a forward slash (/) directly before the element type name. Here, we close the *from* element (we could have not done so, and SGML would have inferred it based on the DTD).

```
<to>
<fname>Mark
<sname>Uplang
</to>
```

Here a **to** element is opened. The first name **fname** of the recipient—Mark—is then supplied. This is followed by a **sname** element—Uplang. The **to** element is then closed.

```
<date YEAR = 1965 MONTH = 04 DAY = 27>
```

Next comes a **date** element. This example uses an SGML facility known as *attributes* to capture the details of the date. An SGML attribute is a way of tacking on some extra information to an individual element so as to further qualify its meaning. Sometimes, as in this example, the information supplied in attributes is all that is required. In other words, there is no need for the **date** element to have any content. This sort of element is known in SGML as an *empty element.* The emptiness or otherwise of an SGML element is one of things specified in the DTD. Just as with

---

2. Of course, this raises the question of how to insert a real ampersand character in the document. As it happens, there are a number of ways to do it but probably the most common is to use an ampersand entity, typically &.

entities, attributes come in a variety of shapes and sizes (see Chapter 6—Elements, Attributes, and Models):

```
<subject>Greeting
<body>
```

Here we open a **subject** element and set its data content—Greeting. We then open a **body** element. As before, SGML can infer that the previous **subject** element has been closed.

```
<para>Hello World!
```

The body of this simple memo consists of a single element: a paragraph of text denoted by the **para** start-tag.

```
</body>
</memo>
```

Finally, we close off both the **body** element and the overall **memo** element.

We now turn our attention to the memo DTD file:

```
C>type memo.dtd

<!-- Memo DTD -->
<!ENTITY mac SDATA "Mac" -- "Son of" in surnames -->
<!ELEMENT memo          - O (from,to+,date,subject,body)>
<!ELEMENT (from,to)     - O (fname,sname)>
<!ELEMENT date          - O EMPTY>
<!ATTLIST date
  YEAR  NUMBER #REQUIRED
  MONTH NUMBER #REQUIRED
  DAY   NUMBER #REQUIRED>
<!ELEMENT subject       - O (#PCDATA)>
<!ELEMENT (fname,sname) - O (#PCDATA)>
<!ELEMENT body          - O (para)+>
<!ELEMENT para          - O (#PCDATA)>
```

Again, we will analyze the contents of the file line by line:

```
<!-- Memo DTD -->
```

A DTD consists of a sequence of constructs known as *markup declarations*. This first line is an example of an SGML comment declaration. There are a number of ways to create comments in SGML, but this is the most common. It starts with the '`<!--`' sequence and ends with the '`-->`' sequence.

```
<!ENTITY mac SDATA "Mac" -- "Son of" in surnames -->
```

This line declares an SGML construct known as an entity. This particular entity is the sequence of characters that denote the "Mc" part of a surname. We have seen that, in the document instance itself, this entity is referenced by prefixing its name with an ampersand and suffixing a semicolon like this:

```
&mac;
```

There are numerous reasons for doing this sort of thing in SGML. The most obvious is that SGML uses only text characters and thus requires notations for typographical constructs such as superscript. When the document is published, we might like this mac rendered as Mc if the platform supports it. Entities give us a way of coding any of the literally thousands of typographical symbols without resorting to proprietary or binary encodings. Plus we can invent our own as has been done here.

Quite apart from this rationale, it turns out to be very useful to be able to address such constructs uniquely when it comes to SGML text processing, over and above straight rendering applications. We will see such an example in Chapter 5—101 Things To Do with an SGML Document.

The text following the second "Mac" in this declaration is another form of SGML comment—one that occurs within a markup declaration. This form makes it easier to move the entity declaration plus its explanatory comment as a single unit.

```
<!ELEMENT memo - O (from,to+,date,subject,body)>
```

Here we start into the meat of the DTD by telling SGML about the root element type (known as the *document element type*) of documents conforming to this DTD. The declaration of the **memo** element type says that a memo consists of a sequence of other elements—namely **from, to, date, subject**, and **body**—occurring in exactly that order. It also says that the **to** element occurs one or more times. This sort of declaration is known as an *element type declaration.*[3] The details of the model for this element type declaration is known as the *content model.*

The dash (-) to the right of the element type name declares that the start-tag for this element must be supplied. The O (capital oh) to the right of that, indicates that the end-tag is optional. In other words, when an SGML application analyzes a document conforming to this DTD, it is allowed to work out for itself that the element has ended, based on what follows it. Thus the end-tag need not be explicitly supplied.

Note that the ability to infer the presence of an end-tag depends on the overall structure of the DTD. There may be times when SGML cannot possibly work it out for itself. If this is the case, SGML applications that analyze DTDs will warn of a markup error.

Furthermore, the start-tag of an element can also be omitted if it can be inferred automatically. This feature is not as often employed as end-tag omission, however. Used with care, tag omission combined with some other features of SGML can greatly reduce the amount of markup required in a document. In situations where documents are being authored by hand (which was invariably the case when the standard was adopted in 1986), this can be a great boon. Today, there are a variety of SGML editing packages that deal with start- and end-tags "behind the scenes," making tag omission less of an issue from an authoring perspective, although it still affects legibility for those who have to read the SGML source (like programmers).

---

3. The SGML standard currently calls it an element declaration, but that term is confusing because it is the element type that is being declared. It will be corrected when the standard is revised.

```
<!ELEMENT (from,to) - O (fname,sname)>
```

This time, we use a feature of SGML that allows the simultaneous definition of more than one element type. Informally it says, "There are element types in this DTD known as **from** and **to**. Their start-tags are mandatory. Their end-tags are optional. They both consist of an **fname** element followed by an **sname** element."

```
<!ELEMENT date - O EMPTY>
```

This line declares the **date** element type. Its structure is different from the previous examples. Informally it says, "A date element is an empty element" (i.e., it has no subelements within it).

```
<!ATTLIST date
    YEAR   NUMBER #REQUIRED
    MONTH  NUMBER #REQUIRED
    DAY    NUMBER #REQUIRED>
```

These lines are also part of the markup declaration for **date** elements and are known as an *attribute definition list declaration*. Here we declare that the **date** element type has three attributes, namely year, month, and day. Informally, the rest of the declaration says that these attributes are numeric and must all be supplied along with every **date** element.

```
<!ELEMENT subject - O (#PCDATA)>
```

This is the declaration for the **subject** element type. As with most of the other element types in this DTD, it has a mandatory start-tag and an optional end-tag. Informally, the notation (#PCDATA) says that the **subject** element contains actual data. As with most other things in SGML, actual data comes in a variety of shapes and sizes, PCDATA being the most common (see Section 13.8—Data Content Variations).

The # before the word PCDATA serves to indicate to that parser that the string "PCDATA" that follows is a special token and not another element type name. Remember the SGML philosophy of soft-coding its syntax discussed earlier. Using the # to flag the special treatment required for the PCDATA token that follows sidesteps the need to *hard-wire* the interpretation of "PCDATA." Thus

```
<!ELEMENT foo - O (pcdata)>
```

is a perfectly valid element type declaration, indicating that a **foo** element contains a single **pcdata** element.

```
<!ELEMENT (fname,sname) - O (#PCDATA)>
```

This declaration is similar to the previous one except that we again use SGML's ability to simultaneously declare multiple element types. Both **fname** and **sname** are declared to contain PCDATA.

```
<!ELEMENT body - O (para)+>
```

This is the declaration of the **body** element type. It says, "A **body** element consists of one or more **para** elements."

```
<!ELEMENT para - O (#PCDATA)>
```

Finally, **para** elements are declared to contain PCDATA.

It is often useful to visualize DTDs and documents instances as hierarchical structures. For example, Figure 2.1 illustrates one possible visualization of the Memo DTD. A number of tools that aid in the construction of such visual DTD models are available.

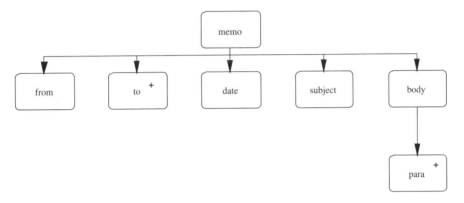

Figure 2.1 Visualization of memo DTD

Documents can be visualized similarly. Perhaps the simplest document visualization is created by simply indenting the text to correspond with the levels in the document hierarchy, much the way source code is often indented:

```
<memo>
  <from>
    <fname>Sean
    <sname>&mac; Grath
  </from>
  <to>
   <fname>Mark
   <sname>Uplang
  </to>
  <date YEAR = 1965 MONTH = 04 DAY = 27>
  <subject>Greeting
  <body>
    <para>Hello World!
  </body>
</memo>
```

Although indenting elements in this way while creating them in a text editor can be tempting, it is important to note that line ends[4] and white space can sometimes be significant in an SGML

---

4. Formally known as "record ends" in SGML to distinguish them from formatted output line ends.

document—specifically in the case of so-called mixed content (see Section 13.14—Mixed-Content Models). By far the easiest way to achieve these visualizations of the structure of an SGML document is to create them using an SGML-aware editing tool.

Now that we have a DTD model and a document instance, our memo document is ready to be parsed for correctness. Much more will be said later about SGML document parsing and the output that parsers produce. For the moment we will briefly examine the output of the NSGMLS parser for this document:

```
>nsgmls memo.sgm

(MEMO
(FROM
(FNAME
-Sean
)FNAME
(SNAME
-\|mac\| Grath
)SNAME
)FROM
(TO
(FNAME
-Mark
)FNAME
(SNAME
-Uplang
)SNAME
)TO
AYEAR TOKEN 1965
AMONTH TOKEN 04
ADAY TOKEN 27
(DATE
)DATE
(SUBJECT
-Greeting
)SUBJECT
(BODY
(PARA
-Hello World!
)PARA
)BODY
)MEMO
C
```

This output format is known as *ESIS* (Element Structure Information Set).[5] We will use it extensively throughout this book. The format is explained in detail in Appendix B—NSGMLS

---

5. Actually it is one particular character string representation of ESIS, which is, as its name suggests, an abstract information set.

Output Format Details. For the moment we will just note a few salient features:

- The output is line oriented, with each line corresponding to an SGML construct recognized by the parser; it is sometimes referred to as an *event*. The first character of each line tells us what type of construct it is (e.g., '(' for opening an element, 'A' for attributes, '-' for data).

- Whether tags were omitted in the original document does not matter (e.g., there is an end of para element event—denoted by ')PARA'—in the preceding output even though no para end-tag was supplied in the original document).

- Constructs such as entities that can occur in the midst of ordinary data are explicitly marked (e.g., \|mac\|).

- The file ends with a 'C' record (C for conforming) in the event that no errors were encountered by the SGML parser.

By way of analogy with programming language compilers, the ESIS format is a bit like a pcode representation of the original document. The SGML parser has dealt with all of the difficult lexical issues, leaving us with a clean, easily processed canonical representation of the original SGML document's Element Structure.

As with the SGML source document, the hierarchical nature of the data is readily visible:

```
(MEMO
  (FROM
    (FNAME
      -Sean
    )FNAME
    (SNAME
      -\|mac\| Grath
    )SNAME
  )FROM
  (TO
    (FNAME
      -Mark
    )FNAME
    (SNAME
      -Uplang
    )SNAME
  )TO
  AYEAR TOKEN 1965
  AMONTH TOKEN 04
  ADAY TOKEN 27
  (DATE
  )DATE
  (SUBJECT
    -Greeting
  )SUBJECT
  (BODY
    (PARA
```

```
      -Hello World!
    )PARA
  )BODY
)MEMO
C
```

This ESIS format will serve as the basis for many of the examples in this book.

## CHAPTER 3

STRUCTURE OF AN SGML SYSTEM

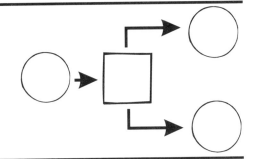

3.1 Introduction

In this chapter we will examine the overall environment in which SGML documents are designed, created, and stored. There is more to an "SGML environment" than simply a collection of SGML-based application software. In many respects, the process of analysis, design, and implementation that goes into the creation of these environments is comparable to that of, say, organization-wide relational database systems. Moreover, much of the literature, knowledge, and technologies concerned with the analysis, design, and deployment of such systems is directly relevant to the SGML world.

There is no magic formula for the creation of a good SGML environment any more than there is one for the creation of a relational database environment. Getting it right, with all the real-world constraints, trade-offs, and technological advances of a constantly moving world is *just plain hard*. Each stage of the process outlined in this chapter merits a book on its own.[1] The aim of this chapter is to provide an overview only, concentrating on the stages and the various technologies likely to be involved (see Figure 3.1).

3.2 Analysis

The field of systems analysis, of which SGML systems analysis (document analysis) is a part, is large and complex, involving a mixture of art and science. The principle purpose of document analysis is to capture knowledge about how an organization's document workflow functions from the various people involved. It involves capturing information about how documents are classified, structured, authored, and ultimately published. It involves requirements analysis to figure out what the system *should* do as opposed to what it currently does do.[2] It involves trade-offs between authoring efficiency on one hand and processing efficiency on the other and so on.

---

1. For example, *README.1ST—SGML for Writers and Editors* in this series covers the process from the writer's perspective.
2. Systems analysts have been known to quip that every system needs to be developed twice—once to implement it and once to implement it the way it *should* have been implemented in the *first* place.

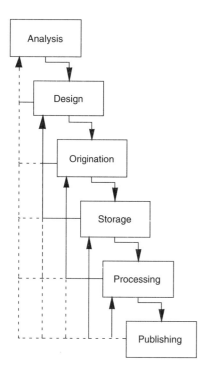

Figure 3.1 Stages in the creation of an SGML environment

One common difficulty in document analysis is finding a common language for the communication of ideas among the wide variety of people likely to be involved. Various techniques—common to any form of systems analysis—can be used. These include data flow diagrams and decision trees. On top of this, DTD diagramming tools can be used as a way of communicating document models as they evolve.

From the developer's perspective, it is very important that good document analysis is performed because decisions made here will have an impact on the ease or even the very feasibility of various processing tasks down the line. The situation is not unlike the difficulties that can arise if a relational database schema or a class hierarchy needs to be modified midproject.[3] It thus goes without saying that the more time spent on thorough document analysis, the better.

3.3   Design

In this phase, the knowledge gleaned about document classification and structure created during the analysis phase is converted into formal models in the form of DTDs. If DTD creation/visu-

---

3. Analysts also quip that even though there never seems to be time to get it right, there is always time to do it over and over again.

alization tools were used in analysis, the creation of the actual DTDs may be an automatic or semi-automatic process.

In situations where there are a number of DTDs, common subcomponents may be identified. If so, it may be decided to "factor out" the common components into DTD fragments to be included in a number of separate DTDs as illustrated in Figure 3.2.

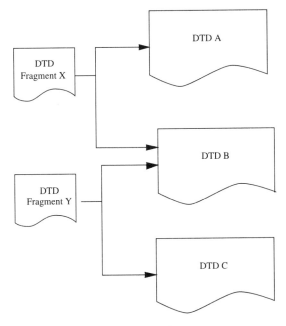

Figure 3.2 Sharing DTD fragments

In some situations. it may be sensible to use an industry standard DTD[4] rather than invent a new one. It might be that an industry standard DTD with some customization will suffice. Either way, there are so many DTDs in use in so many diverse industries, it is unlikely that a design will have to start from scratch.

More often than not, issues that come to light in the design phase will feed back into the analysis phase, causing a fresh bout of analysis. This sort of feedback can, in fact, happen between any of the stages involved in creating an SGML environment, thus the feedback arrows in Figure 3.1.

3.4   Origination

Origination is the process of creating documents that conform to the DTD models produced in the design phase. This is often a mixture of two types of activity, namely, the origination of new content in SGML and the translation of existing content to SGML.

---

4. See Appendix D.6—Some SGML-Related Industry Standards.

3.4.1   New Content

New content can be authored in a variety of ways ranging from simple text editors through to fully blown SGML-aware editing systems.

3.4.1.1   Text Editors

The "clear text" nature of SGML makes it feasible to use any text editor to create SGML files. One of the aims of the SGML standard is to make SGML documents both machine and human readable. Clearly, legibility for humans is directly related to the amount of tagging required. SGML provides a number of features to allow the reduction of the amount of tagging required. This includes features such as start/end-tag omission and short reference maps (see Section 14.6—Markup Minimization Methods).

Markup can be entered manually and/or macros can be developed to add a level of automation to the tagging process. Note that if a text editor is the intended authoring environment, this can have an impact on the DTD design. For example, authors are unlikely to be impressed with the use of PartNumber as an element type if the shorter PNUM would have sufficed. Judicious use of SGML entities for commonly used text not only reduces data redundancy but reduces markup as well. For example, the following two lines are SGML entity declarations. They establish a mapping between the entity names TIA and BTW with the text "Thanks in advance" and "by the way," respectively:

```
<!ENTITY TIA CDATA "Thanks in advance">
<!ENTITY BTW CDATA "by the way">
```

An author can type something like this:

```
<p>&TIA; and &BTW; how are you?
```

This is less onerous to type than

```
<p>Thanks in advance and by the way how are you?
```

SGML allows start- and end-tags to be omitted in situations where their presence can be inferred by the parser. These features can have a significant effect on the amount of markup. For example, the following two SGML documents are equivalent:

```
C>type a.sgm

<!DOCTYPE book [
<!ELEMENT book     - - (prelude,sect+)>
<!ELEMENT prelude - - (#PCDATA)>
<!ELEMENT sect     - - (p)+>
<!ELEMENT p        - - (#PCDATA)>
]>
<book>
```

```
<prelude>
I am the prelude
</prelude>
<sect>
<p>
I am a p in a sect
</p>
</sect>
</book>

C>type b.sgm

<!DOCTYPE book [
<!ELEMENT book O O (prelude,sect+)>
<!ELEMENT prelude O O (#PCDATA)>
<!ELEMENT sect O O (p)+>
<!ELEMENT p - O (#PCDATA)>
]>
I am the prelude
<p>
I am a p in a sect
```

Passing the files through the NSGMLS parser produces identical ESIS:

```
C>nsgmls a.sgm

(BOOK
(PRELUDE
-I am the prelude
)PRELUDE
(SECT
(P
-I am a p in a sect
)P
)SECT
)BOOK
C

C>nsgmls b.sgm

(BOOK
(PRELUDE
-I am the prelude
)PRELUDE
(SECT
(P
-I am a p in a sect
)P
)SECT
)BOOK
C
```

In other words, from the point of view of application software working with the ESIS output produced by the parser, the documents are indistinguishable. Some other methods of reducing the amount of markup required are outlined in Section 14.6—Markup Minimization Methods.

One final point on the use of text editors for SGML authoring: obviously, a text editor will not stop the user from producing invalid SGML, and a stand-alone validating SGML parser (such as NSGMLS) is required to validate the documents. Some text editors such as GNU Emacs have SGML editing modes that facilitate SGML markup and validation from within the editing environment.

3.4.1.2   WYSIWYG Systems

In Section 1.3 we discussed how WYSIWYG systems such as word processors and desktop publishing programs focus on capturing rendition rather than structure and content. Although a certain degree of structure is captured through the use of so-called outline modes and stylesheets, the structure is not enforceable. This, combined with the myriad of typesetting features supported by these systems, poses a challenge for creating SGML.

Text-Only Mode

Trivially, WYSIWYG tools can be used to author SGML as long as the author enters all the markup and saves the files as text-only documents. Some authors may prefer this route to adopting a traditional text editor in order to avoid learning new keystroke combinations, menus, and the like. The macro facility availability in many WYSIWYG editors can also be useful for semi-automating the markup process.

Postprocessing Style Information

Although it involves much more work for the developer, the presentation features of WYSI-WYG systems can be used to automate the creation of markup. The idea is to let the authors work in their WYSIWYG environments in as natural a way as possible and then postprocess the files into SGML.

The least viable way of doing this is to rely on keeping track of paragraph/character formatting codes. A more reliable way is to get the authors to work exclusively with paragraph and character *styles* in their WYSIWYG stylesheets.

The translation process can consist of macros running within the native WYSIWYG system or of separate programs that pick up the file in some known storage format such as RTF. As with text editor editing, the onus is upon the authors to order the content correctly. An external validating SGML parser is required to check the validity of the documents.

Note also that there may be limits to the richness of SGML structure that can be inferred using paragraph and character styles. For example, many WYSIWYG systems prohibit the nesting of character styles, thus limiting you to one level of "tagging" beneath the paragraph level.

SGML "Add-Ons"

A growing number of WYSIWYG systems have either SGML editions or third-party SGML add-ons. Some of these work in a manner analogous to the postprocessing method mentioned previously. Some guide the authoring process via custom dialogs, largely hiding the native usage of the WYSIWYG system underneath.

3.4.1.3   SGML-Aware Authoring Packages

SGML-aware authoring tools have a built-in knowledge of SGML and thus are the most reliable way to author valid SGML documents. As a document is being created, these tools can constantly check that the document fits the structure specified in the DTD. Moreover, at any given point in the creation process, the author can ask the system, "What element types are valid at this point?" Some systems take this one stage farther by inferring what comes next in the structure. For example,

```
<!ELEMENT from        - O (fname,sname)>
<!ELEMENT (fname,sname) - O (#PCDATA)>
```

After the author inserts the **from** element start-tag, an SGML-aware editor can immediately infer that the **fname** element is coming next and that it contains data.

Another common feature is the ability to attach presentation attributes to element types to provide a pseudo-WYSIWYG environment in which changes in presentation style help the author visualize the underlying structure. Some systems take a completely non-WYSIWYG approach using a variety of alternative metaphors to communicate the structure of the SGML document. One such visualization metaphor is shown in Figure 3.3.

SGML-aware editing systems typically work by first compiling DTDs into an internal format for speed and efficiency reasons. This process can require a good knowledge of DTD constructs and is often the domain of SGML technical people rather than authors. Setting up the pseudo-

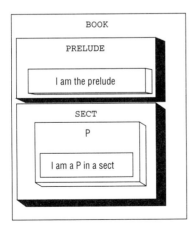

Figure 3.3 Sculpted editing view of an SGML document

WYSIWYG stylesheet, if required, can also require a good knowledge of SGML and is probably best done by a combination of authors and developers.

3.4.2   Translation of Existing Content

It is rare that an SGML environment is installed into a green field site (i.e., a site without an existing collection of non-SGML documents that will require conversion to SGML). This sort of data is known, perhaps somewhat condescendingly, as *legacy data*, and the process of converting it to SGML is known as *up-translation*.

Up-translation is, in general, a difficult problem and one that is attracting a lot of attention from theorists and developers alike. In essence, the challenge is to construct software capable of "reverse engineering" the sort of structural information about a document that a human being recognizes by simply looking at it.

A variety of purpose designed up-translation tools are available. The essential philosophy is to allow the developer to establish a mapping between the presentation-oriented representation of the legacy documents and the corresponding information content–oriented SGML elements.

The extent to which up-translation can be automated is directly related to the consistency of the formatting characteristics applied to the original documents. The consistent use of a stylesheet is the most desirable attribute of legacy documents. However, given that stylesheet mechanisms are not enforced by traditional WYSIWYG systems, statements from users such as, "Oh yes we use the stylesheet for everything," can safely be viewed with some scepticism. Apart from dedicated tools, it is also possible to "roll your own" up-translators in a number of ways.

Direct File Format Access

If you know the file format used by the legacy documents or you know a file format that the documents can be exported to, it may be possible to build applications in C, Perl, or sed, for example to at least semi-automate the up-translation.

Unfortunately, the more powerful the WYSIWIG system that created the files is, the more difficult the task of up-translation. Anything more complex than a collection of search and replace constructs can involve maintaining details of the formatting state, which can involve many variables and is fraught with difficulties.

A common "gotcha" is the presence of formatting codes for invisible content. For example, if you turn all italic text into text bounded by an <emphasis> element, you might find **emphasis** elements consisting solely of white space such as tabs and carriage returns. This can lead to such strange results as the following paragraph:

```
Hello World
```

getting up-translated to

```
<par>
<emphasis>
```

```
Hello
</emphasis>
<bold> </bold>
<emphasis>World
</par>
</emphasis>
```

Another common issue is the extent to which formatting can be redundant or overlapping. For example, the text

B555-*3345* Installation

might look like the following when the formatting codes are directly translated to SGML tags:

```
<bold><para>B555-<italic>3345 </bold></italic>Installation</para>
```

To be valid SGML this would need to look like this:

```
<para><bold>B555-</bold><bold><italic>-3345 </italic>
</bold>Installation</para>
```

The overlapping element structures need to be unraveled. Also, the space would not be considered to be in bold, italic:

```
<para><bold>B555-</bold><bold><italic>-3345</italic></bold> Installation
</para>
```

Finally, to make the SGML more useful we would like

```
<para><PartNumber>B555-3345</PartNumber> Installation</para>
```

Or better yet

```
<installation PartNumber="B555-3345">
```

As can readily be appreciated, this is a nontrivial exercise requiring highly intelligent up-translation software.

Rainbow DTD

One possible launching pad for the development of up-translation software is an interchange DTD known as the rainbow DTD developed by Electronic Book Technologies and released freely to the public (see Appendix D—SGML Resources for Developers).

The idea behind the *rainbow DTD* is to shield the developer from having to know the native file format of the source documents. It achieves this by providing a DTD that encapsulates the formatting capabilities of many common WYSIWYG systems in a single DTD. Applications known as rainbow makers then convert specific WYSIWYG formats to this DTD, as shown in Figure 3.4.

The boon for the developer is that the details of the WYSIWYG file format itself can be ignored and dealt with by the rainbow maker. The result is a valid but rendition-oriented SGML that acts as the starting point for the custom up-translation effort. By building intermediate DTDs for

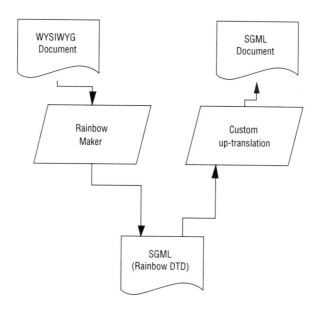

Figure 3.4 Up-translation via the rainbow method

the various stages of up-translation, it is possible to use a validating SGML parser to help monitor the process.

A variety of rainbow makers for formats such as RTF, FrameMaker MIF, and Interleaf have been developed and released into the public domain (see Appendix D.7—Rainbow Makers).

Out-Sourcing Up-Translation

Finally, given the nontrivial nature of the up-translation task, some organizations conclude that the effort involved in performing the up-translation in-house is not worth the time and effort. This might be especially true if the up-translation process is a once-off task. In this situation, out-sourcing the up-translation can be an attractive option.

As with in-house up-translation, SGML's ability to validate documents against their DTDs can be a useful tool for quality assuring the up-translated documents. The DTD itself also acts as an unambiguous schema for communicating the markup requirements to the markup service provider.

3.5   Storage

3.5.1   Straight SGML Files

The simplest way to store SGML is in standard files as provided by the host operating system. This type of storage has the advantage of simplicity but can become unwieldy as the number and volume of SGML documents increases. Storing single SGML documents as many separate SGML files on disk increases the granularity at which they can be accessed but increases the problems of managing the file system, performing backups, and the like. On the other hand, having large SGML files on disk makes it easier to manage the file system but less easy to access components of the documents.

3.5.2   Relational Databases

Relational databases excel at storing and manipulating tabular data. SGML documents have an inherently hierarchical structure that does not cleanly fit the tabular model. The simplest way to store SGML in such a system is to use a (large) text field or, in some databases, a BLOB[5] field.

The granularity of access to the data in the SGML document can be improved by "chopping" the SGML into smaller pieces. This typically involves establishing a mapping between elements and the text fields into which they will be stored. For example, Figure 3.5 shows how an SGML document might get chopped at major structural boundaries to be stored in a relational database. Note that the **body** element is missing and the **sect1** elements are stored as peers of the **front** and **back** elements.

The essential problem of the mismatch between SGML hierarchies and tabular data is the same problem faced in object-oriented systems in which similar hierarchical structures occur that require persistent storage in a database. In object-oriented technology parlance, this is the so-called impedance mismatch. SGML-aware databases are, in fact, often built on top of object-oriented databases.

3.5.3   SGML Databases

Databases in this category "know" SGML and store the inherent hierarchy intact. Access to structure and content is provided down to the individual element level, thus providing the easiest way to capitalize on the granularity of SGML documents for queries, content reuse, and so on.

SGML databases provide easy management due to the centralized storage along with ease of use resulting from the high granularity at which the documents are stored.

3.6   Processing and Publishing

The processing and publishing stages of the simple six stage model are dealt with in the next two chapters.

---

5. **Binary Large OB**ject.

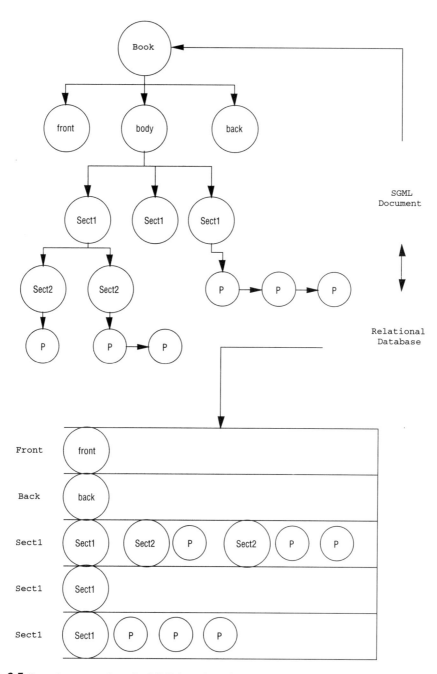

Figure 3.5 Example storage schema for SGML in a tabular format

## CHAPTER 4

PUBLISHING *SGML* DOCUMENTS

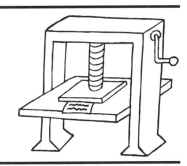

4.1   Introduction

The most obvious thing you can do with an SGML document is to publish it. With SGML, the word *publish* has a wide spectrum of possible interpretations. It can mean typesetting information onto paper, burning it onto a CD-ROM, making it available on the World Wide Web, translating it into sound, or simply listing it to a computer screen. Given that one of the core ideas of SGML is the future-proofing of information, it also includes the possibility of publishing to formats not yet even invented or imagined.

The physical appearance of information on a page or screen can be an important part of the overall message conveyed. Prior to the Desktop Publishing (DTP) revolution such aesthetic control over the appearance of information was largely the domain of specialists in the arts of typography and graphic design. Nowadays, anyone with access to desktop computing power can try their hand at page layout, typeface design, or illustration work, using a wide variety of application software packages. Furthermore, technologies such as the World Wide Web and CD-ROM make it possible to reach a large audience quickly and cheaply.

Advances in origination technologies (word processors, DTP packages, etc.) and dissemination technologies (World Wide Web, CD-ROM, etc.) continue to raise the aesthetic standards expected in the publishing world. Today, even humdrum commercial documents such as invoices and purchase orders are routinely rendered at laser printer resolutions.

The net result is that authors can find themselves spending an increasingly large amount of time *formatting* content as distinct from originating it. Apart from tinkering with the "look" of their content, authors can also spend a significant amount of time performing repetitive formatting tasks. Here are some examples of possible "house rules" for text entry that actually relate to formatting:

"Tab in the first line of each paragraph except in the case where the paragraph immediately follows a bulleted list."

"When creating a cross reference marker for a C++ method use the name of the class, followed by an underscore followed by the name of the method."

"If the warning message is in part of a client-performed maintenance procedure use red text, otherwise, use italic text."

These can be thought of as algorithms that human beings execute in formatting documents. SGML is an enabling technology for the automation of such algorithms via a combination of software and markup.

In some situations, the automated formatting process might produce a completely finished product. In others it might require touching up by a human being prior to publication. The latter scenario is not a failing on the part of SGML or the software that processes it. Rather, it is a by-product of the fact that there is a limit to how much of the aesthetic skills of a human being can be reduced to a set of algorithms. Sometimes, partial automation is the right solution.

4.2   Classifying Formats for Rendered SGML Documents

Prior to the arrival of electronic publishing, the final rendered format of an SGML document was invariably paper. As electronic publishing technology continues to advance, we are seeing more and more purely electronic formats for the final rendering of documents. On top of this trend is the move toward SGML itself as a *final* delivery format. In other words, rendered SGML can itself be SGML. This may be the original SGML markup or some more rendition-centric form of SGML markup. The principle categories of document publishing formats are shown in Figure 4.1.

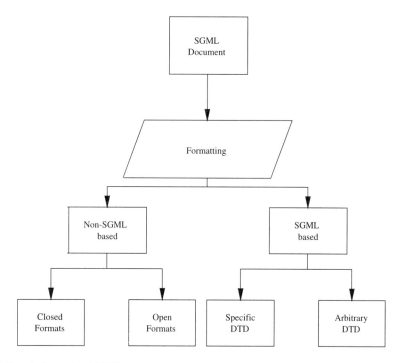

Figure 4.1 Formats for rendered SGML

4.3   Non-SGML-Based Formats

The non-SGML-based formats include PostScript, RTF, MIF, TeX, troff, and CCITT Group 4 Fax. Some of these formats, such as PostScript, predate electronic publishing. However, as screen resolutions have increased, so too has the use of such paper-oriented formats for purely on-line use.

To develop software to convert from SGML to a particular format, the details of the file format must be available to the developer. This may be in the form of open access to the document structure itself such as in TeX or troff. It may be in the form of an intermediate file format such as RTF or MIF. It may also be in the form of an API whereby software is written to link directly to another application that will produce the necessary file format via a set of function calls.

There are a number of systems for both paper and electronic delivery that are either completely or partially closed, which makes the task of targeting them from SGML either difficult or impossible. Thankfully, as the concept of open systems continues to penetrate the document world the way it has penetrated the database world, these are increasingly in a minority.

4.3.1   PostScript

PostScript is a page description language (PDL) developed by Adobe Systems and used extensively in everything from industrial to desktop level printers. It is a stack-based language for describing the construction of rendered pages.[1] A program called a PostScript interpreter typically runs within the printing device executing the PostScript programs sent to it. It expects a sequence of instructions telling it where to move on the page in terms of X,Y coordinations and what to paint.

PostScript is a text-only format intended to be generated rather than authored by hand. However, it is not an attractive format to target *directly* from SGML because it knows nothing about text flows. For example, the following is a PostScript command sequence:

```
0 0 MoveTo
(Hello World) show
showpage
```

This will print a page with string "Hello World" in the top left-hand corner. When a string of characters is rendered as a unit via the show command, the PostScript interpreter will adjust the rendering position in accordance with the escapement direction[2] and the geometry of the active font in order to paint the text correctly. However, PostScript knows nothing about paragraphs or margins and will not wrap text. PostScript is typically generated from SGML via an intermediate page composition system that deals with these issues. For example, RTF might be generated from the SGML and subsequently printed to a PostScript device via a word processor or DTP package.

---

1. For an introduction to PostScript for developers see *Hands on PostScript* by Dr. Michael B. Spring and David Dubin (ISBN: 0-672-30185-7).
2. The direction in which text is flowing (e.g., in English normally left to right and top to bottom).

4.3.2 Rich Text Format

Rich Text Format (RTF) is an interchange format for WYSIWYG systems developed by Microsoft and supported by most word processing and DTP systems. The RTF model is that of a collection of text flows (body text, footnotes, table cells). These text flows can, by and large, contain paragraphs. Paragraphs have associated properties such as margins and justification settings. Within paragraphs, text can have style information such as font, weight, and color.

An RTF interpreter (typically called an import filter) combines the text and the formatting commands to produce paragraphs and pages. RTF uses a stack-based metaphor in which formatting commands can be grouped so as to have local effect as follows:

```
{\fs20\b\i Hello World}
```

In this example, the text Hello World is rendered in 10 point,[3] bold, italic. The opening '{' indicates the start of a formatting state. The '}' at the end causes all modifications to the formatting state to revert to what they were prior to the opening '{'.

RTF is commonly generated directly from SGML. However, some knowledge of the final destination of the RTF is also required because of the differing interpretations of the RTF codes by different systems. This is a result of the fact that, although the syntax of an RTF file is well defined, the semantics are not.

RTF is also used as the base format for a number of electronic delivery formats such as the on-line help format for the Microsoft Windows series of operating systems. In this format, certain RTF formatting codes are interpreted differently from the way they would be on paper (e.g., some footnote types are used for search keywords, hypertext anchors, etc). Chapter 12—Some Processing Examples—includes an example of RTF generation from SGML.

4.3.3 TeX

TeX is a typesetting system developed by the computer scientist and mathematician, Professor Donald E. Knuth. Like RTF, TeX handles text flows and issues of page size, hyphenation, justification, and more. It offers very fine control over typesetting detail and, as one might expect, is particularly strong at mathematics.

Broadly speaking, the TeX model lays out type onto a collection of rectangular areas corresponding to physical pages. These rectangles themselves consist of rectangles corresponding to paragraphs, equations, and so on. These rectangles in turn consist of smaller rectangles consisting of subparagraph or subequation elements. The final rectangle size corresponds to the image of an individual character called a *glyph*.

---

3. RTF measures font size in half-point units.

The end result of a TeX run is one or more files in DVI (DeVice Independent) format. These DVI files can then be processed by so-called DVI drivers to produce a variety of formats such as PostScript, TIFF, and HPGL.

TeX includes a macro programming language that allows extensions to the language to be developed in TeX itself. One popular set of TeX macros is known as LaTex, which provides a higher level of abstraction for TeX and is thus easier to author/generate directly.

An example LaTex document follows:

```
\begin{document}
\abstract{I am the abstract}
\section
Hello World
\end{document}
```

TeX is commonly used in SGML formatting systems. It is freely available on a wide variety of machines with a large variety of support software and a constantly increasing library of DVI drivers.

4.3.4   troff

troff is a document preparation system that was developed as part of the original UNIX system by AT&T. troff is philosophically similar to TeX in many respects. It is programmable and provides a wide degree of control over the typesetting process.

troff was designed around the dual UNIX philosophies of pipes and specialist "little languages."[4] A full troff system consists of a troff process and a collection of little languages acting as troff preprocessors for speciality purposes such as dealing with equations and tables. A number of these little language processors are then chained together to yield pure troff at the far end:

```
cat hello.ms | tbl | eqn | troff -ms
```

This command says, "Pump the hello.ms document through the tbl, eqn, and troff programs in that order. Specify the use of the ms macros for troff."

The following is a simple troff document:

```
.TL
I am a title
.AU
Mark Uplang
Sean Mc Grath
.PP
Hello World from this line
.br
```

---

4. Information on troff and UNIX in general can be found in *The UNIX Programming Environment* by Brian W. Kerneghan and Rob Pike (ISBN 0-13-937681-X).

```
Hello World from this line
.EQ
1 over {(2 pi)}
.EN
```

The uppercase commands are troff macros implemented as part of the popular ms macro set. The lowercase command .br is a raw troff command meaning break the text flow onto a new line. Finally, the text between the .EQ and .EN commands is interpreted by the eqn program to produce

I am a title

Mark Uplang
Sean Mc Grath

Hello world from this line
Hello world from this line

$1/(2\Pi)$

4.4   SGML-Based Formats

SGML-based formats are systems that render SGML documents directly. There are two main types, namely specific and arbitrary DTD systems.

4.4.1   Specific DTD

Specific DTD systems can work directly with SGML as long as a specific DTD has been used.

4.4.1.1   World Wide Web

The World Wide Web is based on the HTML DTD. Publishing arbitrary SGML on the Web can be achieved by cross-translating to this HTML DTD. It is a low-level DTD consisting of a mixture of structural and format-oriented markup. A simple HTML document follows:

```
<!doctype html PUBLIC "-//IETF//DTD HTML//EN">
<HTML>
<HEAD>
<TITLE>I am a title</TITLE>
</HEAD>
<BODY>
<P>Hello World
</BODY>
</HTML>
```

Notice the Document Type Declaration line. It uses a so-called *formal public identifier* (FPI) to identify the DTD. This is an SGML mechanism for uniquely identifying a DTD (or other information object) with a standardized naming convention. FPIs are covered in Section 7.3—System Versus Public Identifiers.

The decision as to how an HTML document will look on the screen is principally under the control of the viewing application. The same HTML document can look different under different viewers. A number of different approaches have been suggested to rectify this, ranging from the addition of more format-oriented tags to separate style sheet languages.

The addition of more format-oriented tags has the benefit of providing closer control over the formatting process for the author at the expense of producing less useful documents. If sufficient formatting elements get added to the documents, they will inherit many of the problems associated with WYSIWYG documents we discuss in this book. Essentially this route runs the risk of making HTML a text flow description language such as RTF.

Style sheet languages work by associating formatting characteristics with particular SGML element types and their attributes. The have the benefit that they separate formatting from content and hold out the possibility of transforming the Web from a specific DTD to an arbitrary DTD system. Style sheet languages will be discussed later in this chapter.

For a detailed treatment of HTML and how it relates to SGML, see *SGML on the Web; Small Steps* by Yuri Rubinsky and Murray Maloney.[5]

4.4.1.2   ICADD

The International Committee for Accessible Document Design (ICADD) is a set of guidelines to enable the transformation of SGML to Braille and for publication in large print and voice formats.[6] The scheme works by encoding ICADD-related information in SGML attributes. These modifications are made solely in the DTD—the SGML document instances themselves do not need to change.

4.4.1.3   IETM

Interactive Electronic Technical Manuals (IETM) is a collection of U.S. military specifications providing guidelines for the creation of interactive manuals. Documents are created in SGML using the MIL-D-87269 DTD.

4.4.2   Arbitrary DTD

Systems in the arbitrary DTD category can work with documents conforming to any SGML DTD. Some work by putting the documents through a compilation phase during which the developer can tailor style issues as required. In the case of on-line systems that use this approach, they may have a "save as SGML" capability to allow users to retrieve the original SGML documents.

---

5. ISBN 0-13-519984-0.
6. ISO 12083 Annex A.8.

4.4.2.1   FOSI

Formatting Output Specification Instance (FOSI) is also a U.S. military specification (MIL-M-28001B). The idea behind FOSI is similar to the idea of a style sheet with the added twist that the style sheet is itself an SGML document conforming to the FOS DTD. A FOSI provides a mechanism for establishing a link between SGML elements and formatting characteristics. The formatting can be fine-tuned by specifying the context(s) in which elements occur. For example, this is a FOSI snippet:

```
<e-i-c gi = "A" context="B">
<font size="24pt">
```

It says, "when the A element occurs within a B element, set the font size to 24 points."

4.4.2.2   HTML Cascading Styles

The HTML cascading styles is a style sheet specification from the World Wide Web Consortium. Although aimed primarily at HTML, the general mechanism is applicable to any SGML DTD. The idea is to allow the association of style properties with SGML elements and to allow those settings to be inherited by subelements. For example,

```
BODY {
color: red;
}
EM {
color:black;
}
```

The first specification says, "everything occurring within a **BODY** element will be in red." The second says, "Everything within an **EM** element will be black." The net effect is that everything in a **BODY** will be red with the exception of **EM** elements, which will be black.

4.4.2.3   DSSSL

We will discuss Document Style Semantics and Specification Language (DSSSL) in more detail in Chapter 16. For now, suffice it to say that DSSSL is a standard way of specifying how an SGML document should be (a) transformed and (b) formatted for publication. The DSSSL standard uses a variation of Scheme[7] as its expression language.

DSSSL-On-line is a specification for a subset of DSSSL that has been designed as a style language for electronic delivery media such as the World Wide Web.

---

7. A Lisp-like language.

## CHAPTER 5

101 THINGS TO DO WITH AN SGML DOCUMENT

5.1 Introduction

In the previous chapter we talked about the most obvious application of SGML, namely automatic publishing in multiple delivery formats from the same source documents. However, this is only part of what SGML has to offer and, in some situations, can be a secondary reason for using it. In this chapter we look at examples of using SGML as a technique for *harvesting* content prior to the publishing process proper. We will also give some examples that do not involve "publishing" at all. Hopefully, the examples will trigger some ideas as to how you might use SGML in your own situation and set the scene for the coming chapters, which detail the nuts and bolts of SGML.

5.2 Data and Derived-Data

The "information" that flows in ever-increasing volume around our information-centric world comes in a number of abstract varieties.

- If a new variety of beetle is discovered and the information about it published, it is *new* information.

- If an analysis of historical data on car sales and the price of oil yields a hitherto unknown correlation between the two, this is new information.

- If someone publishes *The 50 Heaviest Beetles in the World* and *The A to Z of Beetles*, they are making existing information more accessible.

The information about the new species of beetle stands on its own as new information. It is not derived from an analysis of other information (apart perhaps from checking existing information to make sure that the beetle is a genuinely new species). The car-sales-versus-oil-price information is a combination of the analysis of existing information and the intelligence required to research it and spot the correlation. The information in *The A to Z of Beetles* is also derived from existing information but does not require research or intellectual effort. If no one has ever put bee-

tles on a weighing scales before or generated an alphabetical list of their names, then these order-
ings might qualify as new information derived from old.

Apart from the new species of beetle, the other publications feature what is variously known
as derived information, derived-data, or bits about bits.[1] There is no clear dividing line between data
and derived-data, and the terms are somewhat relative to one's viewpoint. What is clear is that
derived-data makes up a significant proportion of the world's publishing corpus. It is also clear that
a large amount of time and effort goes into its creation and dissemination.

The creation of derived-data involves the harvesting and analysis of existing data. Historically, this has been a strong point of the database world and a weak point in the document world.
We are accustomed to the ease with which we can use relational databases and query tools such as
SQL to import interesting information into spreadsheets for further analysis. We are used to the
idea of being able to combine physically separate databases into one logical database for the purposes of generating new views of their collective data content.

Traditional documents, which in reality make up the bulk of the world's information repository, are not as readily harvested. Hence we have a case for a more database-like treatment of documents in the form of SGML. Many of the examples that make up the rest of this chapter illustrate
how SGML can help to close the gap between documents and databases as sources of derived-data.

5.3   Some SGML Opportunities

5.3.1   Normalization

Situation

In the course of document analysis, an organization discovers that its street address occurs in
hundreds of documents and is duplicated every time.

SGML Opportunity

When stored in SGML, the documents can be "normalized."[2] A single document containing
the company's street address, telephone number, and the like can be created. The DTD for this
small document might look something like this:

```
C>type company.dtd

<!ELEMENT company - O (name,addr+,city,state,zip,country)>
<!ELEMENT (name,addr,city,state,zip,country) - O (#PCDATA)>
```

---

1. For a discussion on this topic see *Being Digital* by Nicholas Negroponte (ISBN 0-340-64930-5).

2. Note that *normalization* is used here in the database sense of removing data redundancy. In SGML *normalization*
   refers to the creation of SGML documents that do not use markup minimization features.

The document fragment itself might look something like this:

```
C>type comp.sgm

<company>
<name>Acme Corp.
<addr>Acme House
<addr>555 Smith Street.
<city>Smithsville
<state>MO
<zip>12345
<country>USA
</company>
```

This miniature document can then be included by reference in other SGML documents using SGML entities:

```
C>type foo.sgm

<!DOCTYPE foo SYSTEM "foo.dtd" [
<!ENTITY comp SYSTEM "comp.sgm">
]>
<foo>
<frontmatter>
&comp;
</frontmatter>
...
</foo>

C>type bar.sgm

<!DOCTYPE bar SYSTEM "bar.dtd" [
<!ENTITY comp SYSTEM "comp.sgm">
]>
<bar>
<preface>
&comp;
</preface>
...
</bar>
```

The particular form of entity used here is called an SGML Text Entity. They are covered in detail in Chapter 7—Entities, Notations, and Marked Sections.

Benefits

A single copy of the company's street address etc. is all that is required. If it needs to be modified it only has to be modified *once* and in a single place. Any documents published after the modification will automatically inherit the modified details.

Notice that the model is such that a valid company document instance must have at least 1 address line but can have as many address lines as are required. This unbounded iteration makes street addresses (especially European addresses) easier to deal with in SGML than in relational databases where the number of "fields" per "record" is fixed in the database schema.

5.3.2   Content Addressability

Situation

A company involved in direct mailing is having problems intelligently processing addresses. The following are sample addresses from the company's database:

```
Acme Gmbh
Acmestrasse 654
45324 Acmebitte
Germany

Acme Ltd.
The Moorings
104 Moorings Way
Mooringshire
Wessex WX5 555
England
```

The problem is that the company needs to print addresses exactly as they look here but also to be able to explicitly locate things like City and Zip Code for query purposes.

SGML Opportunity

A flat database approach leaves it up to the processing application to work out which line (or portion of a line) relates to what logical portion of an address (see Figure 5.1). This schema has the disadvantage of making work for the processing applications down the line in locating City, Zip Code, and the like for query purposes. On the positive side, the lines of the address are in the correct order for printing.

An alternative approach is to make the City, Zip Code, State, and Country fields explicit, as

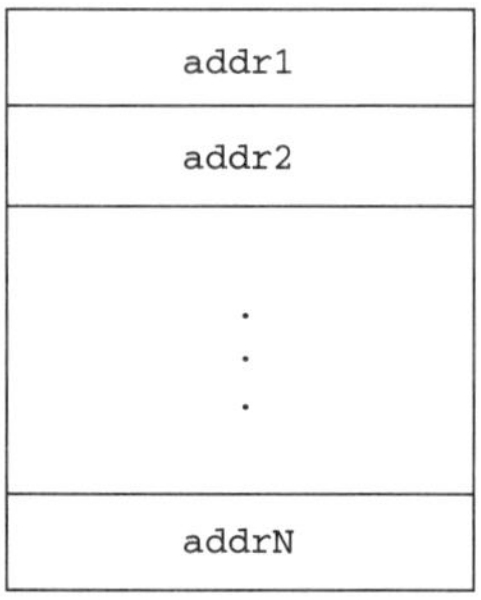

| addr1 |
| addr2 |
| . . . |
| addrN |

Figure 5.1 A flat address schema

shown in Figure 5.2. This model is more content addressable but has lost the knowledge about the order the items should be printed in.

An SGML model that combines the two approaches might look like this:

```
<!ELEMENT address - O (name,addr+,(city|state|zip)*,country)>
<!ELEMENT (name,addr,city,state,zip,country) - O (#PCDATA)>
```

The addresses in SGML might look like this:

```
<address>
<name>Acme Gmbh
<addr>Acmestrasse 654
<zip>45324
<city>Acmebitte
<country>Germany

<address>
<name>Acme Ltd.
<addr>The Moorings
<addr>104 Moorings Way
<addr>Mooringshire
<state>Wessex
<zip>WX5 555
<country>England
```

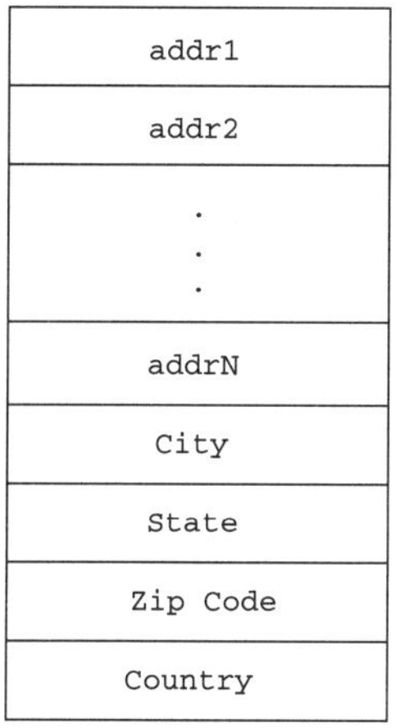

addr1
addr2
.
.
.
addrN
City
State
Zip Code
Country

Figure 5.2 Address schema with explicit content

Benefits

In SGML, the addresses are maintained in a content-addressable way for intelligent queries and the like. SGML's ability to store structured fields in arbitrary orders simplifies capturing the "natural order" of the addresses for such processes as printing.

Note however, that as far as this model is concerned, the following is also a valid address:

```
<address>
<name>Acme Ltd.
<addr>The Moorings
<addr>104 Moorings Way
<addr>Mooringshire
<zip>XYZ 1234
<state>Wessex
<zip>WX5 555
<country>England
<country>Tumbolia
```

Clearly, extra semantic checking is required by the processing application in this example. In general, design decisions must be made as to what semantic checking to build into the SGML models and what semantics to check at the processing stage (see Section 13.3—Levels of Semantic Checking). We could, for example, have used this model:

```
<!ELEMENT address - O (name,addr+,(city?&state?&zip),country)>
```

The ? operator used with the **city**, **state**, and **zip** element types is an occurrence indicator, a unary operator meaning optional (i.e., X? means X can occur once or not at all). The & operator is used to allow permutations (i.e., A & B means A followed by B or B followed by A).

5.3.3   Variant Elements

Situation

During document analysis an organization discovers that, although they have many different products, each of which will logically have its own DTD for documentation purposes, the wording of the legal disclaimer is *almost* identical in every case. The difference boils down to slightly different wording in a single paragraph based on the type of product.

SGML Opportunity

A **variant** element might be used in a DTD fragment specifically created for disclaimers. A single disclaimer document fragment could then be used in multiple documents via an SGML entity reference. The disclaimer might look something like this:

```
<disclaimer>
<para>This product is provided...
<para>In the event that <variant><case product = "Widget">the top of the
      widget...</case><case product = "Grommit">the bottom of the Grommit...
      </case></variant>
</disclaimer>
```

In this model, one or more **case** elements with a **product** attribute are used to specify what text to use to produce the different disclaimer types. A sample document using this disclaimer might look like this:

```
<!DOCTYPE amanual SYSTEM "amanual.dtd" [
<!ENTITY disc SYSTEM "disclaim.sgm">
]>
<amanual>
<FrontMatter>
&disc;
Other front matter...
</FrontMatter>
Body of the manual...
</amanual>
```

Using this scheme, the user would have to specify to the SGML publishing software which variant to use at processing time. As an alternative to specifying the variation required at run-time, the currently active variation might be indicated in the document fragment itself:

```
<FrontMatter>
<disclaimer product = "Widget">
<para>This product is provided...
<para>In the event that <variant><case product = "Widget">the top of the
        widget...</case><case product = "Grommit">the bottom of the Grommit...
        </case></variant>
</disclaimer>
...more front matter
</FrontMatter>
```

Here a **disclaimer** element with a product attribute set to "Widget" has been used. SGML processing software would then use this attribute to reduce the content of the disclaimer to this:

```
<FrontMatter>
<disclaimer>
<para>This product is provided...
<para>In the event that the top of the widget...
</disclaimer>
...more front matter
</FrontMatter>
```

Benefits

The redundancy in the disclaimer text has been removed and is easier to maintain as a result. Adding a new variation is a straightforward process.

5.3.4   Automatic Customization

Situation

A company produces technical reports on desktop computers aimed at volume purchasers of computer equipment. The reports all take the same general form with sections dealing with CPU, memory, hard disk storage, and so on. The company regularly gets requests for reports that deal with a single topic over a *range* of machines (e.g., disk IO performance, CPU clock speeds, etc.). Although the clients are willing to pay a premium for such customized reports, the amount of work involved in assembling and publishing them has proved prohibitive.

SGML Opportunity

By analyzing the reports, it should be possible to produce a DTD that captures the semantic content and structure of the reports (i.e., there might be **HardDiskData** element type for holding content concerned with hard disks). Individual statistics such as **Access Time** and **Number of Platters** might be explicitly tagged also.

For each customized report, a DTD can be defined. For example, a report dealing exclusively with hard disks might start with something like this:

```
<!ELEMENT HardDiskReport - O (HardDiskData)+>
```

An application can be developed that processes the individual computer reports harvesting the **HardDiskData** sections into a single file. A validating SGML parser can then be used to ensure that the derived report conforms to the HardDiskReport DTD.

At this point, additional editorial content might be added manually or the generated report could be published directly (see Figure 5.3).

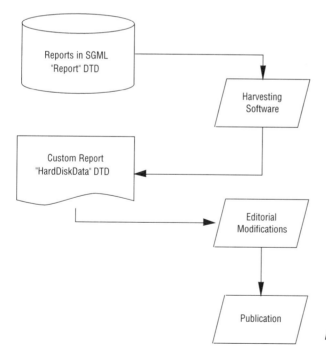

Figure 5.3 Data harvesting example

Benefits

Once the workflow in generating the custom reports is in place, the process is largely both automatic and volume independent (i.e., generating a custom hard disk report based on 10 computers or 1000 computers is merely a matter of CPU time—and hard disk space!—rather than human effort).

This illustrates an important point. A team of humans would have less difficulty with a customized report for 10 computers than the one for 1000. The higher the volume, the larger the number of people who are likely to be involved and the higher the incidence of errors due to communication problems and the like. In this respect, the automated SGML solution, scales up better than the manual one, as illustrated in Figure 5.4.

The cost of SGML is encountered up front with the benefits occurring down the line. Initially the learning curve can be steep and the costs high for no immediate return. In many respects this is a characteristic SGML shares with other technologies concerned with reuse such as object-oriented technology.

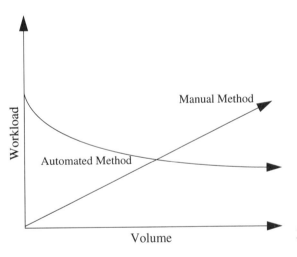

Figure 5.4 Relationship between workload and volume

5.3.5   Customized Anthologies

Situation

A publisher of technical books discovers by polling university professors that, although many of their titles are relevant to the courses taught, no single book covers all the required material for any one course. However, by selecting sections from a *number* of books in their product range, ideal course material could be created.

SGML Opportunity

Store the technical books in SGML. Create a custom anthology "template" that the professors can fill in to specify what sections of what books they require in their custom book. The custom book template is then used to drive SGML processing software that harvests the required sections to create a new SGML document, as shown in Figure 5.5.

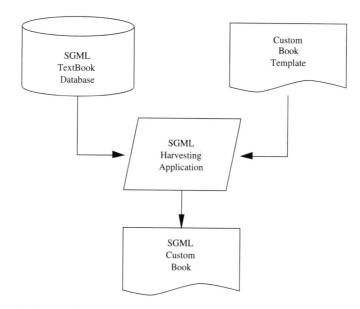

Figure 5.5 Custom book generation

Benefits

The benefits are similar to those in the previous situation. Namely, once the workflow is in place, generating custom books to satisfy exact customer requirements is possible without significant human intervention. This example builds on the last one via the notion of a template that drives the generation of the custom document. This adds another level of "soft-coding" to the information harvester.

Note that the template file could itself be an SGML document! With SGML on hand as a data modeling, capture, and validation tool, developers have less reason to say, "What I need now is a file format…" and "What I need now are some parsing routines…". SGML can be both file format and parser, allowing the developer to concentrate on the specifics of the problem at hand.

5.3.6   Information Filtering

Situation

A vendor of financial information polls its customers and finds that the sheer volume of information is becoming a problem for the clients who simply cannot "take it all in." The vendor finds that at any one time, many of their clients have well-defined areas of interest and would ideally like to receive *only* the information of immediate relevance to them. The vendor also discovers that these areas of interest can change rapidly, requiring a rapid change in the material sent to the customers.

SGML Opportunity

This is similar to the situation in Section 5.3.5 but has more emphasis on the dynamic modification of selection criteria templates. A client interests template could be designed to capture the areas and subareas of interest to a particular client at any one time:

```
<client name = "Smith">
<topic>Information Technology
<urgent>SGML
<urgent>DSSSL
<exclude>Graphical User Interfaces
<exclude>Robotics
</client>
```

This could mean that "Client Smith is interested in the whole area of Information Technology. Any news concerning SGML or DSSSL should be marked as urgent. Anything to do with Graphical User Interfaces or Robotics is to be filtered out. All other Information Technology to be sent to Smith as normal priority news."

Benefits

This method allows for the precise specification of news selection criteria based on individual user requirements. The criteria are easily amended allowing rapid response to changing customer requirements.

5.3.7   Validated Cross References

Situation

A company is involved in the publication of "rules and regulations" books for the Health and Safety sector. These publications are highly structured and highly cross referenced both internally and externally (i.e., the text of Regulation Book A will make frequent references to other parts of Regulation Book A along with Regulation Books C, D, etc.). The company has identified a market for electronic versions of their books making extensive use of hypertext to help users follow the cross references.

SGML Opportunity

In order to facilitate converting cross references into hypertext, the documents could include addresses for every location likely to be the target of a cross reference. In hypertext parlance these addresses are typically known as locators[3] and the objects they locate are known as anchors. A cross-reference element type will be required to allow a cross reference to be included in the text.

One issue raised by using cross references is the need to ensure that all cross references point to a known address. SGML has a mechanism that helps achieve this. Consider the following DTD snippet:

```
<!ATTLIST para id  ID    #IMPLIED>
<!ATTLIST xref ref IDREF #REQUIRED>
```

The first declaration makes id an attribute of the **para** element type. It is declared to have a *declared value*[4] of type ID. ID is an example of an SGML attribute data type. It informs the parser that an attribute's value must be unique within the SGML document in which it occurs. In this example the attribute has been called "id" which is common SGML practice but any valid attribute name can be used.

The second declaration makes ref an attribute of the **xref** element type. It is declared to have a declared value of IDREF. IDREF is another example of an SGML attribute declared value. It informs the parser that values specified for this attribute must exist as values of an ID attribute somewhere else in the document (i.e., if it points somewhere, the thing it points to *must* exist). The net effect of the checking performed by the SGML parser in ID/IDREF pairs is that we have a self-checking basis for cross references.

A sample usage of ID/IDREF between two elements follows:

```
<regbook>
...
<para id = "P88">Pursuant to <xref ref = "P124">paragraph 124</xref>of this...
...
<para id = "P124">...
```

In graphical form, this snippet looks like that in Figure 5.6. Note that the parser checks ID/IDREFs within a *single* document instance. For linking between separate SGML documents, more powerful SGML-based mechanisms are employed (see Chapter 15—The HyTime Standard).

---

3. For more information on SGML as a basis for hypertext, see Chapter 15—The HyTime Standard.
4. See Chapter 6—Elements, Attributes, and Models.

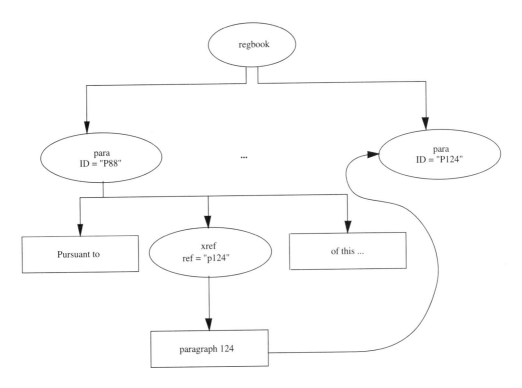

Figure 5.6 ID IDREF cross reference

Benefits

Using SGML frees the designer to describe cross-reference relationships in a way that is independent of the ultimate form in which that cross reference will be rendered (e.g., paper cross reference or hypertext link). SGML's ID/IDREF mechanism helps the process of validating these relationships.

Moreover, the programmable nature of SGML documents makes it feasible to semi-automate the process of creating cross references and locators. For example, an SGML-aware processing application could search for the text

```
Pursuant to Paragraph 2(b)
```

and replace it with

```
Pursuant to <xref ref = "p2b">paragraph 2(b)</xref>.
```

An SGML representation of the paragraph might look like this:

```
<para number = "2(b)">
This is paragraph 2(b)
```

which would make it easy to auto-generate a locator at this point "p2b."

For documents with a lot of cross references, this can represent a significant labor saving.

5.3.8   Print on Demand with Live Links

Situation

A company involved in performing maintenance on engines wishes to streamline the workflow involved. The maintenance procedures involved in a 50,000-mile service include some of the procedures performed for a 100,000-mile service. When the engineers know what level of service they are performing, they photocopy diagrams and procedures from the maintenance manuals to assemble a work schedule. Assembling a complete work schedule is made more difficult by the fact that the procedures to be performed are subject to constant update from the engine manufacturers.

SGML Opportunity

Uniquely identify each procedure and each diagram in the maintenance manuals. Design a DTD for the different levels of service, each consisting of a collection of references into the core maintenance manuals. (See Figure 5.7.)

Use SGML processing software to turn the service detail documents into work schedule documents that include everything required. After the maintenance, throw the document away and regenerate again as required. This ensures that all modifications made to maintenance procedures are taken into account each time the work schedules are generated.

Benefits

The benefits include a streamlined workflow via "print on demand" and reduced risk of using out-of-date information. The work schedules need not even be printed. They may be used to create simple electronic books or Interactive Electronic Technical Manuals (IETMs).

5.3.9   Automated Statistics Gathering

Situation

An organization that produces hundreds of hardware products and installation manuals is attempting to increase documentation quality. By polling clients, they find that a common complaint is the number of steps involved in the installation procedures. Management tells the documentation department that the following statistics will henceforth be required every month:

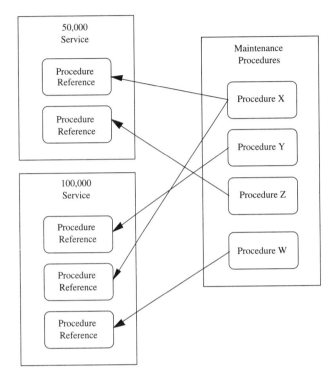

Figure 5.7 Linked service and
maintenance manuals

- Total number of installation procedures

- Total number of installation steps

- Average, maximum, and minimum number of installation procedures per product

- Average, maximum, and minimum number of steps in installation procedures

Management cannot understand why the technical writers say it will take several days *every month* to gather this data.

SGML Opportunity

When in SGML, with the notions of installation procedure and step made explicit via element types, gathering these statistics can be automated. A rudimentary model for an installation procedure might look like this:

```
<!ELEMENT instproc     - O (title,(step)+)>
<!ELEMENT (title,p)    - O (#PCDATA)>
<!ELEMENT step         - O (p)+>
```

When viewed as a hierarchical data structure, it is readily seen how an SGML-aware processing application could count the number of steps per **instproc** element, as shown in Figure 5.8.

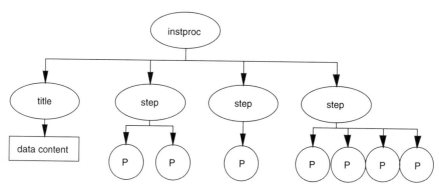

Figure 5.8 Hierarchical view of an installation procedure

Benefits

Automation of an otherwise time consuming and error prone manual task is possibly the greatest benefit. Conceptually, the process required to generate this report can be applied to any of the myriad of reports that can be contemplated once the SGML system is in place.

5.3.10   Electronic Forms

Situation

A government agency wishes to streamline the filing of forms related to company filings. It wishes to dispense with paper forms completely in favor of an electronic system. It has ruled out a relational database solution as not all the data fall easily into a rigid field structure (i.e., chairman's report, notes attached to the financial statements, etc.).

The agency wishes to

- Reduce the amount of time spent checking for forms that have not been correctly filled in.

- Be able to query the data on the forms intelligently.

- Publish a subset of the data for public consumption on the World Wide Web.

SGML Opportunity

The agency produces a DTD or perhaps a collection of DTDs that capture the structure of the various forms required. This DTD is then made publicly available. The agency establishes a rule that only documents that conform to this DTD will be accepted. Once accepted, the SGML documents are loaded into an SGML database for querying.

Benefits

The use of SGML allows the agency to "off-load" some of the problems relating to incorrectly completed forms back onto the filer. Because the DTD makes the semantic components of the forms content explicit, intelligent queries are possible (i.e., find all references to X that occur within a footnote to the accounts but not within the chairman's report).

Finally, by having the forms data in SGML, publishing a subset of the data to the Web is a straightforward down-translation.

5.3.11   Data-Feed Standardization

Situation

A company involved in the trading of financial instruments takes a number of different financial price "feeds" from various vendors. The feed formats are all proprietary to their respective vendors. The feeds are broadcast across the LAN with client software interpreting all the different feed formats at each workstation, as shown in Figure 5.9.

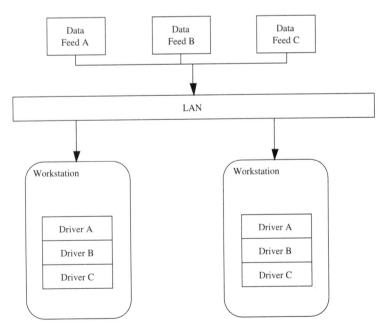

Figure 5.9 Data feed distribution architecture

When a new price feed is added, all the client software applications need to be updated. The organization is looking for a way to avoid downtime at the workstation end when new feeds are added to the system.

SGML Opportunity

All the proprietary feeds could be converted into a common structure in the form of an SGML document conforming to a price-feed DTD. A typical price feed might consist of prices for various commodities interspersed with time stamps. An individual price might be either a bid or an offer. A possible DTD for this price feed follows:

```
<!ELEMENT feed          - O (price|time)+>
<!ELEMENT price         - O (bid|offer)>
<!ATTLIST price
          COMM CDATA #REQUIRED
          UNITS (U16 U32 U10 U1) U1>
<!ELEMENT time          - O EMPTY>
<!ATTLIST time
          DD NUMBER #REQUIRED
          MM NUMBER #REQUIRED
          YY NUMBER #REQURIED
          HH NUMBER #REQUIRED
          MM NUMBER #REQURIED
          SS NUMBER #IMPLIED>
<!ELEMENT (bid,offer) - O (#PCDATA)>
```

There are a number of new things in this DTD. The SS attribute of the price element type is declared to have a *default value* of #IMPLIED (see Chapter 6—Elements, Attributes, and Models). This means that if a value for it is not supplied, that fact will be made known to the processing application, which can provide a value as it sees fit.

The units attribute of the **bid** and **offer** element types is declared to take one of four possible values, namely, U16, U32, U10, and U1. Furthermore, it defaults to the value U1.

With the DTD in place, converters can be developed that transform the proprietary feeds into price-feed documents. As always, the SGML parser can be used to validate the files that are up-translated from proprietary formats to SGML.

Next, a single price-feed handler can be installed in the client software that can deal with price-feed documents. The situation is shown in Figure 5.10.

Benefits

When a new feed is added, there is no need to modify client-side software or bring the system "down." Any data, irrespective of its source, will be handled by the client applications as long as it is a conforming price-feed document.

In developing a new filter application for a new price feed, developers can filter perhaps hundreds of megabytes of test data through to a price-feed document and then use an SGML parser to

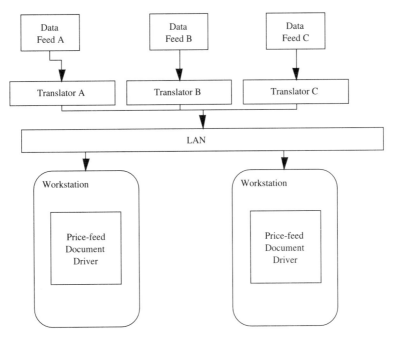

Figure 5.10 Data feed distribution architecture

validate it. Assuming that the client-side software handles price-feed documents correctly, developers can be confident that if it is acceptable to the parser, it will be acceptable to the client software as well.

Note, however, that there are obviously limits to the semantic checks the parser can perform automatically. For example, the parser will not complain if it sees a time stamp like this:

```
<time DD = 27 MM = 4 YY = 1965 HH = 4 MM = 61 SS = 234>
```

There will be more on this subject later on (see Section 13.3—Levels of Semantic Checking).

5.3.12   Multicultural Conventions

Situation

A multinational company is having problems with the interpretation of the content of office memoranda traveling between offices in different countries due to linguistic and cultural differences.

Mr. X Y from the Middle Eastern office is annoyed at the European office for thinking that his family name is Y when in fact it is X.

The French office gets confused when fractional figures are quoted using a decimal character (.) instead of a comma (,).

The English office is never sure what date the American office means when they get a fax dated 01/02/95. Does it mean the first day of February or the Second day of January?

SGML Opportunity

These problems are simple examples of how the interpretation of information implicit in the content of a document can change between languages and cultures. Making the content explicit is easy with SGML:

```
<person order = "FG"><Title>Mr.<GivenName>Y<FamilyName>X</person>
<person order = "GF"><Title>Mr.<GivenName>Mark<FamilyName>UpLang</person>
```

Here, an order attribute is used that can take the values "FG," denoting family name – given name order, or "GF," denoting given name – family name order.

We might capture dates this way:

```
<date day = "01" month = "02" year = "1995">
```

or alternatively this way:

```
<date><day>01<month>02<year>1995</date>
```

or even this way:

```
<date><day>01<month>02<century>19<year>95</date>
```

To solve the fractional figures problem we might use

```
<money>345<point>55</money>
```

or alternatively

```
<money units = "345" fraction = "55">
```

Benefits

SGML's information content–oriented representation of the data removes the possibility of an erroneous interpretation due to human assumptions inferred from the way the data have been formatted.

SGML-aware formatting applications can be used to guarantee correct ordering when the documents are published in different countries.

5.3.13   Context Preservation

Situation

A market research organization conducts research on everything from parser development tools for software developers to animal husbandry. They find that searching their database of information is producing irrelevant information (e.g., searches for words like *Bison* produce many irrelevant hits).

SGML Opportunity

This is somewhat similar to the last situation in that the normal full text search software hasn't got the context information required to distinguish between *bison* the compiler tool and *bison* the four-legged animal.

At this stage it will come as no surprise that the way to improve the utility of the search is to use SGML and explicitly tag the different contexts in which words are used:

```
<para>There are over 30 species of <animal>Bison</animal> in existence.
```

Also at this stage, it will be no surprise to know that there is more than one way to do it in SGML. A (possibly preferable) alternative is

```
<article domain = "Husbandry">
<para>There are over 30 species of Bison in existence.
<para>Not many users of the <domain = "software">Bison</domain> package know
      that.
```

In the first form, we explicitly mark the terms based on the interpretation we deem correct. In the second form, we mark the entire article based on its logical domain and mark only those terms where interpretation via the logical domain would be erroneous. Searching for all uses of the word *bison* in the context of husbandry can then be paraphrased as, "Find all **article** elements with domain="Husbandry" containing the word 'Bison.' Exclude those in which the node containing the word 'Bison' has a **domain** element ancestor."

Benefits

We benefit from a more intelligent searching of text than would be possible without SGML's information content adressability.[5]

5.3.14 Paper Document Computerization

Situation

An organization has a large collection of paper documents that it wishes to computerize. The documents are old legal texts and share a common structure, although there are many typographical differences and inconsistencies.

---

5. A search for *bison* on the World Wide Web yielded over 27,000 hits in over 60,000 documents. Hits 1 to 6 were for bison the software tool; hit 7 was for bison the animal.

The organization has tried OCR tools on the documents, but the results have not been satisfactory. They wish to outsource the data entry of the documents. However, they are worried about the amount of work that will be involved in checking the documents for accuracy when they return.

SGML Opportunity

The documents are of a single class—legal texts—and share a common structure. This should translate readily into a DTD. This DTD can then be supplied to the data entry vendor to use as a checking tool to monitor the structural accuracy of the documents.

Although no DTD will be capable of capturing all the semantics you may wish to enforce and will certainly not catch spelling mistakes and the like, validating a document is a useful first check and can be performed without human intervention.

Moreover, once in SGML, various document metrics can be computed that might help to locate data entry problems. For example, a heuristic analysis of the legal texts might yield some of the following rules of thumb:

Expect to find 3 footnotes for every 50 numbered paragraphs.
Level 3 headings never have more than 20 numbered paragraphs.
The average length of a sentence is 20 words.

Such rules can be translated into SGML queries to find exceptional situations, some of which may turn out to be the result of data-entry errors.

Benefits

The DTD provides the organization with a way of expressing the structure it wants the documents to conform to. Furthermore, the DTD acts as a way of communicating that structure to the data-entry vendor. Finally, the DTD acts as a partial but useful QA tool.

5.3.15   General-Purpose Data Validation

Situation

A developer is confronted with a 50-MB text file consisting of company name and contact information. There is no documentation available for the file format. A sample of the contents looks like this:

```
C:Acme
F:Sean
S:Mc Grath
C:UpLang Inc.
E:Smith@uplang.com
W:www.uplang.com
C:Acme Holdings
```

```
S:Smith
F:John
```

By analyzing a sample of the file the developer has guessed that the structure is as follows:

Every record consist of a company name (C), followed by either:
a) a first name (F) and a surname (S), in any order; or
b) an e-mail address (E) and a World Wide Web (W) address in any order.

The problem is to test if this hypothesis is correct and to provide documentation of the structure for future developers who will work with the file.

SGML Opportunity

SGML parsers can compare documents of arbitrary size against the DTDs they conform to. In other words, SGML parsers are useful, general-purpose data validation tools.

The first task is to convert the basic tagging in the file (e.g., C: for company name and F: for first name) into more typical SGML as follows:

```
<cname>Acme
<fname>Sean
<sname>Mc Grath
<cname>UpLang Inc.
<email>Smith@uplang.com
<www>www.uplang.com
```

This can trivially be achieved with a wide variety of tools ranging from text editors to awk, sed, Perl, python, and so on.

The next stage is to turn the English description of the reverse-engineered structure into an SGML DTD:

```
<!ELEMENT comps - O (cname,((fname&sname)|(email&www)))+>
<!ELEMENT cname - O (#PCDATA)>
<!ELEMENT fname - O (#PCDATA)>
<!ELEMENT sname - O (#PCDATA)>
<!ELEMENT email - O (#PCDATA)>
<!ELEMENT www   - O (#PCDATA)>
```

For convenience, the DTD and the data can be concatenated in the same physical file as follows:

```
C>type comps.sgm

<!DOCTYPE comps [
<!ELEMENT comps - O (cname,((fname&sname)|(email&www)))+>
<!ELEMENT cname - O (#PCDATA)>
<!ELEMENT fname - O (#PCDATA)>
<!ELEMENT sname - O (#PCDATA)>
<!ELEMENT email - O (#PCDATA)>
<!ELEMENT www - O (#PCDATA)>
]>
```

```
<comps>
<cname>Acme
<fname>Sean
<sname>Mc Grath
<cname>UpLang Inc.
<email>smith@uplang.com
<www>www.uplang.com
<cname>Acme Holdings
<sname>Smith
<fname>John
...
</comps>
```

The structure of the file can now be validated using a validating SGML parser:

```
C>nsgmls comps.sgm

(COMPS
(CNAME
-Acme
)CNAME
(FNAME
-Sean
)FNAME
(SNAME
-Mc Grath
)SNAME
(CNAME
-UpLang Inc.
)CNAME
(EMAIL
-Smith@uplang.com
)EMAIL
(WWW
-www.uplang.com
)WWW
(CNAME
-Acme Holdings
)CNAME
(SNAME
-Smith
)SNAME
(FNAME
-John
)FNAME
)COMPS
C
```

Note the C record at the very end of the ESIS output indicating conformance (i.e., no parser errors were encountered).

In situations where our interest centers around the presence or absence of errors, the ESIS records themselves are not of interest. The UNIX command

```
$nsgmls comp.sgm >/dev/null
```

ensures that the only output is the errors encountered, if any. An equivalent in DOS is

```
C>nsgmls comp.sgm >nul
```

Benefits

SGML allows us to rapidly develop models and automatically check the validity of these models against data. An alternative would be to hard-wire a structure-checking program in something like Perl. Apart from the extra time consumed by the latter approach, there can be the extra worry about errors introduced while creating the hard-wired structure checker.

5.3.16   Algorithmic Processing Support

Situation

A publisher is planning to publish a book on various family names detailing the history of the names. The book will have a number of different tables of contents breaking the names down by geography and frequency as well as listing them alphabetically. Names beginning with separate prefixes such as "Mc" and "Mac" are proving troublesome. So too are those that have rolled the prefix into a single word such as "Macken" and "Macey."

Part of the algorithm to be used follows: "Names with the prefix 'mac' rolled into the name are sorted based on their fourth letter. Names beginning with 'Mc' or 'Mac' are both to be treated as 'Mc' and sorted on the first letter of the main part of the name."

SGML Opportunity

There are a number of ways in which we might use SGML to solve this problem depending on how "intelligent" we want the SGML to be as opposed to the processing software. This is a common tension in SGML systems. Simply put, the question is, "Should the semantics be explicit in the SGML or is the implicit information sufficient to allow the processing application to work it out for itself?"

For example, we could use markup like this:

```
<name prefix = "Mac" main = "Grath">
<name prefix = "Mc" main = "Grath">
<name main = "Macgrath" >
```

This form of markup simply makes the prefix part explicit. It allows the processing application to work out the intended sort order.

Alternatively, the sortstring logic could be encoded in the SGML document itself:

```
<name prefix = "Mac" main = "Grath" sortas = "grath">
<name prefix = "Mc" main = "Grath" sortas = "grath">
<name main = "Macgrath" sortas = "grath">
```

Here a human being has determined the sorting order, thus making the processing software that much easier. This approach makes life simpler for the developer at the expense of complexity/ time at the authoring stage.

Note that this is not necessarily an "either/or" situation (i.e., processing software could encode the logic of the sort order but allow the SGML document to provide an override in situations where the sort order algorithm is found wanting). Natural language is a tricky data structure! It may prove more cost effective to use the algorithm to deal with the common cases and human intelligence for the exceptions.

Benefits

A sorting algorithm is easier to implement, thanks to the tokenization of the awkward names.

5.4   Classification of SGML Usage Strategies

In this and the preceding chapter, we have seen a variety of strategies for using SGML. One possible classification of these strategies is shown in Table 5.1.

Table 5.1: Classification of SGML usage strategies

Usage Strategy	Examples
Same content, different delivery formats	Automatic production of paper. World Wide Web and CD-ROM versions of documentation from a single set of source documents.
Same content, multiple occurrences	Data Normalization. Removal of duplicated content and "linking" a single copy back to the documents that require it.
Generated content	Combining authored text with text generated by SGML processing software.
Derived content	Creation of documents consisting purely of component parts of other documents.
Modeling/validation	Creation of data models with DTDs. The ability to use an SGML parser to automate the validation of data against models.

## CHAPTER 6

ELEMENTS, ATTRIBUTES, AND MODELS

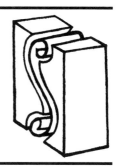

Note that we deal with the syntactical details of SGML in some detail in this and the following chapter. You may wish to read through them briskly as a first pass and return to the details as required later on.

6.1   Introduction

One of the things that can make SGML difficult to define succinctly is that, although it is very definitely a language in its own right—possessing its own syntax and semantics—it functions as a vehicle for the creation of *other* languages. A full SGML document consisting of an SGML declaration, a DTD, and a document instance is actually a language definition followed by a sentence in that language.

At the core of SGML's ability to define languages are the closely related ideas of *elements*, *attributes,* and *models.* We will look at them more closely in this chapter. Before doing so, it is important to understand how the syntax of SGML has been constructed and how it differs from syntax definitions of traditional programming languages.

6.2   The Philosophy of SGML Syntax

Part of the mission of SGML is to provide a machine-independent way of representing information. To do this requires a mechanism of dealing with the variety of native character sets likely to be encountered on different computers (i.e., ASCII, Extended ASCII, EBCDIC, and Unicode). The variety of character sets in existence, or likely to exist in the future, makes it desirable to avoid assigning particular significance to any one character code or character sequence. In other words, although the < character is typically used to designate SGML markup constructs, it is desirable that this not be hard-wired within the standard.[1]

---

1. The ANSI C standard addresses character set issues to some extent through the use of *trigraph sequences*, the three-letter codes that map to single-letter delimiters (i.e., "??=include <stdio.h>" is the same as "#include <stdio.h>").

To achieve this goal, SGML uses the notion of an *abstract syntax,* as illustrated in Figure 6.1.

The standard itself uses abstract names for delimiters. For example, the delimiter used to denote the opening of a start-tag is Start Tag Open known by the mnemonic STAGO. A given real-world implementation of SGML must provide a mapping from the abstract notion of an STAGO to a character sequence that will serve the required role. A collection of these mappings along with some other necessary information is referred to as a *concrete syntax.* The standard defines a particular concrete syntax known as the *Reference Concrete Syntax*, which is the one we will use in this book. The important thing to bear in mind is that whenever you see something like

```
<!ELEMENT foo - O (#PCDATA)>
```

much of the syntactic structure is under the control of the concrete syntax and can be changed if required. A document's concrete syntax is defined in its SGML declaration, which is discussed in detail in Appendix A—The SGML declaration.

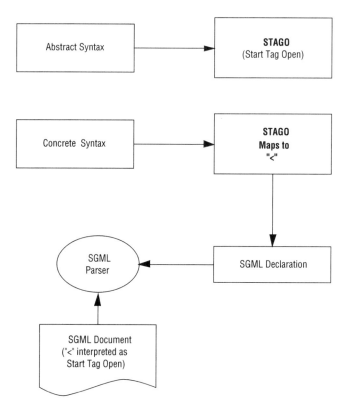

Figure 6.1 SGML's abstract syntax model

6.3   Element Type Declarations

In SGML, elements can be thought of as *keywords* or *primitive tokens* of the language being defined. Part of the definition of an element type is its *permissible content*. This spells out what elements and/or primitive text content is permitted within an element of the type and in what order the subcomponents can occur.

The overall syntax of an element type declaration is shown in Figure 6.2.

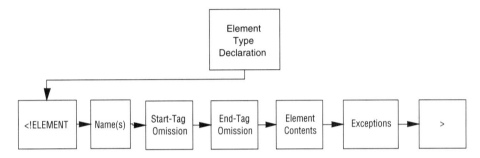

Figure 6.2 Structure of an element type declaration

6.3.1   Element Type Names

Element type names establish class identifiers by which the markup of elements of the type can subsequently be recognized. For example, after the definition

```
<!ELEMENT foo ...
```

the parser will be aware of the special meanings that may subsequently apply to the <foo> and </foo> character sequences.

The permissible length of element type names (also known as Generic Identifiers or GIs) is ultimately under the control of parser implementation and can be modified downward from any system limit via the SGML declaration if required. The case sensitivity of element type names is also controlled by the SGML declaration, although case-sensitive element type names are rarely used in practice. If case sensitivity is not enabled (the default) then element names are treated as if they were all uppercase:

```
C>type foo.sgm

<!DoctyPE test [
<!ELEment test   - O (AnElem)+>
<!eleMENT anelem - O empTY>
]>
<test>
<ANELEM>
```

```
<anelem>
<anELEM>
</test>

C>nsgmls foo.sgm

(TEST
(ANELEM
)ANELEM
(ANELEM
)ANELEM
(ANELEM
)ANELEM
)TEST
C
```

Note that the element type name length specified in the SGML declaration is *enforced* by the parser. This contrasts with the behavior of many programming languages that impose similar constraints on the length of identifiers *silently* (i.e., if the maximum identifier length is **N** then only the first **N** characters are significant for symbol table purposes and the rest are discarded). This is not the case with SGML.

6.3.2   Start/End-Tag Omission

Following the element type name and one or more parameter separator characters[2] comes the start-tag minimization field. This must be either a dash (-) meaning no omission allowed or O (capital oh) meaning omission allowed. The end-tag omission field that immediately follows it is handled similarly.

6.3.3   Element Contents

The meat of the element type declaration begins here. We have encountered the two main forms of element content prescription already. First, we have seen element types whose instances contain nothing (i.e., the so-called "empty" elements[3]) as well as the element types that can contain something (i.e., a mixture of text denoted by the keyword #PCDATA[4] and additional elements). The latter case is the most common and is known as a *content model*. The content model consists of a *model group* along with optional exceptions to the model group known as *inclusion* and *exclusion* exceptions. We will return to these later; for now we concentrate on the core model.

---

2. Essentially white space.
3. Technically, an EMPTY element is an example of an element with a *declared content* as opposed to an element with a content model. We will return to this topic later in this chapter.
4. There will be more on the precise interpretation of #PCDATA later.

In order to allow elements to represent the rich hierarchical and recursive structures found in documents, model groups may themselves contain other model groups and can also be recursive. The syntax used is reminiscent of that used in regular expressions with some important differences. In Table 6.1, we will start with some examples to give you a feel for how content models work and then move on to the details.

Table 6.1: Content model examples

Example	Interpretation
X*	Zero or more Xs
X+	One or more Xs
X?	One or zero Xs
X , Y	X followed by Y
X | Y	X or Y
X & Y	X followed by Y **or** Y followed by X
(X , Y , Z?)	X followed by Y followed by an optional Z
(X | Y+ | Z)	X or one or more Ys or Z
(X | (Y? , Z))	One of: X Optional Y followed by Z
(Z? | (X , B+))	One of: Optional Z X followed by one or more Bs
(X | Y)+	One or more occurrences of: Either X or Y
#PCDATA	PCDATA (basically data content)
(#PCDATA | X)*	Zero or more occurrences of: PCDATA or X

A simplified BNF-like description of the production rules used to define model groups follows:

```
mgroup      ::= content ( connector , content )* occurr?
content     ::= primitive | mgroup
primitive   ::= #PCDATA | (GenericIdentifier , occurr?)
connector   ::= AND | OR | SEQ
occurr      ::= OPT | PLUS | REP
OPT         ::= "?"
PLUS        ::= "+"
REP         ::= "*"
AND         ::= "&"
OR          ::= "|"
SEQ         ::= ","
```

6.3.3.1   Connectors

The connector types provided are shown in Table 6.2.

Table 6.2: Connector types

Connector	Example	Explanation
SEQ	A , B	A followed by B
OR	A I B	A or B
AND	A & B	(A , B) I (B , A)

Note in Table 6.2 that, even though the examples use two operands A and B, any number of operarands > 2 are allowed. Note also that all connectors must be the same at any one level in a model group. For example,

```
A | B , C
```

is illegal. The standard does not use precedence rules to disambiguate the connectors, which, in this example, could be construed to mean

```
(A | (B , C))
```

or

```
((A | B) , C)
```

The precedence between connectors must always be made explicit through the use of brackets.

6.3.3.2   Occurrence Indicators

Unlike connectors, occurrence indicators are unary operators operating on a single element or model group, as shown in Table 6.3. They have higher precedence than connector operators. For example,

```
A | B +
```

is interpreted as

```
(A) | ((B)+)
```

Table 6.3: Occurrence indicators

Occurrence Indicator	Example	Explanation
OPT	A?	A or nothing
PLUS	A+	A, one or more times
REP	A*	A, zero or more times

6.3.3.3　*Primitive Content Token*

A primitive content token is either the name of an element type or #PCDATA. The keyword #PCDATA stands for Parsed Character Data and indicates the presence of data characters after parsing for all markup.

6.3.4　Exceptions

Exceptions come in two flavors, inclusions and exclusions.

6.3.4.1　*Inclusions*

Inclusions provide a convenient way of specifying that a given element type can occur anywhere within a hierarchy of elements. It must be said that they can also be an accident waiting to happen because of the far-reaching implications they have for the overall structure of the DTD (more on this topic later). In the following document model (DTD), an **A** element can occur at *all* levels within the **body** element:

```
<!DOCTYPE test [
<!ELEMENT test -    O (BODY)>
<!ELEMENT BODY - O (A)*>
<!ELEMENT A    - O (A | B)*>
<!ELEMENT C    - O (A | B | C)*>
<!ELEMENT D    - O (A | B | C | D)*>
]>
<test>
<BODY>
<A>
</test>
```

The same effect can be achieved by factoring **A** out of the individual element type declaration levels and including it once at the **body** level as follows:

```
<!DOCTYPE test [
<!ELEMENT test -    O (BODY)>
<!ELEMENT BODY - O (A)* +(A)>
<!ELEMENT A - O (B)*>
<!ELEMENT C - O (B | C)*>
<!ELEMENT D - O (B | C | D)*>
]>
<test>
<BODY>
<A>
</test>
```

Note the far-reaching effect of the inclusion. Essentially every model group occurring below the inclusion point in the hierarchy *inherits* the inclusion.

Debate on the merits/demerits of inclusions is an institution in the SGML world. It is reminiscent in some ways of the perennial debate about the use of goto statements in programming languages. The issues are discussed further in a number of sections in Chapter 13.

6.3.4.2   Exclusions

Exclusions are analogous to inclusions but have the effect of excluding specified element types from model groups. Perhaps their most common application is the removal of unwanted recursion in model groups. The following example illustrates a situation where an exclusion is useful:

```
<!DOCTYPE test [
<!ELEMENT test   - O (block)+>
<!ELEMENT block  - O (para|table)+>
<!ELEMENT table  - O (cell+)>
<!ELEMENT cell   - O (block+)>
<!ELEMENT para   - O (#PCDATA)>
]>
<test>
<block>
<para>Paragraph text
<table>
<cell><block><para>Cell  1</block></cell>
<cell><block><para>Cell  2</block></cell>
</table>
</block>
</test>
```

Here the reuse of the **block** element type as the **cell** component opens up the possibility of tables within tables, which is not desirable. An exclusion can remedy the situation cleanly:

```
<!ELEMENT cell - O (block+) -(table)>
```

Note that, as with inclusions, exclusions are inherited by every model group and every piece of PCDATA occurring below the exclusion point in the document hierarchy.

6.3.5   Comments

Comments within markup declarations start and end with a **COM** delimiter (-- in the Reference Concrete Syntax):

```
<!ELEMENT foo - O EMPTY -- This is a comment about foo -->
```

A markup declaration with nothing but comments, known as a comment declaration looks like this:

```
<!-- This declaration is a comment declaration -->
```

6.4 Attributes

We have already encountered some simple examples of attributes. In broad terms, attributes are used to hold auxiliary information that further qualifies the meaning of an element. Deciding whether to make a piece of information an attribute or an element is not subject to any hard and fast rules. For example, if a document contains details of apples and oranges each of which have associated varieties and weights, we might use this markup:

```
<!DOCTYPE test [
<!ELEMENT test - O (apple,orange)+>
<!ELEMENT (apple,orange) - O EMPTY>
<!ATTLIST (apple,orange)
      variety CDATA #REQUIRED
      weight  CDATA #REQUIRED>
]>
<test>
<apple  variety = "Granny Smith" weight = "10">
<orange variety = "Orange Glory" weight = "14">
</test>
```

Here, the distinction between apple and orange is established at the element level. An alternative document type follows:

```
<!DOCTYPE test [
<!ELEMENT test  - O (fruit)+>
<!ELEMENT fruit - O EMPTY>
<!ATTLIST fruit
      type    CDATA #REQUIRED
      variety CDATA #REQUIRED
      weight  CDATA #REQUIRED>
]>
<test>
<fruit type ="apple"  variety = "Granny Smith" weight = "10">
<fruit type ="orange" variety = "Orange Glory" weight = "14">
</test>
```

This time the distinction between apple and orange is made by qualifying a more general element type **fruit**. A third alternative that dispenses with attributes altogether follows:

```
<!DOCTYPE test [
<!ELEMENT test  - O (fruit)+>
<!ELEMENT fruit - O (type,variety,weight)>
<!ELEMENT (type,variety,weight) - O (#PCDATA)>
]>
<test>
<fruit><type>apple<variety>Granny Smith<weight>10
<fruit><type>orange<variety>Orange Glory<weight>14
</test>
```

One factor that can influence the element-or-attribute decision is the amount of semantic checking the parser can perform on documents. A limited variety of attribute types are available. They allow the parser to ensure that values are supplied, that they are of the correct data type, and so on.

The (slightly simplified) general form of attribute definitions is shown in Figure 6.3.

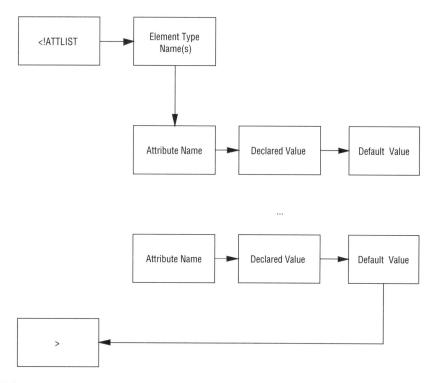

Figure 6.3 Structure of an attribute list declaration

Element Type Name(s)

The element type name specifies the name or names of element types that this attribute definition list declaration refers to. If there is more than one element type name they are surrounded by parentheses and are separated by any of the connectors *AND*, *OR*, or *SEQ*. For example,

```
<!ATTLIST foo ...
<!ATTLIST (foo,bar)...
<!ATTLIST (foo|bar)...
```

The last two examples are equivalent.

Attribute Name

The attribute name is the name of the attribute being declared.

Declared Value

The declared value specifies the allowable "data types" for the value of an attribute.

Default Value

The default value provides control over the mechanisms whereby an attribute value can be specified or inferred either within the SGML document itself or when the application processes the SGML document after it is parsed.

We now look at declared values and default values in greater detail.

6.4.1   Attribute Declared Values

SGML provides 15 "data types" for specifying the permissible values of attributes.

6.4.1.1   CDATA ("character data")

CDATA is the most common form of attribute declared value. Essentially it says that the attribute value consists of a string of characters.

```
C>type foo.sgm

<!DOCTYPE test [
<!ELEMENT test - O (#PCDATA)>
<!ATTLIST test t1 CDATA #REQUIRED>
]>
<test t1 = "foo">
</test>

C>nsgmls foo.sgm

AT1 CDATA foo
(TEST
)TEST
C
```

Note that CDATA attribute values can be empty:

```
C>type foo.sgm

<!DOCTYPE test [
<!ELEMENT test - O (#PCDATA)>
<!ATTLIST test t1 CDATA #REQUIRED>
]>
<test t1 = "">
</test>
```

```
C>nsgmls foo.sgm

AT1 CDATA
(TEST
)TEST
C
```

Note also that, if the value does not contain characters that could be misconstrued as separators, the quotes can be omitted:

```
C>type foo.sgm

<!DOCTYPE test [
<!ELEMENT test - O (#PCDATA)>
<!ATTLIST test t1 CDATA #REQUIRED>
]>
<test t1 = Hello>
</test>

C>nsgmls foo.sgm

AT1 CDATA Hello
(TEST
)TEST
C
```

However, the following is invalid:

```
C>type foo.sgm

<!DOCTYPE test [
<!ELEMENT test - O (#PCDATA)>
<!ATTLIST test t1 CDATA #REQUIRED>
]>
<test t1 = Hello World>
</test>

C>nsgmls foo.sgm

foo.sgm:5:23:E: 'WORLD' is not a member of a group specified for any attribute
```

6.4.1.2   *ID/IDREF/IDREFS*

The ID and IDREF declared values provide a mechanism for referencing one element in a document from another in the same document so that the parser can validate the reference. In other words, the parser can ensure that, for every value in an IDREF or IDREFS attribute, there is an ID attribute in the document with the same value.

```
C>type foo.sgm

<!DOCTYPE test [
<!ELEMENT test - O (#PCDATA|P1|P2)+>
<!ELEMENT P1   - O (#PCDATA)>
<!ATTLIST P1 id ID #REQUIRED>
```

```
<!ELEMENT P2    - O EMPTY>
<!ATTLIST P2 idref IDREF #REQUIRED>
]>
<test>
<p1 id = "id1">I am known by the ID "ID1"
<p2 idref = "id1">I am a reference to the element with ID "ID1"
</test>
C>nsgmls foo.sgm

(TEST
AID TOKEN ID1
(P1
-I am known by the ID "ID1"
)P1
AIDREF TOKEN ID1
(P2
)P2
-I am a reference to the element with ID "ID1"
)TEST
C
```

Note that by default NSGMLS reports the attribute as being of type TOKEN. NSGMLS reports TOKEN attributes for a large subset of the permissible declared values. There will be more on this later.

If the P1 element's id attribute is changed as follows:

```
<p1 id = "id2">I am known by the ID ID2
<p2 idref = "id1">I am a reference to ID "ID1"
```

the parser produces an error message at the p2 element because it cannot "resolve" the reference from p2 to an ID with the value ID1:

```
C>nsgmls foo.sgm

foo.sgm:10:14:E: IDREF = "ID1" IDREF attribute ignored: referenced ID does not
      exist
```

An attempt to assign the same value to two ID attributes also produces an error:

```
C>type foo.sgm
<!DOCTYPE test [
<!ELEMENT test - O (#PCDATA|P1|P2)+>
<!ELEMENT P1    - O (#PCDATA)>
<!ATTLIST P1 id ID #REQUIRED>
<!ELEMENT P2    - O EMPTY>
<!ATTLIST P2 id ID #REQUIRED>
]>
<test>
<p1 id = "id1">I am known by the ID location ID1
<p2 id = "id1">I am also known by the ID location ID1
</test>
```

```
C>nsgmls foo.sgm

foo.sgm:10:11:E 'ID1' already defined
foo.sgm:9:11: ID 'ID1' first defined here
```

6.4.1.3   ENTITY/ENTITIES

ENTITY/ENTITIES can be used to specify that an attribute contains a single ENTITY or multiple ENTITY names. The entity must be either a subdocument entity (discussed in Section 14.5) or a data entity (discussed in Chapter 7).

6.4.1.4   NUMBER/NUMBERS

NUMBER/NUMBERS can be used to specify that an attribute's value is a number or a list of numbers. For example,

```
<!DOCTYPE test [
<!ELEMENT test - O (#PCDATA)>
<!ATTLIST test n NUMBER #REQUIRED>
]>
<test n = 12345689>
</test>
```

Note that attribute value types are lexical types, not data types. Therefore, declaring an attribute to be of type NUMBER restricts the characters allowed within the value to the digits 0–9 but does not impose a numerical interpretation on the attribute value. For example,

```
C>type foo.sgm

<!DOCTYPE test [
<!ELEMENT test - O (A,A)>
<!ELEMENT A - O EMPTY>
<!ATTLIST a n NUMBER #REQUIRED>
]>
<test>
<a n = 1>
<a n = 01>
</test>

C>nsgmls foo.sgm

(TEST
AN TOKEN 1
(A
)A
AN TOKEN 01
(A
)A
)TEST
C
```

Both instances of the attribute n are checked to be numbers but the 01 is not reduced to the numerically equivalent token 1. Quotation marks can be used to delimit NUMBER attributes if required. In the case of NUMBERS—a list of NUMBER tokens—the quotation marks are mandatory.

Note also that negative real numbers are not supported and that the maximum size of a number is dictated by a parameter in the SGML declaration.

6.4.1.5   *NMTOKEN/NMTOKENS (Name Tokens)*

Name tokens are used for attribute values that must contain only so-called name characters. These characters are valid in the creation of names such as element type names and attribute names. The exact characters allowed are determined by the SGML declaration (see Appendix A—The SGML Declaration).

6.4.1.6   *NUTOKEN/NUTOKENS (Number Tokens)*

Number tokens are used for attribute values that must begin with a digit but thereafter can contain any name characters. For example,

```
<!DOCTYPE TEST [
<!ELEMENT TEST - O EMPTY>
<!ATTLIST test
        A1 NUTOKEN #REQUIRED
        A2 NUTOKEN #REQUIRED
        A3 NUTOKEN #REQUIRED>
]>
<TEST a1 = "12" a2 = "1qqq" a3 = "1-foo">
```

6.4.1.7   *NAME/NAMES*

NAME is similar to NMTOKEN but with some further restrictions on the first character. Essentially, it must begin with either a lowercase or uppercase letter.

6.4.1.8   *Name Token Group*

The name token group is the form of attribute declared value that has the following general format:

```
<!ATTLIST e a (v1,v2...vn)>
```

Here, **e** is the element type, **a** is the attribute name, and **v1** to **vn** are a list of permissible NMTOKENS for the attribute. For example,

```
C>type foo.sgm

<!DOCTYPE test [
<!ELEMENT test - O (#PCDATA)>
```

```
<!ATTLIST test fruit (apple,orange,banana) #REQUIRED>
]>
<test fruit = apple>
</test>

C>nsgmls foo.sgm

AFRUIT TOKEN APPLE
(TEST
)TEST
C
```

Attempting to use any value other than those prescribed produces a parser error:

```
C>type foo.sgm

<!DOCTYPE test [
<!ELEMENT test - O (#PCDATA)>
<!ATTLIST test fruit (apple,orange,banana) #REQUIRED>
]>
<test fruit = grape>
</test>

C>nsgmls foo.sgm
foo.sgm:5:15:E FRUIT = "grape" attribute value defaulted: token not in group
```

6.4.1.9   NOTATION

NOTATION specifies that the attribute is a NOTATION name. NOTATIONs are discussed in Chapter 7.

6.4.2   Attribute Default Value

The attribute default value provides control over two things. First, it allows control over when an attribute must be specified and when it can be omitted. Second, it allows control over what the default value will be if it *is* omitted, as shown in Figure 6.4.

6.4.3   #REQUIRED as Default Value

#REQUIRED is the default value we have encountered most often so far. It makes it imperative that a value be supplied for an attribute. A parser error will be generated if it is omitted.

6.4.4   Attribute Value Specification as Default Value

By specifying an attribute value specification, the attribute is given a default value in the event that the document instance does not supply one. For example,

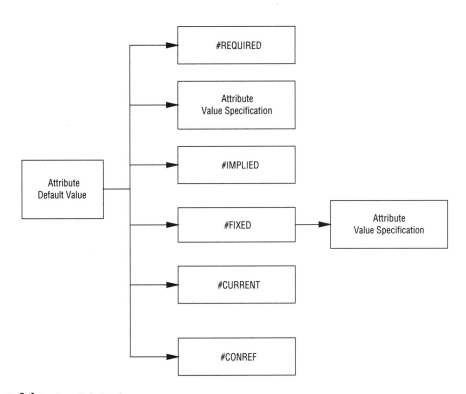

Figure 6.4 Attribute default value syntax

```
C>type foo.sgm

<!DOCTYPE test [
<!ELEMENT test - O (#PCDATA)>
<!ATTLIST test fruit (apple,orange,banana) apple>
]>
<test>
</test>
```

Here the fruit attribute is declared to take values from the name token group (apple, orange,banana). In the event that no value is supplied, it defaults to apple:

```
C>nsgmls foo.sgm

AFRUIT TOKEN APPLE
(TEST
)TEST
C
```

6.4.5   #IMPLIED as Default Value

#IMPLIED leaves it up to the processing application to imply a suitable value for an attribute in the event that one is not supplied. For example,

```
C>type foo.sgm

<!DOCTYPE test [
<!ELEMENT test - O (t)*>
<!ELEMENT t - O EMPTY>
<!ATTLIST t foo CDATA #IMPLIED>
]>
<test>
<t>
<t foo = "bar">
</test>

C>nsgmls foo.sgm

(TEST
AFOO IMPLIED
(T
)T
AFOO CDATA bar
(T
)T
)TEST
C
```

Note that the side effect of the #IMPLIED attribute is that the ESIS stream does not contain a declared value (in this case CDATA) when the attribute is not specified.

6.4.6   #FIXED as Default Value

#FIXED specifies that the value of the attribute is to be fixed to the value supplied in the DTD. Any attempt to specify a value other than the fixed value within the document is flagged as an error:

```
C>type foo.sgm

<!DOCTYPE test [
<!ELEMENT test - O (t)*>
<!ELEMENT t - O EMPTY>
<!ATTLIST t foo CDATA #FIXED "24">
]>
<test>
<t>
<t foo = "22">
</test>

C>nsgmls foo.sgm >nul

foo.sgm:8:13:E: value of fixed attribute 'FOO' not equal to default
```

The following example is valid. The assignment to foo in the second **t** element is valid because the value assigned is equal to the value fixed in the DTD.

```
C>type foo.sgm

<!DOCTYPE test [
<!ELEMENT test - O (t)*>
<!ELEMENT t - O EMPTY>
<!ATTLIST t foo CDATA #FIXED "24">
]>
<test>
<t>
<t foo = "24">

C>nsgmls foo.sgm

(TEST
AFOO CDATA 24
(T
)T
AFOO CDATA 24
(T
)T
)TEST
C
```

6.4.7   #CURRENT as Default Value

#CURRENT is used to allow an attribute to "inherit" the most recently assigned value in the event that none is supplied:

```
C>type foo.sgm

<!DOCTYPE test [
<!ELEMENT test - O (t)*>
<!ELEMENT t - O EMPTY>
<!ATTLIST t foo CDATA #CURRENT>
]>
<test>
<t foo = "3">
<t>
<t foo = "4">
<t>
</test>
```

In this example, the value of foo is initialized to "3" in the first occurrence of the **t** element. The second occurrence will inherit the "3." The third establishes a new value for foo of "4," which is then inherited by the fourth occurrence of **t** as can be seen in the ESIS:

```
C>nsgmls foo.sgm

(TEST
AFOO CDATA 3
(T
)T
AFOO CDATA 3
(T
)T
AFOO CDATA 4
(T
)T
AFOO CDATA 4
(T
)T
)TEST
C
```

Note that the use of #CURRENT makes it an error not to specify a value for the attribute's first occurrence. In effect, the attribute is #REQUIRED for its first occurrence, and the latest value assigned is used thereafter.

```
C>type foo.sgm

<!DOCTYPE test [
<!ELEMENT test - O (t)*>
<!ELEMENT t - O EMPTY>
<!ATTLIST t foo CDATA #CURRENT>
]>
<test>
<t>
<t foo = "4">
</test>

C>nsgmls foo.sgm >nul

foo.sgm:7:3:E: first occurrence of current attribute 'FOO' not specified
```

6.4.8   #CONREF as Default Value

#CONREF is used in situations where it is required to allow/disallow content in an element based on whether or not one of its attributes has been assigned a value. This is best explained by example.

Imagine a situation where a glossary is being marked up in SGML. The terms "PC" and "Personal Computer" are encountered in the text. The desired format for the glossary follows:

Personal Computer - A desktop based machine consisting of…

…

PC- see "Personal Computer"

Clearly, some glossary elements will consist of definitions while others will consist solely of a *reference* to another glossary element.

The text is marked up as follows:

```
C>type gloss.sgm

<!DOCTYPE test [
<!ELEMENT test  - O (gloss)*>
<!ELEMENT gloss - O (#PCDATA)>
<!ATTLIST gloss
          term    CDATA #REQUIRED
          id      ID #IMPLIED
          termref IDREF #IMPLIED>
]>
<test>
<gloss TERMREF = "G-PERCOM" term = "PC">
<gloss id = "G-PERCOM" term = "Personal Computer">A desktop based machine
        consisting of...
</test>

C>nsgmls gloss.sgm

(TEST
ATERM CDATA PC
AID IMPLIED
ATERMREF TOKEN G-PERCOM
(GLOSS
)GLOSS
ATERM CDATA Personal Computer
AID TOKEN G-PERCOM
ATERMREF IMPLIED
(GLOSS
-A desktop based machine consisting of...
)GLOSS
)TEST
C
```

The problem is that, as it stands, nothing prevents the first gloss element from actually having content, as shown here:

```
C>type gloss.sgm

<!DOCTYPE test [
<!ELEMENT test  - O (gloss)*>
<!ELEMENT gloss - O (#PCDATA)>
<!ATTLIST gloss
          term    CDATA #REQUIRED
          id      ID #IMPLIED
          termref IDREF #IMPLIED>
]>
<test>
<gloss TERMREF = "G-PERCOM" term = "PC">A computer with...
```

```
<gloss id = "G-PERCOM" term = "Personal Computer">A desktop based machine
      consisting of...
</test>
```

By modifying the definition of the termref attribute from #IMPLIED to #CONREF we can get the parser to catch this problem for us. Informally, the use of #CONREF allows us to say, "If the attribute is given a value, then there can be no content in the element. In other words, the element will be treated as if its declared content is EMPTY." The document now looks like this:

```
C>type gloss.sgm

<!DOCTYPE test [
<!ELEMENT test  - O (gloss)*>
<!ELEMENT gloss - O (#PCDATA)>
<!ATTLIST gloss
           term    CDATA #REQUIRED
           id      ID    #IMPLIED
           termref IDREF #CONREF>
]>
<test>
<gloss TERMREF = "G-PERCOM" term = "PC">A Personal Computer is a...
<gloss id = "G-PERCOM" term = "Personal Computer">A desktop based machine
      consisting of...
</test>

C>nsgmls gloss.sgm

gloss.sgm:10:41:E Character data not allows here.
```

Removing the erroneous text after the first gloss element yields the correct document:

```
C>type gloss.sgm

<!DOCTYPE test [
<!ELEMENT test  - O (gloss)*>
<!ELEMENT gloss - O (#PCDATA)>
<!ATTLIST gloss
           term    CDATA #REQUIRED
           id      ID    #IMPLIED
           termref IDREF #IMPLIED>
]>
<test>
<gloss TERMREF = "G-PERCOM" term = "PC">
<gloss id = "G-PERCOM" term = "Personal Computer">A desktop based machine
      consisting of...
</test>
```

The ESIS output looks like this:

```
(TEST
ATERM CDATA PC
AID IMPLIED
ATERMREF TOKEN G-PERCOM
```

```
(GLOSS
)GLOSS
ATERM CDATA Personal Computer
AID TOKEN G-PERCOM
ATERMREF IMPLIED
(GLOSS
-A desktop based machine consisting of...
)GLOSS
)TEST
C
```

6.5   Some Details

6.5.1   Attribute Definition List Declaration

There can be only one attribute definition list declaration for a given element. The following declaration is illegal:

```
<!DOCTYPE test [
<!ELEMENT test -    O EMPTY>
<!ATTLIST test A CDATA #IMPLIED>
<!ATTLIST test B CDATA #IMPLIED>
]>
<test>
```

The correct declaration looks like this:

```
<!DOCTYPE test [
<!ELEMENT test -    O EMPTY>
<!ATTLIST test A CDATA #IMPLIED
              B CDATA #IMPLIED>
]>
<test>
```

6.5.2   Duplicate Name Token Values

The following attribute definition list declaration is illegal:

```
C>type foo.sgm

<!DOCTYPE test [
<!ELEMENT test - O (#PCDATA)>
<!ATTLIST test a (yes,no) yes
              b (yes,no) yes>
]>
<test a = "yes" b = "no">
</test>

C>nsgmls foo.sgm >nul
```

```
foo.sgm:4:25:E: token 'YES' occurs more than once in attribute definition list
foo.sgm:4:25:E: token 'NO' occurs more than once in attribute definition list
```

The rule is that a name token can only be a valid name token for one attribute of a given element. This rule is a consequence of an SGML markup minimization feature, which allows a parser to *infer* which attribute is being assigned a value from a syntax such as:

```
<test yes>
```

In the example, "yes" satisfies both attributes a and b and thus the parser would not be able to decide which one the "yes" refers to (see Section 14.6—Markup Minimization Methods).

A workaround using entities will be presented in the next chapter.

6.5.3   Minimum Size of #PCDATA

The keyword #PCDATA means 0 or more parsed character data characters. There is no way to guarantee that data will be entered into a #PCDATA segment of a document. For example,

```
<!DOCTYPE test [
<!ELEMENT test - O (#PCDATA)>
]>
<test></test>
```

is a perfectly valid document.

6.5.4   Attribute Value Delimiters

In this chapter we have used double quote characters to delimit attribute values. Single quotes may also be used:

```
C>type foo.sgm

<!DOCTYPE test [
<!ELEMENT test - O (#PCDATA)>
<!ATTLIST test a1 CDATA #REQUIRED
               a2 CDATA #REQUIRED>
]>
<test a1 = "Hello's World" a2 = 'Hello"s World'></test>

C>nsgmls foo.sgm

AA1 CDATA Hello's World
AA2 CDATA Hello"s World
(TEST
)TEST
C
```

Technically, the attribute value delimiters are known by the abstract syntax names LIT and LITA.

6.5.5   Modular DTDs

DTDs can get large and can benefit from the modularization techniques typically found in programming languages and preprocessors. In the next chapter we will see ways of doing this with SGML entities.

6.5.6   Document Type Declaration Subset

In the short examples used in this chapter, we have used the syntax in which the DTD and the document both physically exist in the same file. It is more usual to find the DTD stored externally using a syntax such as this:

```
<!DOCTYPE test SYSTEM "test.dtd">
<test>
...
</test>
```

Even when this form of syntax is used, it is possible to declare elements/attributes and a variety of other things for use *solely* within the confines of the document at hand:

```
C>type test.dtd

<!ELEMENT test - O (#PCDATA)>

C>type test.sgm

<!DOCTYPE test SYSTEM "test.dtd" [
<!ATTLIST test local CDATA #REQUIRED>
]>
<test local = "foo">
</test>
```

Here the **test** element type is modified with the addition of a local attribute in what is known as the *document type declaration internal subset*.

6.5.7   The ANY Keyword

The use of the ANY keyword instead of a model group in an element type declaration indicates to the parser that the content model of the element is effectively

```
(#PCDATA | e1 | e2 |...en)*
```

where **e1** to **en** are all the element types declared in the DTD. For example,

```
<!DOCTYPE test [
<!ELEMENT test -     O ANY>
<!ELEMENT (apple,orange,banana) - O (#PCDATA)>
]>
```

```
<test>
<apple>
<banana>
<apple>
<apple>
```

is a valid document. The ANY keyword is typically used solely during DTD development.

6.5.8   Declared Content Variations

Apart from the keyword EMPTY indicating that an element contains no content at all, it is possible to declare elements with a declared content of CDATA or RCDATA. An element type with CDATA declared content is one in which the parser does not look inside the content for special characters such as the various SGML delimiters. The only character sequence interpreted by the parser is the one that will *terminate* an element:

```
C>type foo.sgm

<!DOCTYPE test [
<!ELEMENT test - O CDATA>
]>
<test>This is not a <tag></test>

C>nsgmls foo.sgm

(TEST
-This is not a <tag>
)TEST
C
```

An element with RCDATA declared content is similar except that as well as recognizing the sequence required to terminate an element, it also recognizes entity and character references (discussed in the next chapter).

Note that as a result of tags not being recognized in elements with CDATA and RCDATA declared content, inclusions are not valid as part of their declaration.[5] (More information on CDATA/RCDATA declared content appears in Section 13.8—Data Content Variations.)

6.5.9   Priority of Inclusions and Exclusions

If a "Race Condition" exists between an inclusion and an exclusion (i.e., if an element X is both included and excluded from an element Y), it is treated as an exclusion of Y.

---

5. Naturally, inclusions and exclusions are also inapplicable to EMPTY elements.

6.5.10   Ordering of Attribute Value Specifications

The order in which attribute values are supplied in a document instance is not significant. They will be passed to the SGML-processing application in the order they were defined in the DTD:

```
C>type foo.sgm

<!DOCTYPE test [
<!ELEMENT test - O (t)+>
<!ELEMENT t - O EMPTY>
<!ATTLIST t
    a CDATA #IMPLIED
    b CDATA #IMPLIED
    c CDATA #IMPLIED>
]>
<test>
<t>
<t b = "b val">
<t c = "c val" a = "a val">
</test>

C>nsgmls foo.sgm

(TEST
AA IMPLIED
AB IMPLIED
AC IMPLIED
(T
)T
AA IMPLIED
AB CDATA b val
AC IMPLIED
(T
)T
AA CDATA a val
AB IMPLIED
AC CDATA c val
(T
)T
)TEST
C
```

6.5.11   Declared Values Passed Through by NSGMLS

Of the 15 attribute declared values, only CDATA, NOTATION, and ENTITY are passed through by NSGMLS by default. All others receive the more generic term TOKEN.

6.5.12   End-Tag Omission for EMPTY Elements

Element types with a declared content of EMPTY should be declared with end-tag omission enabled:

```
C>type foo.sgm

<!DOCTYPE TEST [
<!ELEMENT TEST - - EMPTY>
]>
<TEST>
```

This document will parse with NSGMLS. However, if full warnings are enabled with the -w all option we get an error message:

```
C>nsgmls -w all test.sgm

test.sgm:2:20:W: end-tag minimization should be 'O' for element with declared
          content of EMPTY
```

Note also that end-tags *are* supplied for empty elements in the ESIS:

```
C>type foo.sgm

<!DOCTYPE TEST [
<!ELEMENT TEST - O EMPTY>
]>
<TEST>

C>nsgmls foo.sgm

(TEST
)TEST
C
```

6.5.13   Order of Declarations in DTDs

Note that the entire DTD is scanned prior to the interpretation of content models. As a result, element type declarations can be provided in whatever order seems most natural as opposed to the order implied by the hierarchy. There is no need to "forward declare" constructs as there are in some programming languages. However, some DTD-processing applications prefer the first element type declaration provided to be the "root" element of the document (i.e., the document element type). This is the one with the same name as the DTD:

```
C>type foo.sgm

<!DOCTYPE foo - [
<!ELEMENT bar - O (#PCDATA)>
<!ELEMENT foo - O (bar)>
]>
<foo>
```

In this example, the **foo** element is the document element type because its name occurs in the document type declaration. It does not matter that it is not declared first.

CHAPTER 7

ENTITIES, NOTATIONS, AND MARKED SECTIONS

Note: In this chapter, we deal with the syntactical details of SGML in some detail. You may wish to read through it briskly as a first pass and return to the details as required later on.

7.1 Introduction

In computing, the word *file* is so ubiquitous that one would expect it to be easy to define. Unfortunately, the fundamental notion of a file is a very slippery one. At the hardware level, there is typically no such thing as a file. There is merely the notion of storage space that can be allocated in fixed size chunks.[1] By chaining chunks together to build larger "logical chunks" we get to the most basic definition of a file.

Above the hardware, there are typically many additional layers of abstraction provided by operating system software before we arrive at the notion of a word processor file or a database file. Files can *pretend* to be other files (symbolic links or shortcuts). Files can pretend to be hardware devices as in /dev/kb, which is typically the keyboard on UNIX machines, or NUL, which is a black hole on DOS machines.[2] A word processing application file might contain a mixture of text and links to other files, which might be spreadsheets, Web pages, or more word processor files.

Typically, files can be considered singular, homogenous units at the base operating system level. Irrespective of what the constituent bit patterns represent, or how/where they are stored, they can be manipulated as single independent entities. For example, they can be copied from a hard disk onto a floppy disk, transferred down a phone line with a modem, or chopped into pieces without regard to the nature of the content.

To do more application-specific work such as query an accounts system, print a report, or calculate a sales forecast requires that higher levels of semantics be layered above the basic notion of a file. In most operating system architectures, files are physically independent of the application programs that created them. After a graphics file comes into existence, the connection between it and the application that created it is severed. Subsequent processing of such files relies upon heuristics

---

1. Commonly known as sectors or blocks.
2. In the "Plan 9" Operating System from AT&T Bell Labs even CPUs are considered files.

such as file-naming conventions and magic bytes[3] to reassociate the file with the application or class of application that created it. For example .doc files are typically documents. However the files a.doc and b.doc may have been created by different word processing applications and be mutually incompatible. This fact is typically discovered late in the day when an application program reports the dreaded "invalid file format" message.

Documents represent an increasingly broad categorization of the notion of a file. Everything from a graphic image to a spreadsheet to a video clipping falls within its remit. Hypermedia has added new dynamic forms of information such as hypertext and interactive scripts. Each of these different information types are valid candidates to be constituent parts of documents. For reasons of pragmatism and/or system limitations, we may choose to store these various component parts as separate "files."

The issues raised here give rise to two fundamental questions that SGML needs to address:

1. How can documents to be stored in separate "files" without introducing system dependencies into the documents?

2. How can we unambiguously denote the types of data content in component files.

In SGML, the concept of an *entity* is used to address the former question, and the notion of a *notation* addresses the latter. Entities provide ways of factoring out collections of information content and giving them their own symbolic, platform-independent names. Notations provide a way of unambiguously declaring what sort of content is to be found within such entities.

7.2   Logical Storage

The SGML standard eschews the notion of file in favor of logical objects known as *entities* that inhabit a purely logical storage space. When physically stored on some real-world computer system, a subsystem known as an *entity manager* is responsible for performing the mapping from logical to physical storage, as shown in Figure 7.1. Given that the entity manager is, by definition, system-specific, its implementation is not part of the standard.

7.3   System Versus Public Identifiers

There are two ways to make the association between entity names and the physical objects onto which the entities are mapped: system identifiers and public identifiers. System identifers effectively "pass through" SGML parsers unaffected to be interpreted by the system's entity manager. They may or may not be portable across systems.

---

3. Microsoft Windows executable files, for example, typically have an .EXE extension and always start with the "magic" 2-byte combination MZ. The operating system uses this to identify the file as executable.

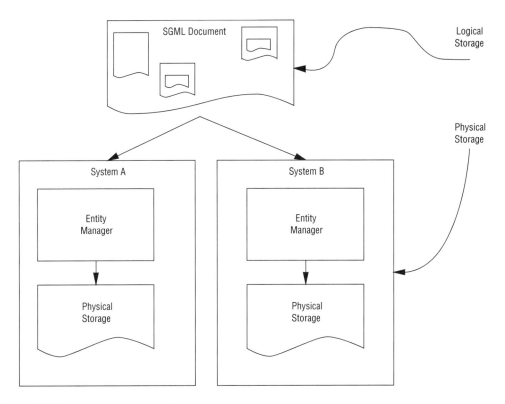

Figure 7.1 Mapping logical to physical storage

Public identifiers, on the other hand, are "logical names" intended to be converted to physical locations by the entity manager. A public identifier effectively provides a "table lookup" key string for the entity manager to use in arriving at the physical address, as shown in Figure 7.2.

An optional feature of SGML is the ability to formalize the structure of such public identifier strings. See Section 7.9.8.

As can be seen in Figure 7.3, entities come in two principle flavors—those intended to be used purely as an aid to markup declaration (parameter entities) and those intended for use in creating document instances (general entities). Another level of classification distinguishes those that are completely housed within their own declarations (internal) and those stored in other objects (external).

7.4   Internal Parameter Entities

Internal parameters are the simplest form of entity. They are used to provide a simple text substitution facility, typically within DTDs. For example,

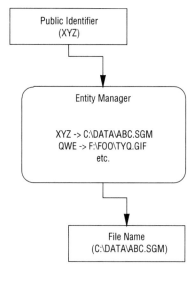

Figure 7.2 Mapping a public identifier to a system identifier

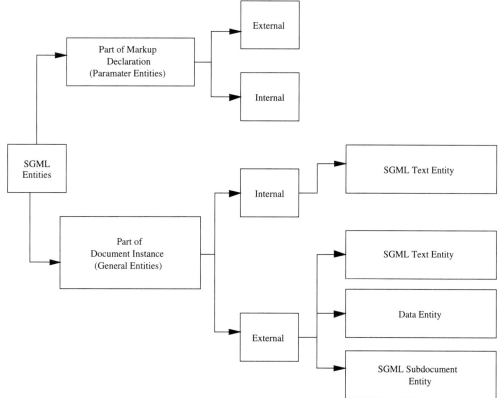

Figure 7.3 Entity classification

```
<!DOCTYPE test [
<!ENTITY % letter "A | B | C | D">
<!ENTITY % digit "one | two | three | four">
<!ELEMENT test - O (var)>
<!ELEMENT (%letter;) - O EMPTY>
<!ELEMENT (%digit;) - O EMPTY>
<!ELEMENT var - O (first , other) >
<!ELEMENT first - O (%letter;)>
<!ELEMENT other - O (%letter; | %digit;)*>
]>
<test>
<var>
   <first>
     <a>
   </first>
   <other>
     <one>
     <two>
   </other>
</var>
```

Parameter entities can be thought of as preprocessors or macro expansion languages.[4] As far as the core SGML parser is concerned, the foregoing element type declarations look like this:

```
<!DOCTYPE test [
<!ELEMENT test - O (var)>
<!ELEMENT (A | B | C | D) - O EMPTY>
<!ELEMENT (one | two | three | four) - O EMPTY>
<!ELEMENT var - O (first , other) >
<!ELEMENT first - O (A | B | C | D)>
<!ELEMENT other - O (A | B | C | D | one | two | three | four)*>
]>
```

By analogy with the C programming language the SGML statement

```
<!ENTITY % foo "bar">
```

is similar in effect to

```
#define %foo; bar
```

7.5   External Parameter Entities

External parameter entities are stored "externally" in order to be referenced from multiple documents. Imagine a situation in which the content model for an address has been standardized across a range of DTDs:

---

4. There are some subtle differences. See Section 13.13—Obfuscatory Entity References.

```
c>type address.dtd

<!ELEMENT addr - O (street,city,zip,country)>
<!ELEMENT (street,city,zip,country) - O (#PCDATA)>

C>type foo.sgm

<!DOCTYPE test [
<!ENTITY % AdModel SYSTEM "address.dtd">
%AdModel;
<!ELEMENT test - O (addr)>
]>
<test>
<addr>
<street>XYZ Street
<city>Erewhon
<zip>123 ABC
<country>Tumbolia
</addr>
</test>

C>nsgmls foo.sgm

(TEST
(ADDR
(STREET
-XYZ Street
)STREET
(CITY
-Erewhon
)CITY
(ZIP
-123 ABC
)ZIP
(COUNTRY
-Tumbolia
)COUNTRY
)ADDR
)TEST
C
```

As far as the core parser is concerned, it is as if the content model of the **addr** element is physically part of the preceding DTD. By analogy with the C programming language, the SGML statements

```
<!ENTITY % AdModel SYSTEM "address.dtd">
%AdModel;
```

are similar in effect to

```
#include "address.dtd"
```

7.6   Internal General Entities

A general entity is one that is intended to be used within a document instance as opposed to a DTD. The simplest form of general entity is the internal type

```
C>type foo.sgm

<!DOCTYPE test [
<!ENTITY StdDisc "<p>This product is provided...</p>">
<!ELEMENT test - O (p)>
<!ELEMENT p - O (#PCDATA)>
]>
<test>
&StdDisc;
</test>

C>nsgmls foo.sgm

(TEST
(P
-This product is provided...
)P
)TEST
C
```

Here, an SGML text entity called StdDisc (Standard Disclaimer) has been declared and sub-sequently used with the **test** element. Note that it is perfectly legal for the replacement text to contain markup, as in this case.

These entities are analogous to C language macros intended for use within code as opposed to within data definitions. For example,

```
#define assert(exp) \
( (exp) ? (void) 0 : _assert (#exp , __FILE__,__LINE__))
```

Most C compilers provide the assert macro. It uses a test on a specified condition parameter to decide if the program should call the _assert() function or continue on. Given that it contains code, it can only be sensibly referred to within a function. Similarly, internal general entities can contain text/markup and can be referred to only from within a document instance.

7.7   External General Entities

7.7.1   SGML Text Entity

These are external entities that contain SGML text. For example,

```
C>type stddisc.sgm

<p>This product is provided...</p>

c>type test.sgm
```

```
<!DOCTYPE test [
<!ENTITY StdDisc SYSTEM "stddisc.sgm">
<!ELEMENT test - O (p)>
<!ELEMENT p - O (#PCDATA)>
]>
<test>
&StdDisc;
</test>
```

When parsed, this produces exactly the same result as the previous example. Again, the advantage of the external approach is that the contents of the standard disclaimer are available for reuse by any number of documents.

Note that once included in the document, the contents of stddisc.sgm are treated exactly as if they had been included there directly (i.e., markup characters occurring within stddisc.sgm will normally be interpreted by the parser). In some situations, this is not what you want and the standard provides a way of "shielding" the content of an external entity from the parser (see Section 7.7.2—Data Entities).

This form of entity is often used to simplify managing large documents such as books by breaking them into chapter-sized chunks. The following construct is so common as to be an SGML idiom:

```
<!DOCTYPE ABOOK SYSTEM "ABOOK.DTD" [
<!ENTITY chap01 SYSTEM "chap01.sgm">
<!ENTITY chap02 SYSTEM "chap02.sgm">
<!ENTITY chap03 SYSTEM "chap03.sgm">
<!ENTITY chap04 SYSTEM "chap04.sgm">
]>
<BOOK>
&chap01;
&chap02;
&chap03;
&chap04;
</BOOK>
```

7.7.2   Data Entities

Data entities are used to allow SGML documents to refer to content that is not itself necessarily SGML. Examples include other text markup languages such as troff, TeX, and RTF and binary encodings such as graphics, sound, and video formats. They come in a variety of flavors. Here we give an example of the NDATA type (see Section 13.12—Data Entity Variations—for details of the others). An NDATA data entity contains non-SGML data:

```
C>type foo.sgm

<!DOCTYPE test [
<!ENTITY e1 SYSTEM "e1.txt" NDATA BMP>
```

```
<!NOTATION GIF      SYSTEM "GIF Format" >
<!NOTATION BMP      SYSTEM "BMP Format" >
<!ELEMENT test - O (#PCDATA)>
<!ATTLIST test img ENTITY #REQUIRED>
]>
<test img = e1>
</test>
```

This document declares GIF and BMP as NOTATIONs known locally on this system as "GIF Format" and "BMP Format," respectively. The element type **test** has an img attribute with a declared value of ENTITY.

```
C>nsgmls foo.sgm

sBMP Format
NBMP
se1.txt
f<OSFILE FIND>e1.txt
Ee1 NDATA BMP
AIMG ENTITY e1
(TEST
)TEST
C
```

Note the s and N records in the ESIS output. The N indicates that the parser has recognized BMP as a NOTATION. The s indicates that the NOTATION is known locally on this system as "BMP Format."

In the preceding example, we refer to the data entity via an attribute. We can also refer to them from within data content as follows:

```
C>type foo.sgm

<!DOCTYPE test [
<!NOTATION foo SYSTEM>
<!ENTITY e1 SYSTEM "e1.txt" NDATA foo>
<!ELEMENT test - O (#PCDATA)>
]>
<test>
Hello &e1; World
</test>

C>nsgmls foo.sgm

(TEST
-Hello
NFOO
se1.txt
f<OSFILE FIND>e1.txt
Ee1 NDATA FOO
&e1
```

```
- World
)TEST
C
```

Next, we examine some of this ESIS output line by line.

```
NFOO
```

The N record indicates that the parser has recognized FOO as a NOTATION.

```
se1.txt
```

The s record indicates that e1.txt has been recognized as an SGML system identifier.

```
f<OSFILE FIND>e1.txt
```

The f record indicates that the entity manager has generated the physical file name e1.txt from the system identifier. For details see Appendix B.9—Formal System Identifiers.

```
Ee1 NDATA FOO
```

The E record indicates that e1 is an NDATA entity with notation FOO.

```
&e1
```

The & record indicates that the entity e1 has been referenced.

7.7.3   SGML Subdocument Entities

SGML subdocument entities are themselves valid SGML documents with their own DTD. This DTD may be different from the DTD of the parent document if desired. Subdocuments are an optional feature of SGML which we return to in Section 14.5.

7.8   Marked Sections

The SGML concept of a marked section is closely related to the issues addressed by entities and notations; thus this chapter is a natural place to discuss them. Essentially a marked section is a section of text that requires special handling by the parser. It can be used to signal that a section of text is to be excluded from the text passed on by the parser and/or to control the extent to which the parser "looks inside" the section for further markup.

Figure 7.4 illustrates the overall structure of a marked section (using the delimiters from the Reference Concrete Syntax).

The most common usage of a marked section is to flag to the parser whether or not a section of text should be considered part of the document.

The following document illustrates a simple use of a marked section:

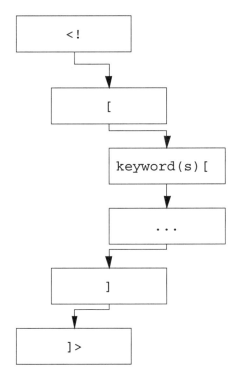

Figure 7.4 Overall structure of a marked section

```
C>type foo.sgm

<!DOCTYPE test [
<!ELEMENT TEST - O (#PCDATA)>
]>
<test>
Hello
<![ INCLUDE [
I may or may not be here
]]>
World
</test>

C>nsgmls foo.sgm

(TEST
-Hello\nI may or may not be here\nWorld
)TEST
C
```

By replacing the keyword INCLUDE with EXCLUDE, we can get the parser to pretend the section of text is not there:

```
C>type foo.sgm

<!DOCTYPE test [
<!ELEMENT TEST - O (#PCDATA)>
]>
<test>
Hello
<![ IGNORE [
I may or may not be here
]]>
World
</test>

C>nsgmls foo.sgm

(TEST
-Hello\nWorld
)TEST
C
```

One of the most common uses of this technique is to support conditional text. Switching between INCLUDE and EXCLUDE is commonly achieved via a parameter entity:

```
C>type foo.sgm

<!DOCTYPE test [
<!ELEMENT TEST - O (#PCDATA)>
<!ENTITY % VAR1 "INCLUDE">
<!ENTITY % VAR2 "IGNORE">
]>
<test>
Hello
<![ %VAR1; [
I may or may not be here
]]>
<![ %VAR2; [
I also may or may not be here
]]>
World
</test>
```

The parameter entities VAR1 and VAR2 are used to control the inclusion/exclusion of the marked sections.

```
C>nsgmls foo.sgm

(TEST
-Hello\nI may or may not be here\nWorld
)TEST
C
```

There are a number of other keywords apart from the INCLUDE and IGNORE keywords covered in this section. These keywords are concerned with exerting control over the extent to which the parser "looks inside" the marked section for further markup. These are covered in Section 13.9—Marked Section Variations.

7.9   Some Details

7.9.1   Variations on General Entities

There are a number of variations on the general entity mechanism presented in this chapter. We will return to them later (in Section 13.11—Text Entity Variations). For now it is sufficient to note that the interpretation of a general entity by the parser can be modified with a number of keywords. The SDATA keyword, for example, indicates that the entity contains characters that are system-specific and should be made available to the processing application. The CDATA keyword indicates that the entity text should be interpreted as pure character data without attaching special connotations to any characters within it that might look like markup (i.e., < and &).

7.9.2   Standard Entity Sets

One common use of entities is to provide access to special characters (glyphs) used in typesetting such as fractions, mathematical symbols, and accent characters. These codes typically do not form part of the native character set used to create the SGML documents and entities provide a way of keeping the documents system independent.

A number of entity collections have been published in an annex to the SGML standard (ISO 8879). For example, suppose that a lowercase alpha character from the Greek alphabet is required in a document. The following line will declare ISOgrk1 as an external parameter entity:

```
<!ENTITY % ISOgrk1 PUBLIC "ISO 8879:1976//ENTITIES Greek Letters//EN">
```

Now it can be included in the DTD with the corresponding entity reference:

```
%ISOgrk1;
```

This file includes many definitions for various Greek characters. The definition for lowercase alpha looks like this:

```
<!ENTITY agr SDATA "[agr ]">
```

The document proper can now refer to a lowercase alpha character via this agr internal general entity:

```
Here is a small alpha character : &agr;
```

Parsing this snippet through NSGMLS would produce

```
-Here is a small alpha character : \|[agr ]\|
```

Note the \| codes housing the entity replacement text. This is the NSGMLS parser's way of denoting internal SDATA entities (see Section 17.9.1—Variations on General Entities).

7.9.3   Defaulting Undefined Entities

The standard allows a special entity known as the *default entity* to be declared to catch the situation where a general entity is used but not defined. For example,

```
C>type foo.sgm

<!DOCTYPE test [
<!ENTITY #DEFAULT "Error : Entity Reference found for non-existent Entity">
<!ELEMENT test - O (#PCDATA)>
]>
<test>
&foo;
</test>

C>nsgmls foo.sgm

(TEST
-Error : Entity Reference found for non-existent Entity
)TEST
C
```

Without the default entity declaration, the parser produces an error message:

```
C>type foo.sgm

<!DOCTYPE test [
<!ELEMENT test - O (#PCDATA)>
]>
<test>
&foo;
</test>

C>nsgmls foo.sgm > nul

foo.sgm:5:2:E: general entity 'foo' not defined and no default entity
```

7.9.4   Multiple Definitions of the Same Entity

Defining the same entity more than once is not flagged as an error by the parser. The first definition of a multiply defined entity takes precedence, definitions supplied in the document type declaration internal subset taking precedence over the external DTD. This allows a document to override entities defined in its DTD if required as long as the DTD is stored externally. For example,

```
C>type foo.sgm

<!DOCTYPE test [
<!ENTITY x "Hello">
<!ENTITY x "Hello Again">
<!ELEMENT test - O (#PCDATA)>
]>
<test>
&x;
</test>

C>nsgmls foo.sgm

(TEST
-Hello
)TEST
C
```

In other words, the second definition of the entity X is ignored. However, if the DTD component is separated out into an external entity y.dtd,

```
C>type y.dtd

<!ENTITY x "Hello">
<!ELEMENT test - O (#PCDATA)>
```

and we have the document instance y.sgm

```
C>type y.sgm

<!DOCTYPE test SYSTEM "y.dtd"[
<!ENTITY x "Hello Again">
]>
<test>
&x;
</test>

C>nsgmls y.sgm

(TEST
-Hello Again
)TEST
C
```

7.9.5　Entity Name Spaces

Parameter and general entities have separate name spaces (i.e., the same SGML document can have a parameter entity foo and a general entity foo).

7.9.6 Character Set for Public Identifiers

Because public identifiers cannot have anything system-specific about them, they use a reduced character set known in SGML as minimum data characters. This set is basically upper- and lowercase letters + digits + some special characters. For details see **ISO 8879, §10.1.7.**

7.9.7 Duplicate Attribute Values

In the last chapter, we saw that

```
<!ATTLIST x    HEAVY (YES,NO) YES
               VOLATILE (YES,NO) NO>
```

is invalid. Parameter entities are commonly used to work around this as follows:

```
<!ENTITY % yesorno "NUMBER">
<!ENTITY % yes "1">
<!ENTITY % no  "0">
```

Now we can have

```
<!ATTLIST x
    HEAVY     %yesorno; %yes;
    VOLATILE  %yesorno; %no;>
```

Obviously, the parser will not be able to flag an error on encountering, say,

```
<x HEAVY="0" VOLATILE = "42">
```

However, as in many programming languages, any nonzero value is typically interpreted as TRUE.

7.9.8 Formal Public Identifiers

An optional feature of the standard is the ability to enforce a formal naming convention for public identifiers. A simplified[5] depiction of the structure of a formal public identifier (FPI) is shown in Figure 7.5.

An FPI that starts with the string "ISO" is ISO owned. For example, the formal public identifier for the SGML standard document itself is "ISO 8879:1986."

An FPI starting with "+//" indicates an identifier with a prefix that has been registered with the ISO.[6] For published material with an associated ISBN number, the ISBN number can be used. For example,

---

5. See **ISO 8879, §10.2** for full details. Also see Appendix A.3—Referencing a Character Set—for details of how formal public identifiers are used to identify character sets.
6. ISO 9070 deals with registration of public text owner identifiers for SGML.

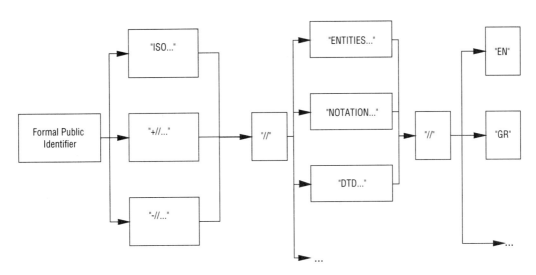

Figure 7.5 Structure of formal public identifiers (simplified)

```
<!NOTATION TEX     PUBLIC "+//ISBN 0-201-13448-9::Knuth//NOTATION
The TeXbook//EN" >
```

An FPI starting with a "-//" indicates an unregistered identifier:

```
<!NOTATION ULYSSES PUBLIC
"-//ISBN 0-19-282866-5::Joyce//NOTATION Ulysses//EN"

<!DOCTYPE HTML PUBLIC "-//IETF//DTD HTML//EN">
```

7.9.9   Character References

Although the use of entities to include characters outside a document's basic character set is highly recommended, it is possible to bypass the entity mechanism and hard-code the system-specific numeric value of the character required. For example, the following are taken from the HTML2 DTD:

```
<!ENTITY amp  CDATA  "&#38;"    -- ampersand        -->
<!ENTITY gt   CDATA  "&#62;"    -- greater than     -->
<!ENTITY lt   CDATA  "&#60;"    -- less than        -->
<!ENTITY quot CDATA  "&#34;"    -- double quote     -->
```

Note that referencing characters this way compromises the portability of documents to different character sets.

7.9.10   Data Attributes

Just as with elements, attributes can be attached to NOTATIONs. The attributes can then be set when a data entity is used as shown here:

```
C>type foo.sgm

<!DOCTYPE test [
<!NOTATION nota SYSTEM>
<!ATTLIST #NOTATION nota var CDATA #REQUIRED>
<!ENTITY e1 SYSTEM NDATA nota [ var="foo" ]>
<!ELEMENT test - O (#PCDATA)>
]>
<test>
&e1;
</test>
```

Notice how the attribute var is delimited within the entity declaration by square brackets.[7]

```
C>nsgmls foo.sgm

(TEST
NNOTA
Ee1 NDATA NOTA
De1 VAR CDATA foo
&e1
)TEST
C
```

Notice the use of D as opposed to A for attributes associated with data entities.

7.9.11   NOTATION Declared Values

When an attribute is defined with a declared value of NOTATION, a group of NOTATION names is supplied to specify the allowable values of the attribute. For example,

```
C>type foo.sgm

<!DOCTYPE test [
<!NOTATION A SYSTEM "A NOTATION">
<!NOTATION B SYSTEM "B NOTATION">
<!ELEMENT test - O (#PCDATA)>
<!ATTLIST test notype NOTATION (A,B) A>
]>
<test>
</test>
```

---

7. Technically, the attributes are housed between **DSO** (declaration subset open) and **DSC** (declaration subset close) characters. These are [and] in the Reference Concrete Syntax and can be modified in the SGML declaration.

Here, the **test** element type has a notype attribute with a declared value of NOTATION. The permissible values for the attribute are A or B, both of which have been declared as NOTATIONs. Finally, the default value for the attribute is A.

```
C>nsgmls foo.sgm

sA Notation
NA
ANOTYPE NOTATION A
(TEST
)TEST
C
```

Note that the following is also valid SGML!

```
C>type foo.sgm

<!DOCTYPE test [
<!NOTATION A SYSTEM "A Notation">
<!NOTATION B SYSTEM "B Notation">
<!ELEMENT test - O (#PCDATA)>
<!ATTLIST test NOTATION (A,B) A>
]>
<test>
</test>
```

Here, the author has forgotten to name the attribute, and the parser has interpreted the word NOTATION as the name. However, it does not recognize the attribute as a NOTATION attribute.

```
C>nsgmls foo.sgm

ANOTATION TOKEN A
(TEST
)TEST
C
```

7.9.12   General Entities in Attribute Values

General text entities can be referenced from within attribute value specifications as shown here:

```
<!DOCTYPE TEST [
<!ENTITY foo "bar">
<!ELEMENT TEST - O EMPTY>
<!ATTLIST test A CDATA #REQUIRED>
]>
<TEST a = "&foo;">
```

This produces the following ESIS:

```
AA CDATA bar
(TEST
)TEST
C
```

The use of CDATA as a declared content for an element type inhibits the interpretation of markup such as entity references. However, entity references occurring in CDATA attribute value specifications *are* parsed as shown here:

```
C>type foo.sgm

<!DOCTYPE TEST [
<!ENTITY foo "bar">
<!ELEMENT TEST - O (TEST1)>
<!ATTLIST test A CDATA #REQUIRED>
<!ELEMENT TEST1 - O CDATA>
]>
<TEST a = "&foo;">
<TEST1>
&foo;
</TEST1>

C>nsgmls foo.sgm

AA CDATA bar
(TEST
(TEST1
-&foo;
)TEST1
)TEST
C
```

The reason for this is that the keyword CDATA, when used with attributes, refers to the *attribute value*. An attribute value is defined as the thing that the parser derives by interpreting an *attribute value literal*. The attribute value literal is what is entered within quotes in the SGML document. For example,

```
C>type foo.sgm

<!DOCTYPE test [
<!ENTITY num "123">
<!ELEMENT test - O (#PCDATA)>
<!ATTLIST test n NUMBER #REQUIRED>
]>
<test n = "&num;456">

C>nsgmls foo.sgm

AN TOKEN 123456
(TEST
```

```
-\n
)TEST
C
```

Here, the attribute n has the attribute value literal "#456." This is clearly not a NUM-BER. However the attribute value after the parser has resolved the entity reference is a NUMBER.

7.9.13   Entities Declared Before Referenced

Unlike element types, entities must be declared before they are referenced.

```
C>type foo.sgm

<!DOCTYPE test [
<!ENTITY % fruit "(apple,orange,pear)">
<!ELEMENT test - O (#PCDATA)>
<!ATTLIST test f %fruit; #REQUIRED>
]>
<test f = apple>

C>nsgmls foo.sgm

AF TOKEN APPLE
(TEST
-\n
)TEST
C

C>type foo.sgm

<!DOCTYPE test [
<!ELEMENT test - O (#PCDATA)>
<!ATTLIST test f %fruit; #REQUIRED>
<!ENTITY % fruit "(apple,orange,pear)">
]>
<test f = apple>

C>nsgmls foo.sgm >nul

foo.sgm:3:19:E parameter entity 'fruit' not defined
```

7.9.14   Case Sensitivity

Unlike element and attribute names, which are case-insensitive by default, entity names are case-sensitive. The entity name and the entity reference must have matching case.

```
C>type foo.sgm

<!DOCTYPE test [
<!ENTITY % fruit "(apple,orange,pear)">
```

```
<!ELEMENT test - O (#PCDATA)>
<!ATTLIST test f %frUIt; #REQUIRED>
]>
<tESt f = apple>

C>nsgmls foo.sgm >nul

foo.sgm:4:19:E: parameter entity 'frUIt' not defined
```

CHAPTER 8

SGML AS A FORMAL LANGUAGE

8.1   Introduction

With all the talk about SGML "languages" and analogies with programming languages in earlier chapters, you are probably wondering what the relationship is between SGML and language compilers.

This is a vast subject, nearly all of which is beyond the scope of this book. In this chapter we simply skim the surface of the subject. A list of references is supplied at the end of the chapter for those who wish to delve further.

8.2   Using Grammars to Describe Languages

In the 1950s, the linguist Noam Chomsky introduced a classification of languages that has lead to the development of a vast field of theory relating to the processing of language by computer. The key to Chomsky's classification system for languages is the idea that languages can be formally defined using grammars and that these grammars fall into a number of general categories. We will get to the categories in a moment. First, we will define what is meant by a *grammar*.

A grammar has four components:

- Terminal symbols

- Nonterminal symbols

- Productions

- A starting symbol

Terminal symbols (or tokens) are component parts of the "written" language. In English, words such as *hello* and punctuation such as the comma (,) are examples of terminal symbols. In the C programming language, keywords such as *while* and operators such as != are also terminal symbols.

Nonterminal symbols are names used to describe particular sequences of tokens. Nonterminals do not appear in the "written" language, rather they say things about the higher abstract structure of the language. For example, the concepts of a sentence and a paragraph are nonterminals of natural languages such as English. Expression and condition are nonterminals in C.

Productions or rewrite rules detail the ways in which combinations of terminals and nonterminals can be transformed into other combinations of terminals and nonterminals. For example, a production rule like this:

```
A ::= b C  | D e
```

might be interpreted as meaning an A is either a b followed by C, or a D followed by e. By convention, nonterminals are denoted in uppercase and terminals, in lowercase. Thus in this example, C and D are nonterminals and would have their own production rules. Intuitively, all nonterminals must "resolve" to terminals at some stage or another to yield concrete expressions in the language.

Finally, a *starting symbol* is a nonterminal used to kick off the grammar (i.e., to provide the production rules with a place to start). For example, the starting symbol for ANSI C is translation-unit which has the following production:

```
translation-unit ::=  external-declaration
                    | translation-unit external-declaration
```

Chomsky's classification of grammars is based on the nature of the production rules used in a grammar. The nature of the production rules controls the complexity of the "machine" required to recognize collections of tokens that fit the grammar, as shown in Figure 8.1.

Chomsky divides these machines into four classes known as regular, context-sensitive, context-free, and phrase grammar machines. These constitute a hierarchy of grammar types from the least to the most expressive, as illustrated in Figure 8.2.

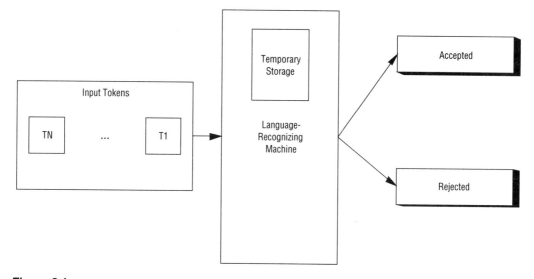

Figure 8.1 Model of a language-recognizing machine

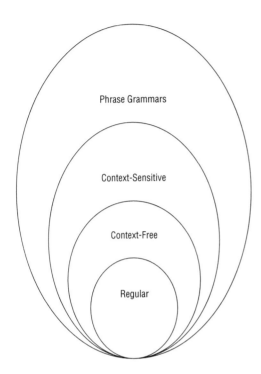

Figure 8.2 Chomsky classification of grammar types

Regular Grammars

These grammars have the simplest production rules and take the general form

```
A :== xB
A :== Bx
```

where A and B denote nonterminals and x denotes any terminal symbol.

A machine to handle grammars of this form is easily built because it can deduce precisely what to do next whenever it consumes an input symbol (i.e., it does not require any temporary storage space). Lexical analyzers typically work with grammars in this category.

Regular grammars are also known as **type 3** grammars.

Context-Free Grammars

These grammars have productions with the general form

```
A :== s
```

where s is any combination of terminals or nonterminals.

In the event that the machine for a context-free grammar cannot deduce what to do at a given point, it can "push" the current token onto the temporary store and read further ahead into the input stream. However, at some point it will be able to tell what to do by simply working with the current token and the most recently pushed token. These machines are also known as push-down automata and as **type 2** grammars.

Context-Sensitive Grammars

Context-sensitive grammars have the same sort of production rules as type 2 grammars but may require access to more than just the most recently pushed token in order to deduce what to do. In other words, they require random access as opposed to stack-based access to the temporary store.

Context-sensitive grammars are also known as **type 1** grammars.

Turing or Phrase Grammars

Phrase grammars are the most general and most powerful form of language grammar. Machines to process these grammars require random access to the temporary store and the ability to modify its contents as well. They are also the most resource-intensive to implement and of little practical use in compiler design.

Phrase grammars are also known as **type 0** grammars.

8.3   Classifying SGML as a Grammar

Before discussing where SGML fits into this hierarchy of grammars. it is important to bear in mind SGML's design criteria. As computer-based languages go, SGML has one foot in each of two camps. First, it is intended to be human readable.[1] Second, it is intended to be processed mechanically. These requirements are at opposite ends of the Chomsky classification, and compromises had to be reached between making SGML easy for humans and machines to read.

SGML is a context-sensitive (type 1) grammar as are many popular programming languages such as Perl or Pascal. Context sensitivity in programming languages is handled by a variety of techniques ranging from rearranging the grammar to embedding extra state variables within the grammar-recognizing machine.

However, such "tweaking" of the machine is more difficult for SGML largely as a result of concessions made to make markup readable for humans. Specifically, in SGML the notion of a token is more dynamic than it is in programming languages.

For example, at one point in an SGML document, a < character might represent an STAGO delimiter, whereas in another it might represent itself. Although analogous situations can happen in, say C, they are limited to simple lexical rules such as "Am I in a string?" or "Is the following

---

1. It will come as no surprise that human language is invariably type 0 and very difficult to process mechanically. How would you get a computer to recognize that the phrases "fat chance" and "slim chance" are semantically equivalent as opposed to semantic opposites!

character an equals sign?" In SGML, the interpretation of a < character as itself as opposed to an STAGO might have been a result of a short reference (see Section 14.6—Markup Minimization Methods) or its occurrence in a CDATA entity. It might also have been because it occurred in a marked section or in an element with a declared content of CDATA or RCDATA.

8.4   SGML and Language Grammar Software Tools

A variety of software tools have been developed to help in the development of language processing applications. The most prevalent are lexical analysis tools such as Lex and parser generators such as Yacc. It is natural to ask if these tools can be brought to bear on the development of SGML-aware applications. Indeed, a constraint in the SGML standard would seem to indicate that SGML should be "yacc'able":

"An element...must be able to satisfy only one primitive content token without looking ahead in the document instance."[2]

This means that at this level, SGML is context-free. In other words, an SGML language machine must be able to consume input tokens one by one without storing them and to know exactly what to do next. For example, the grammar in this DTD

```
<!DOCTYPE test [
<!ELEMENT test   - O (A | (A,B))>
<!ELEMENT (A,B) - O EMPTY>
]>
<test>
<a><b>
```

is invalid and will be rejected by the parser. The reason is that, having consumed an A element, the parser has to decide—without looking ahead—if this is a single A or an A to be followed by a B. In order to work, this model needs to be recast to remove the look-ahead requirement as follows:

```
<!DOCTYPE test [
<!ELEMENT test   - O (A,B?)>
<!ELEMENT (A,B) - O EMPTY>
]>
<test>
<a><b>
```

That said, being context-free (or reasonably context-free) is only one of the requirements for a yacc'able language grammar. Tools like Yacc have been specifically designed to suite a pipeline approach to language processing (i.e., building language processors in layers). Lexical analysis

---

2. ISO 8879, §11.2.4.3.

yields a stream of tokens. This stream of tokens is fed into the parser, which produces an abstract syntax tree. The abstract syntax tree is fed into…, and so on. The human readability features of SGML require feedback between the parser and the lexical analyzer in a way that does not fit this pipeline model.

For a particular DTD, it may well be possible to produce a lexer and parser for documents that conform to it using Lex and Yacc. However, doing this in the general case and supporting the full suite of SGML features severely stretches the design metaphor of Lex and Yacc style tools.

8.5   Comparing SGML with Programming Languages

SGML is a *meta-language* (i.e., a language for expressing the structure and semantics of other languages). In this respect, it is closer by analogy with Yacc or BNF than it is with, say, Perl or C++. Both Perl and C++ can be described in the meta-language syntax provided by Yacc and BNF. In fact, the most common way to implement the parsing of these languages is via tools like Yacc.

C++ and Perl, for example, can be thought of as languages that are (partially at least) described by Yacc or BNF syntax. Similarly, an SGML DTD is an example language described by SGML syntax. A C++ program is an instance conforming to the C++ grammar as defined by Yacc constructs. An SGML instance similarly conforms to its DTD as defined by the SGML DTD constructs. See Figure 8.3.

We typically think of a programming language as something that emerges at the far end of a creation process that enshrines the syntax and semantics of the programming language "in stone." In other words, given a Perl interpreter, there will be an executable program that "understands" a *while* loop. The word *while* will be a keyword or token of the language. It will be expected to be followed by a condition and a statement.

In order to change the syntax and semantics, we need to change the source code of the compiler. In SGML, on the other hand, there is no predefined syntax and no predefined set of keywords for the descriptive languages it creates. There are no hard-wired Lex and no hard-wired Yacc files. These things are soft-coded in the form of an SGML declaration and a DTD. In effect, the combination of an SGML declaration and a DTD can be thought of as a parameterization of the information necessary to *bootstrap* a language. They bear a passing resemblance, philosophically at any rate, to the tasks addressed by tools such as Lex and Yacc.

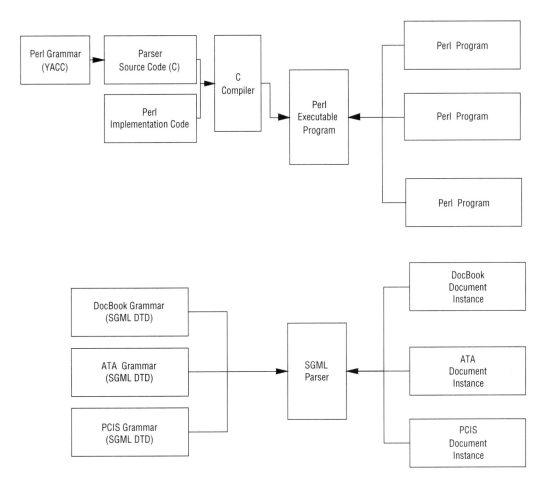

Figure 8.3 SGML parser compared to a programming language interpreter

8.6   References

A. Aho, R. Sethi, and J. Ullman, *Compilers: Principles, Techniques and Tools*, ISBN 0-201-10194-7.

SGML Handbook, Annex H.

A.I. Holub, *Compiler Design in C*, ISBN 0-13-155045-4.

An implementation of a lexical analyzer for a subset of SGML can be found at http://www.w3.org/pub/WWW/TR/WD-sgml-lex.

## CHAPTER 9

ANATOMY OF AN
SGML PARSER

9.1   Introduction

In the last chapter, SGML was discussed in the context of formal language grammars and grammar-processing tools such as the ubiquitous Lex and Yacc. In this chapter, we look more closely at the overall anatomy of an SGML parser and identify the principle phases that all validating SGML parsers share. We then look at how these phases have been implemented in one particular parser, namely, NSGMLS.

9.2   Bird's Eye View of an SGML Document

An SGML document logically consists of a trilogy of components, known as

- the SGML declaration,

- the prolog, and

- the document instance set.

See Figure 9.1. In the simple case, the prolog consists solely of a single document type definition, and the document instance set consists of a single document instance. They may contain other components when certain optional features of SGML are used (see Chapter 14).

A fully specified SGML document takes the following general textual form:

```
<!SGML "ISO 8879:1986"
Details of the SGML declaration here...
>
<!DOCTYPE foo [
Details of the Document Type Definition here
]>
<foo>
The Document Instance here
</foo>
```

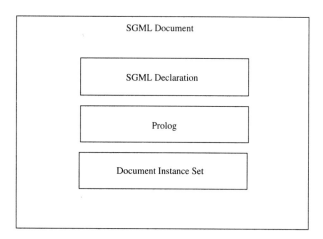

Figure 9.1 SGML document components

In practice, SGML documents are rarely so self contained. This occurs for a variety of reasons, which we will discuss in the next three sections.

9.2.1   The SGML Declaration

SGML declarations are normally stored separately from other SGML components because they tend to change infrequently. It is common for a single SGML declaration to be shared across a range of DTDs. There may even be a single SGML declaration in use in an entire SGML system, as shown in Figure 9.2.

9.2.2   Document Type Definition

A *document type definition* defines a model for at least one document instance, but typically for a *class* of them. The model is typically shared by a range of documents—just as C++ class declarations are typically shared by a range of source files. Sharing of DTDs can happen with or without sharing of SGML declarations, as shown in Figure 9.3.

9.2.3   Document Instance

The *document instance* may itself be stored in multiple storage entities. This may be done to ease document management, reuse components, or reference non-SGML-encoded data from within SGML documents, as shown in Figure 9.4.

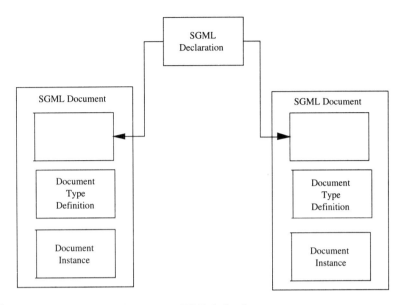

Figure 9.2 Two SGML documents sharing the same SGML declaration

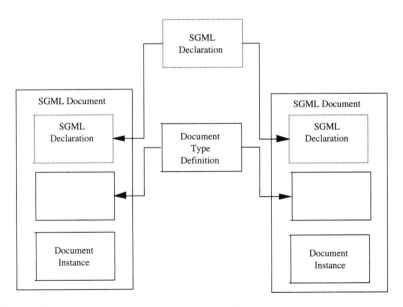

Figure 9.3 Two SGML documents sharing a document type definition

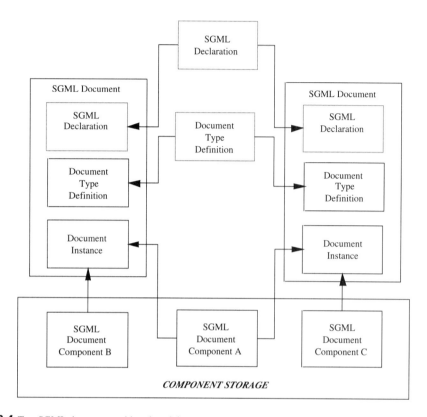

Figure 9.4 Two SGML documents with a shared document component

There are a number of ways in which the segregation mechanisms mentioned here can contain more levels than we have discussed so far. DTDs can be split into components using external parameter entities. For example, SGML declarations can refer to external character sets. General entities can themselves contain other entity references and so on. Resolving all the levels of indirection is the responsibility of the *entity manager*, which we will discuss in detail later in this chapter.

9.3   Bird's Eye View of an SGML Parser

Figure 9.5 is a (very simplified) illustration of the correspondence between SGML document component parts and the activities of the SGML parser. The SGML declaration roughly corresponds to the process of defining the lexical structure of the language to be parsed (i.e., defining how to chop the input data stream into tokens). The document type definition is analogous to a set of semantic rules that control how tokens can be grouped and interpreted as larger structures.

Finally, the document instance corresponds to the subject matter to be parsed in the context of the lexical and semantic rules defined in the preceding two components.

It is instructive to compare Figure 9.5 with Figure 9.6, an analogous illustration for a tradi-

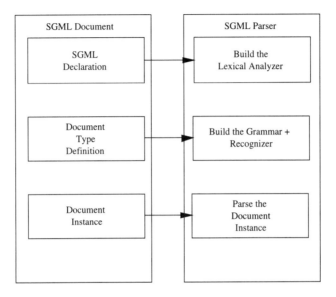

Figure 9.5 Components of an SGML document aligned to parser components

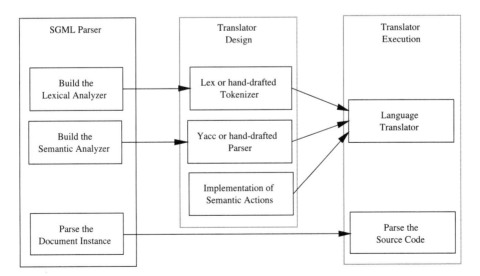

Figure 9.6 Components of an SGML parser aligned to programming language translator components

tional high-level language translator.[1] As can be seen from Figure 9.6, an SGML parser is effectively a high-level language designer, constructor, and executor rolled into one. Indeed, SGML can lay a stronger claim to the term *Compiler Compiler* than Yacc!

9.4 The NSGMLS Parser

9.4.1 Some History

The first SGML parser—known as ARCSGML—was developed by Dr. Charles F. Goldfarb at IBM. He made it freely available through the International SGML Users Group. James Clark used this parser as a base to produce the SGMLS parser. SGMLS is written in C and is freely available on a wide variety of computer systems. The output produced by the SGMLS parser is ESIS, as described in Annex G of *The SGML Handbook*, which is organized into a lexical structure defined by James Clark. Over the years, SGMLS became so popular and prevalent that its way of structuring ESIS became synonymous with the term *ESIS* itself.

In 1995, James Clark released for free use an entirely new SGML parser developed in C++ known as SP. The SP parser improves on SGMLS is many ways. It implements more of the optional features of SGML[2] and allows more facilities of the SGML declaration to be used.

SP provides an architecture for the development of SGML-parser-based applications. To illustrate how SP can be used, James Clark developed NSGMLS—an SP-based application that produces (essentially) the same output ESIS format as SGMLS, thence the name NSGMLS. The set of information that goes into the generation of ESIS from NSGMLS is only a subset of the information that SGML describes and SP can provide to applications. Another SP-based application from James Clark known as SPAM (SP Add Markup), uses SP to transform one SGML document to another, resolving entity references, inserting omitted start- and end-tags, and the like.

9.4.2 Entity and Storage Management in NSGMLS

Entity management and physical storage management in NSGMLS are provided at a number of levels as discussed in the following sections.

9.4.2.1 Omitting the SGML Declaration

The SGML declaration can be omitted from a document, and NSGMLS will infer a default declaration (see Appendix A—The SGML Declaration).

---

1. For the purposes of this comparison, it does not matter whether the translator is a compiler, an interpreter, or some other translator.

2. At the time of writing, NSGMLS supports all the optional SGML features with the exception of CONCUR and DATATAG. See Chapter 14—Optional SGML Features.

9.4.2.2   Concatenation of Files

A collection of file names can be specified on the command line. These files are concatenated together to create the *document entity*, which is then input to the parser:

```
C>type foo.sgm

<!DOCTYPE foo [
<!ELEMENT foo - O (#PCDATA)>
]>
<foo>

C>NSGMLS foo.sgm

(FOO
)FOO
C
```

The same result can be achieved with two files:

```
C>type foo1.sgm

<!DOCTYPE foo [
<!ELEMENT foo - O (#PCDATA)>
]>

C>type foo2.sgm
<foo>

C>NSGMLS foo1.sgm foo2.sgm

(FOO
)FOO
C
```

9.4.2.3   Segregating the Document Type Definition

In an SGML document, the DTD is specified by markup declarations that logically occur in the document type declaration. The declaration can refer to an externally stored set of markup declarations (the external subset) and/or it can contain markup declarations in what is known as the document type declaration internal subset.

In many of the examples we have used in preceding chapters, only the internal form of a DTD has been used (i.e., the markup declarations have been entered entirely into the internal subset):

```
C>type foo.sgm

<!DOCTYPE foo [
<!ELEMENT foo - O (#PCDATA)> <!-- This is the Document Type Declaration
Subset -->
]>
<foo>
```

```
C>NSGMLS foo.sgm

(FOO
)FOO
C
```

The DTD can be segregated into separate storage and located with a system or public identifier. In the following example, a system identifier is used:

```
C>type foo.sgm

<!DOCTYPE foo SYSTEM "foo.dtd">
<foo>

C>type foo.dtd

<!ELEMENT foo - O (#PCDATA)>

C>NSGMLS foo.sgm

(FOO
)FOO
C
```

This two-file combination parses with the same command as before and yields exactly the same ESIS output. But how did the parser locate the file foo.dtd? This mechanism is part of the wider issue of resolving entity references and is discussed in section 9.4.2.4.

9.4.2.4 Entity Catalogs

In Chapter 7, we saw how SGML allows document components to be named using either names (public IDs) or addresses (system IDs). We also saw that the translation from these to physical storage IDs is the responsibility of the entity manager. Because entity management is not part of the SGML standard, a variety of parser-specific ways have been implemented. The mechanism used in the NSGMLS parser is based on the one advocated by the SGML Open Consortium.[3]

Essentially the idea is to use a "mapping file" known as a *catalog* to map various SGML identifiers to physical file names.

The following document uses a public identifier as a logical name for its DTD:

```
C>type foo.sgm

<!DOCTYPE foo PUBLIC "-//Acme//DTD Acme Foo DTD//EN">
<foo>
```

Attempting to parse file foo.sgm with NSGMLS produces an error:

```
C>NSGMLS foo.sgm
foo.sgm:1:53:W: cannot generate system identifier for entity 'FOO'
```

---

3. SGML Open Technical Resolution 9401:1994. See Appendix D—SGML Resources for Developers.

The necessary mapping to resolve the public identifier can be provided with a catalog file entry like this:

```
C>type catalog

PUBLIC "-//Acme//DTD Acme Foo DTD//EN" "foo.dtd"

C>NSGMLS -mcatalog foo.sgm

(FOO
)FOO
C
```

The overall effect of this mapping process is shown in Figure 9.7. We will look at catalogs in more detail later in this chapter.

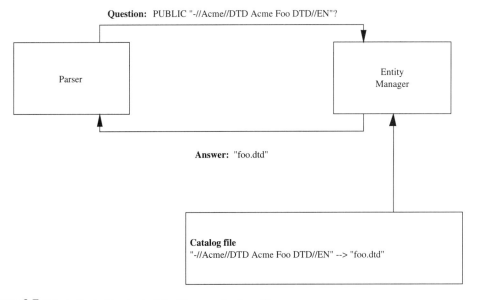

Figure 9.7 Effect of logical to physical identifier mapping by entity manager

9.5 Defining the Lexical Structure

In order to be able to differentiate markup from content, the SGML parser requires a syntactic framework in which to work. It needs to know what characters or character sequences will be used to denote tags, entity references, comments, and the like. It needs to know what characters to allow in element type names, attribute values, and the like. It needs to know, among other things, if these names are case-sensitive. Syntactic details such as these and more are addressed in the SGML declaration, which is covered in detail in Appendix A.

The NSGMLS parser—like most SGML parsers—will infer a suitable SGML declaration if you do not provide one with your document. In the majority of cases, this default declaration is fine. Many SGML users (and developers) can function without in-depth knowledge of the components of the SGML declaration.

9.6 Defining the Grammar

Armed with the details of the syntax to be used in the SGML document, the parser can proceed to interpret the document type definition declarations. This may be provided within the document type declaration (the internal subset) or may require sending a request to the entity manager to resolve the system or public identifier for the external subset.

The entity manager may also be called upon during DTD processing to resolve parameter entity references. When the parser is happy with the contents of the DTD declarations, it can proceed to build a *state machine* to guide the process of parsing documents with respect to the specified grammar. The state machine consists of a collection of states and a collection of transitions from one state to another. These transitions are triggered by the recognition of various constructs in the SGML document. The details of this process are complex, but the principle is simple. Figure 9.8 shows a simple state machine for the content model

```
<!ELEMENT A - - (B,C+,D)>
```

The machine starts out in the START state. The arrival of a B event triggers a move from the START state to the S1 state. From here, a C event will trigger a move to the S2 state. Additional Cs will leave the state as before while the arrival of a D event causes a transition to the END state, which completes recognition of the A element.

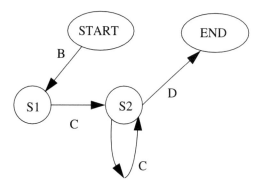

Figure 9.8 Simple state machine

9.7   Some NSGMLS Command-Line Options

In this section, we look at some of the options provided by the NSGMLS parser. Note that a subset of the available options are discussed, and the descriptions have been simplified in a number of places. For full details see the documentation that accompanies NSGMLS.

Command Syntax

NSGMLS [-mpswDefg] [file...]

The input to NSGMLS is a series of files that are to be concatenated together to form an SGML document entity.[4] In the absence of any input file names, NSGMLS will read from the standard input.

The principal output of NSGMLS is the Element Structure Information Set of the document, which is generated on the standard output device by default. (A detailed description of the output format is provided in Appendix B—NSGMLS Output Format Details.) The command-line options are detailed in Table 9.1.

Table 9.1: Some command-line options to NSGMLS

Option	Explanation
-m filename	Specifies a catalog file for the entity manager to use. The principle use of the catalog is to provide a way of mapping public identifiers and entity names to system-level file names. This option is discussed in Section 9.8.
-p	Tells NSGMLS to parse the prolog and then stop. This is useful for debugging SGML declarations and document type definitions.
-s	Tells NSGMLS to throw away normal output and just report errors.
-w	Allows certain optional warning messages to be enabled. For example -wunused-param enables the generation of an error message if a parameter entity is defined but not used. The command -wduplicate enables the generation of an error message if multiple declarations for the same entity are found. (There are numerous others; see NSGMLS documentation for full details.)
-D	Allows the specification of a directory to be searched to resolve system identifier names. Multiple -D options are allowed.
-e	Instructs NSGMLS to include details of open entities in error messages. This option is useful in tracking markup errors in situations where entities are nested within other entities.
-f	Specifies a file name for error messages.
-g	Instructs NSGMLS to include the generic identifiers of open elements in error messages

---

4. More accurately, the input to NSGMLS is a series of system identifiers, which may be a simple file name or formal system identifiers. See Appendix B.9—Formal System Identifiers.

9.8   The NSGMLS Catalog Format

The catalog file generally consists of a series of lines.[5] Lines can take a number of forms, some of which are detailed in Table 9.2.

Table 9.2: Some NSGMLS catalog entry formats

Catalog Entry	Explanation
PUBLIC <pubid> <sysid>	Specifies that the public identifier <pubid> should be mapped to the system identifier <sysid>.
ENTITY <name> <sysid>	Specifies that the general entity <name> should be mapped to the system identifier <sysid>. The standard allows general entities to be declared without either a public or system identifier. This format allows such entities to be mapped to system identifiers.
DOCTYPE <name> <sysid>	This form is used to map a document type name to the system identifier of the entity containing the external subset. A document type name occurs in a document type declaration. As with other entities, the standard allows a document type declaration to leave out an identifier.
SGMLDECL <sysid>	This form is used to provide a system identifier for the SGML declaration that should be used in the event that the document does not provide one.
SYSTEM <sysid1> <sysid2>	This form allows one system identifier to be mapped to another system identifier in a manner not unlike *symbolic links* under UNIX.

9.9   Some NSGMLS Examples

9.9.1   Generating a List of Parser Errors

On platforms that support redirecting of standard error, an error report can be generated by telling the command interpreter where to route standard error. The following works for some CSH-like UNIX shells:

```
NSGMLS foo.sgm 2>foo.err
```

Alternatively, the -f switch can also be used as follows:

```
NSGMLS -ffoo.err foo.sgm
```

---

5. Use whatever definition of *line* is appropriate for the host system.

9.9.2   Search Paths for Files

Multiple -D options can be used to specify directories in which NSGMLS will search for files it cannot find by other means. For example,

```
C>NSGMLS -Dc:\sgml foo.sgm
```

will instruct NSGMLS to search the c:\sgml directory if it cannot find foo.sgm in the current directory.

Alternatively, a set of directories can be specified in the SGML_SEARCH_PATH environment variable. The list is colon delimited on UNIX and semicolon-delimited on DOS.

9.9.3   Including Open Entity Names in Error Messages

The following three files are used to illustrate the effect of the -e switch, which tells NSGMLS to include details of open entities in error messages:

```
C>type test.sgm

<!DOCTYPE test [
<!ENTITY foo SYSTEM "foo.sgm">
<!ENTITY bar SYSTEM "bar.sgm">
<!ELEMENT test - O (#PCDATA)>
]>
<test>
I am test. I include foo here &foo;

C>type foo.sgm
I am foo. I include bar here &bar;

c>type bar.sgm

I am bar. I have an unknown element <here>

C>NSGMLS test.sgm

test.sgm:1:42:E: element 'HERE' undefined
```

Adding the -e option causes NSGMLS to produce more context in the error message:

```
C>NSGMLS -e test.sgm

In entity foo included from test.sgm:7:36
In entity bar included from foo.sgm:1:35
test.sgm:1:42:E: element 'HERE' undefined
```

9.9.4   Including the Element Hierarchy in Error Messages

The following document is used to illustrate the effect of the -g switch, which causes NSGMLS to include generic identifiers of open elements in error messages:

```
C>type test.sgm

<!DOCTYPE test [
<!ELEMENT test  - O (test1)>
<!ELEMENT test1 - O (test2)>
<!ELEMENT test2 - O (test3)>
<!ELEMENT test3 - O (#PCDATA)>
]>
<test>
<test1>
<test2>
<test3>
I am test 3 with an <error>

C>NSGMLS test.sgm

test.sgm:11:27:E: element 'ERROR' undefined
```

Adding the -g option causes NSGMLS to add more context:

```
C>NSGMLS -g test.sgm

test.sgm:11:27:E: element 'ERROR' undefined
test.sgm:11:27: open elements: TEST TEST1 TEST2 TEST3 (#PCDATA)
```

The second line lists the open elements from the root element (TEST) to the point where the error occurs (#PCDATA).

9.9.5   Using ENTITY Lines in Catalog Files

The following example illustrates how ENTITY lines can be used in catalog files:

```
C>type test.dtd

<!ELEMENT test - O (#PCDATA)>
<!ENTITY foo SYSTEM>

C>type test.sgm

<!DOCTYPE test SYSTEM "test.dtd">
<test>
I contain an entity reference &foo;.

C>type test.cat

ENTITY "foo" "foo.sgm"

C>type foo.sgm

I am foo

C>NSGMLS -mtest.cat test.sgm
```

```
(TEST1
-I contain an entity reference I am foo\n.
)TEST1
C
```

In this example, the parser encounters the entity reference foo. The parser asks the entity manager to resolve the reference and receives back the file foo.sgm.

9.9.6   Using DOCTYPE Lines in Catalog Files

The following example illustrates how DOCTYPE lines can be used in catalogs:

```
C>type test.sgm

<!DOCTYPE test system>
<test>

C>type test.dtd

<!ELEMENT test - O (#PCDATA)>

C>type test.cat

DOCTYPE test test.dtd

C>NSGMLS -mtest.cat test.sgm

(TEST
)TEST
C
```

In this example, the parser encounters the document type declaration which does not specify a public or system identifier for the test DTD. The parser asks the entity manager to resolve the reference and receives back the file test.dtd.

9.9.7   Using SYSTEM Lines in Catalogs

The following example illustrates using the SYSTEM entry in a catalog:

```
C>type test.sgm

<!DOCTYPE test [
<!ENTITY foo SYSTEM "foo.sgm">
<!ELEMENT test - O (#PCDATA)>
]>
<test>
I have a general entity reference &foo;

c>type foo.sgm
```

```
I am foo

C>type bar.sgm

I am bar

C>type test.cat

SYSTEM foo.sgm bar.sgm
```

First we parse without a catalog file:

```
C>NSGMLS test.sgm

(TEST
-I have a general entity reference I am foo\n
)TEST
C
```

Next we parse with the catalog file:

```
C>NSGMLS -mtest.cat test.sgm

(TEST
-I have a general entity reference I am bar\n
)TEST
C
```

9.10 Some Common Error Messages

Message: An entity end in a literal must terminate an entity reference in the same literal.

This sort of message, especially if it is associated with a location close to the end of a file, normally means you are missing a delimiter somewhere. For example,

```
<!DOCTYPE test [
<!ENTITY % foo "Definition of foo>
<!ELEMENT test - O (#PCDATA)>
]
<test>
</test>
```

This document is missing a double quote to close off the string (literal) for the parameter entity foo. The parser reaches the end of the file (i.e. the entity) without finding an end to the literal and effectively reports that literals cannot span entities.

Message: Name start character invalid: only s and comment allowed in comment declaration.

The s in the error message is a reference to the SGML syntax definitions in ISO 8879 in which an s is used to denote blank space.

The document probably contains a malformed comment declaration. For example,

```
<!-- First Line
  -- Second Line -->
<!DOCTYPE test [
<!ELEMENT test - O (#PCDATA)>
]>
<test>
</test>
```

This command is invalid in SGML because the comment is terminated by the first occurrence of the COM delimiter ("--" in the Reference Concrete Syntax).

The line on which this error occurs can sometimes be surprising. Consider the following example:

```
<!-- A bad comment >
<!DOCTYPE test [
<!-- Another comment -->
<!ELEMENT test - O (#PCDATA)>
]>
```

Here, the first line opens a comment declaration but fails to close it. Line 3 contains a perfectly valid comment yet the error message will point to the A of line 3 because the first -- on line 3 closes the comment originally opened on line 1.

Message: Content model is ambiguous.

This message indicates that a content model in the DTD would require the parser to look ahead into the document in order to be able to determine how to parse it correctly. Looking ahead to resolve this sort of ambiguity is forbidden by the standard. See Section 13.16—Ambiguous Content Models.

Message: Character '<' not allowed in declaration subset.

You probably have not properly terminated the document type declaration. For example,

```
<!DOCTYPE test [
<!ELEMENT test - O (#PCDATA)>
<test>
Hello
```

Here the author has forgotten to close off the document type declaration prior to opening the **test** element. It should be

```
<!DOCTYPE test [
<!ELEMENT test - O (#PCDATA)>
]>
<test>
Hello
```

Message: Character '<' invalid: only delimiter '>', inclusions, exclusion, and parameter separators allowed.

The final > character is probably missing on an element declaration as is the case in the following test element:

```
<!DOCTYPE test [
<!ELEMENT test - O (foo)+
<!ELEMENT foo - O (#PCDATA)>
]>
```

Message: Digit invalid: only delimiter '-', 'O' and parameter separator allowed.

You probably have used a 0 (zero) instead of an O (oh) for a minimization field in an element type declaration.

Message: Element 'EMPTY' undefined.

You may have an element type declaration with a declared content of EMPTY with round brackets around it like this:

```
<!ELEMENT foo - O (EMPTY)>
```

The opening round bracket causes the parser to look for a content model for the element **foo**, thus causing EMPTY to be treated as an element type name rather than a keyword.

Message: Delimiter # invalid: only 'CDATA', 'ENTITIES', 'ENTITY', 'ID'…allowed.

You may be missing either an element type name or an attribute name in an attribute definition list declaration. For example,

```
<!ATTLIST foo CDATA #REQUIRED>
```

In this example, the parser treats foo as the element type name and CDATA as the attribute name. At that point it is expecting a declared value type keyword and therefore complains at the # sign.

Message: :1:E character '<' not allowed in prolog.

You may be missing the document type declaration or missing the ! in the declaration. Both of the following lines cause this sort of error:

```
<doctype foo....
```

```
<foo>....
```

## CHAPTER 10

SGML
PROCESSING
PARADIGMS

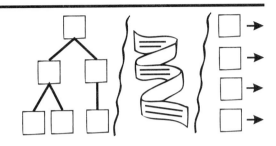

10.1 Introduction

SGML concerns itself with capturing both the structure and content of documents in a way that will facilitate subsequent processing of that structure and content by software. As we saw in Chapter 5—101 Things To Do with an SGML Document, this processing can result in anything from a fully typeset book, to a CD-ROM, to a World Wide Web site.

However (with the possible exception of an optional feature known as Link Process Definitions[1]) the standard does not say anything about *how* SGML documents should be processed by software. Annex G (Page 588 of *The SGML Handbook*) talks about "structure-controlled applications" as distinct from "markup sensitive SGML applications." The former is defined as an application that operates only on the element structure that is described by SGML markup, not the markup itself. Annex G goes on to define ESIS as the element structure information such applications are permitted to act upon.

Over the years, a wide variety of SGML-processing tools and techniques have been developed. Some tools have built-in SGML parsers; others rely on external parsers to generate ESIS. Some tools process markup directly but make no attempt to validate the markup they find. Still other tools process SGML text using nothing more "SGML aware" than regular expression matching.[2] Everything from Lisp to Assembler, from Prolog to Visual BASIC has been used to process SGML in one form or another.

In this chapter, an attempt is made at classifying these techniques. The classification is neither the only one possible nor complete. The focus here is on illustrating the range of approaches rather than listing all of them. Also, it is important to bear in mind that no single SGML data structure or processing paradigm is "correct" in any meaningful sense. Different problems lend themselves to different data structures and different algorithmic approaches. SGML programming regularly involves mixing and matching structures and techniques. The fact that this is easy to do with SGML is one of the big benefits of SGML's open systems philosophy.

---

1. See Section 14.4—The LINK Feature.
2. The variety of techniques and the variance in levels of SGML awareness has prompted Charles Goldfarb to pose the extremely nontrivial question: What does it mean to be SGML aware? See http://www.sgmlsource.com/goldfarb/purity.

10.2   Abstract Data Structures for SGML Documents

When contemplating developing software to process SGML documents, it is natural to start by asking what abstract data structure (or structures) best match SGML from a programming perspective.

10.2.1   SGML Documents as Text Files

The most trivial abstract data structure of an SGML document is to view it as a text file that happens to contain a mixture of "real" text and markup text. The processing possibilities presented by this simple model are exemplified by the variety of tools that originated on the UNIX operating system that work with files at this level. Tools such as wc, grep, and sed can all be used to good effect with SGML documents, as long as due care is taken.

For example, it may be tempting to count the number of **para** elements in an SGML document with a simple grep command such as this:

```
grep -c "<para>" test.sgm
```

Applied to the following simple SGML document, this command generates the correct answer, namely 2:

```
C>type test.sgm

<!DOCTYPE test [
<!ELEMENT test - O (para+)>
<!ELEMENT para - O (#PCDATA)>
]>
<test>
<para>I am para 1
<para>I am para 2
```

However, various features of SGML that may be employed in documents can easily cause such grep commands to yield erroneous answers. The following document illustrates how this can happen:

```
C>type test.sgm

<!DOCTYPE test [
<!ENTITY foo "<question>This is a standard question</question>">
<!ELEMENT test - O (question,answer)+>
<!ELEMENT (question,answer) O O (#PCDATA)>
]>
<test>q1<answer>a1</answer><question>q2<answer>a2</answer>
&foo;
<answer>
a3
</answer>
&foo;
```

```
<answer>
a4
```

Although not immediately obvious, this document contains four **question** elements. One is inferred via start-tag omission, and two are entered indirectly via an entity reference.

Numerous other SGML features can similarly upset this text file approach to SGML processing. These "gotchas" notwithstanding, there are times when direct access to the markup is the quickest way to get the job done. Especially when the job involves simple batch modification of SGML markup to yield other SGML documents. For example, if the task is to rename **chap** elements to **h1** elements, a sed script such as this may well suffice:

```
1,$s/<chap>/<h1>/g
1,$s/<\/chap>/<\/h1>/g
```

Note that this *may* suffice. Various tag minimization features, which we will encounter in Section 14.6, can make this approach problematic. Note also that the following **chap** start-tag is perfectly valid!

```
<chap

>
```

10.2.2   SGML as a Sequence of Events

A more solid approach to SGML processing is to work with a set of tokens or events produced by an SGML parser,[3] as shown in Figure 10.1. In this model, the lexical and semantic issues of SGML are dealt with by the parsing program. It generates a sequence of events into an event queue that is communicated to the SGML-processing application. Such an event stream is easily modeled in software as a collection of records with associated record type fields.

A variety of SGML parsers have been developed—both commercial and freely available—each with their own way of representing SGML events and communicating the event stream to applications. The ESIS event stream produced by NSGMLS is one example.

Using tools such as grep to count elements is clearly easier when we work with records/events rather than the preparsed document. Take the preceding Question and Answer example for instance. The command

```
nsgmls test.sgm | grep -c "^(QUESTION$"
```

yields the correct answer of four question elements. The -c option tells grep to output the number of matching lines. The ^ character anchors the pattern to match only at the beginning of a line. The $ pattern anchors it to the end of a line.

---

3. One could, of course, implement an SGML parser from scratch. However, an SGML parser is a nontrivial piece of software!

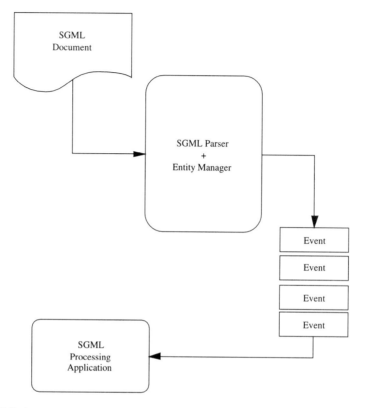

Figure 10.1 SGML document as a sequence of events

The event-based approach is probably the most popular starting point for the development of SGML-processing applications. Many potentially difficult SGML issues are handled transparently to the processing application, which receives a stream of easily parsed records. These records can be readily processed with a variety of text-processing tools.

On the down side, converting an event stream *back* into an SGML document is not straightforward because of the large set of event types required.[4] For this reason, event-based approaches typically generate SGML output by *hand-coding* the output markup. We will see some examples of this in Chapter 12.

---

4. In theory, an SGML parser could communicate sufficient events to allow a processing application to recreate byte for byte the original SGML document. This topic is discussed further in Chapter 16.

10.2.3   SGML as a Hierarchical Data Structure

SGML documents represent a hierarchy in which elements, data content, and the like form nodes in tree structures. A simple document and one possible representation of its tree structure is illustrated next:

```
<!DOCTYPE test [
<!ELEMENT test - O (A,B+,C)>
<!ELEMENT    A - O (#PCDATA)>
<!ELEMENT    B - O (#PCDATA|D)+>
<!ELEMENT    D - O (#PCDATA)>
<!ELEMENT    C - O EMPTY>
<!ATTLIST    C   C1 CDATA #REQUIRED>
]>
<test>
<a>I am A
<b>I am first B
<b>I am second B with <d>D element</d> inside.
<c C1="I am C1">
```

Note that the level of granularity of the tree structure is under the control of the implementor and is limited only by the structure information made available by the parser. For example, in Figure 10.2, attributes are stored in their own node structure and linked back to their parent. They could equally have been stored directly in the element node to which they belong.

Markup that can occur "in-line" with PCDATA content provides a good example of this. For instance, in Chapter 2—Structure of an SGML Document, we had an example of an SDATA entity:

```
<!DOCTYPE test [
<!ENTITY mac SDATA "mac">
<!ELEMENT test - O (#PCDATA)>
]>
<test>
Sean &mac; Grath
```

NSGMLS indicates the presence of such entities by delineating them with the \| sequence and placing them *in-line* with their surrounding content as shown here:

```
(TEST
-Sean \|mac\| Grath
)TEST
C
```

One possible hierarchical representation would be to leave the encoding of the entity as part of the PCDATA content, as shown in Figure 10.3. Alternatively, the entity can be stored in its own node structure, as shown in Figure 10.4.

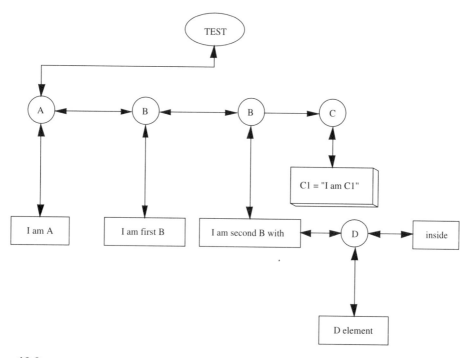

Figure 10.2 Simple tree representation of an SGML document

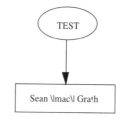

Figure 10.3 SDATA entity and PLDATA

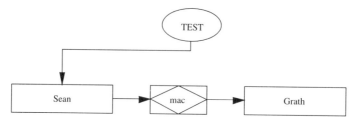

Figure 10.4 SDATA entity and PLDATA separated

10.3   Processing Paradigms

In the previous section, we saw three very different approaches to modeling SGML data structures. In this section we discuss some of the ways in which software can be constructed to work with the latter two of these data structures, namely, events and hierarchies.

10.3.1   Sequential Event Processing

In this approach, events are "read" from the SGML parser and processed in the order in which they arrive.

The approach is typified by the following pseudo-code:

```
e = GetEvent();
while (e.type != END_EVENT) {
  switch (e.type) {
    case ELEMENT_OPEN:
      ...
    break;
    case DATA:
      ...
    break;
  }
  e = GetEvent();
}
```

Typically, individual event types are either processed in-line or dispatched to subroutines.

10.3.2   Recursive Descent Event Processing

In this approach, subroutines are written to handle various SGML constructs represented in the event stream. These subroutines are responsible for analyzing and consuming the input corresponding to the constructs they handle. They are also responsible for calling subroutines to handle the constructs they themselves contain. If a given construct is recursive, then the handling routine will itself be recursive. The general approach is very much like that used in top-down recursive descent parsing, which is commonly used for programming languages such as Pascal.

Take the following DTD for example:

```
<!DOCTYPE test [
<!ELEMENT test - O (para|list)+>
<!ELEMENT para - O (#PCDATA)>
<!ELEMENT list - O (A|B)+>
<!ELEMENT (A,B) - O (#PCDATA) >
]>
```

The top-down recursive descent pseudo-code to handle documents conforming to this model might look something like this:

```
e = PeekEvent();
while (e.type != "C") {
    if (e.type == "(LIST")
        HandleList();
    else if (e.type == "(PARA")
        HandlePara();
    else
        Message "Unexpected event",e.type
    e = PeekEvent();
}

HandlePara()
{
    e = GetEvent(); // Consume "(PARA
    e = GetEvent(); // Consume "-" data event
    // data processing code goes here
    e = GetEvent(); // Consume ")PARA"
}

HandleList()
{
    e = GetEvent(); // Consume "(LIST"
    do {
        e = PeekEvent();
        if (e.type == "(A")
            HandleA();
        if (e.type == "(B")
            HandleB();
        else
            Message "Unexpected event in list element " , e.type
    } while (e.type != ")LIST")
    e = GetEvent(); // Consume ")LIST"
}
```

Note that, in order for this approach to work cleanly with attributes, attribute events need to *follow* the element open event to which they belong. This is the reverse of the way NSGMLS outputs attributes. For example,

```
C>type foo.sgm

<!ELEMENT A - O (EMPTY)>
<!ATTLIST A
          A1 CDATA #IMPLIED
          A2 CDATA #IMPLIED>

C>nsgmls foo.sgm

AA1 CDATA IMPLIED
AA2 CDATA IMPLIED
(A
```

whereas recursive descent parsing is easier if the ESIS looks like this:

```
(A
AA1 CDATA IMPLIED
AA2 CDATA IMPLIED
```

The process of structuring the code in recursive event handlers is a mechanical exercise, and skeleton code can in fact be automatically generated. Next, we look at the various connectors and occurrence indicators that can occur in element type declarations and illustrate how they could map onto processing code.

SEQ Connector

```
<!ELEMENT A - O (B,C)>

handle_a()
{
    e = GetEvent(); // Consume "(A"
    e = PeekEvent();
    if (e.type != "(B")
        Message "Expected (B after (A"
    else
        handle_b();
    e = PeekEvent();
    if (e.type != "(C")
        Message "Expected (C after (B"
    else
        handle_c();
    e = GetEvent(); // Consume "(A"
}

handle_b()
{
    e = GetEvent(); // Consume "(B"
    // Handle B here
    e = GetEvent(); // Consume ")B"
}

handle_c()
{
    e = GetEvent(); // Consume "(C"
    // Handle C here
    e = GetEvent(); // Consume ")C"
}
```

OR Connector

```
<!ELEMENT A - O (B|C)>

handle_a()
{
    e = GetEvent(); // Consume "(A"
    e = PeekEvent();
```

```
    if (e.type == "(B")
        handle_b();
    else if (e.type == "(C")
        handle_c();
    else
        Message "Expected B or C after A"
    e = GetEvent(); // Consume ")A"
}
```

AND Connector

```
<!ELEMENT A - O (B&C)>

handle_a()
{
    e = GetEvent(); // Consume "(A"
    e = PeekEvent();
    if (e.type == "(B") {
        handle_b();
        e = PeekEvent();
        if (e.type != "(C")
            Message "Expected (C after (B"
        else
            Handle_c();
    }
    else if (e.type == "(C") {
        handle_c();
        e # PeekEvent();
        if (e.type != "(B")
            Message "Expected (B after (C"
        else
            Handle_b();
    }
    else
        Message "Expected B or C after A"
    e = GetEvent(); // Consume ")A"
}
```

OPT Occurrence Indicator

```
<!ELEMENT A - O (B?)>

handle_a()
{
    e = GetEvent(); // Consume "(A"
    e = PeekEvent();
    if (e.type == "(B") {
        Handle_b();
        e = PeekEvent();
    }
    if (e.type != ")A")
```

```
        Message "Expected )A"
}
```

PLUS Occurrence Indicator

```
<!ELEMENT A - O (B)+>

handle_a()
{
    e = GetEvent(); // Consume "(A"
    do {
       e = GetEvent();
       if (e.type != "(B")
           Message "Expected B element"
        else
            Handle_b();
    } while (e.type == "(B");
    e = GetEvent(); // Consume ")A"
}
```

REP Connector

```
<!ELEMENT - O A (B)*>

handle_a()
{
    e = GetEvent(); // Consume "(A"
    e = PeekEvent();
    while (e.type == "(B") {
        Handle_b();
    }
    e = GetEvent(); // Consume ")A"
}
```

10.3.3   Event Handlers

Probably the most common way of dealing with events coming from an SGML parser is to use event-handling routines. These routines are registered with, and then called by, the parser to handle particular event types. This contrasts with the recursive descent approach in that handlers do not consume input themselves. Instead, they wait to be called by the event dispatcher.

The philosophy is directly analogous to the sort of event-driven model frequently seen in graphical user interfaces (i.e., the developer declares a collection of handlers, makes them known to the system, and then yields control to the system, which then dispatches events to individual event handlers as needed). In the case of SGML parsers, control is most often yielded to the parser, which acts as the event dispatcher.

In SGML systems it is often convenient to establish handlers at the individual element type level (i.e., a handler for PARAs and a handler for LISTs). Furthermore, it is often convenient to use the same handler for both the "open element" and "close element" events, as depicted in Figure 10.5.

Take the following DTD for example:

```
<!DOCTYPE test [
<!ELEMENT test - O (para|list)+>
<!ELEMENT para - O (#PCDATA)>
<!ELEMENT list - O (A|B)+>
]>
```

Pseudo-code event-driven handlers for this DTD are shown next:

```
element para
open {
// Handle paragraph open event here
}
close {
// Handle paragraph close event here
}

element list
open {
// Handle list open event here
}
close {
// Handle list close event here
}

element a
open {
// Handle a open event here
}
close {
// Handle a close event here
}
data {
// Handle data events here
}
```

Event handling is a powerful and natural way to approach a large class of SGML-processing applications. It can be particularly strong in typesetting applications as a result of the ease with which state modifications can be put into effect and then reversed. For example, imagine an application in which the contents of **note** elements are to be formatted with red text and with an extra 1 inch added to the left margin:

```
global oldcolor; // Global variable
element note
open {
    oldcolor = SaveTextColor();
```

```
    SetTextColor(RED);
    SetLeftMargin(GetLeftMargin() + 1.0 );
}
close {
    SetTextColor(oldcolor);
    SetLeftMargin(GetLeftMargin() - 1.0);
}
```

10.3.4 Hierarchical Navigation

Hierarchical-based paradigms for SGML processing provide either full or partial access to the document hierarchy so that software can navigate around the tree. Many event-driven systems are partially hierarchical in the sense that they record details of certain *prior* nodes and make these available to the processing software. The following pseudo-code illustrates the idea:

```
element PARA
open {
    if (Parent() == LIST)
      // handle PARA within LIST
else
      // Handle other PARA contexts
}
```

The provision of the Parent() function to return the generic identifier of the parent node saves the developer from writing code to track this state variable. Other state variables commonly recorded automatically include ancestors, prior siblings, attribute values of immediate ancestors, and so on. To get a feel for the sort of state information that may be maintained, think of an event-driven system as a depth-first, left-right traversal of the SGML tree structure. Figure 10.6 illustrates a hierarchy in which the nodes have been numbered in the order in which they are traversed using a depth-first, left to right tree walk.

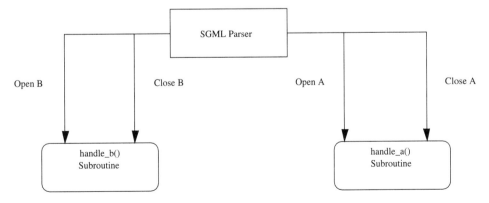

Figure 10.6 SGML parser dispatching events to handlers

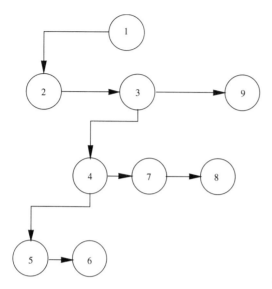

Figure 10.5 SGML tree traversal

Assuming that processing is currently at node 8, the hexagonal nodes in Figure 10.7 illustrate the nodes prior to node 8 that most event-driven SGML-processing systems will store information about. In other words, an event handler might be able to ask, "What was my parent element called?" or "Have I an ancestor element with an attribute 'Security' set to the value 'Classified'?"

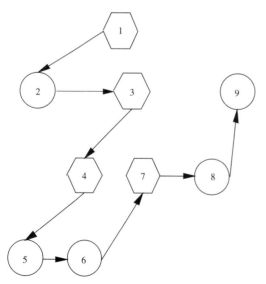

Figure 10.7 Typical history storage for an SGML processor

The more general form of hierarchical system allows the software to navigate at random throughout the document hierarchy. Thus the software can ask, "How many right siblings have I?" or "Do I have an element below me with a 'Security' attribute set to the value 'Classified'?" among other things. Unlike historical hierarchy systems, this random access hierarchy requires a two-pass approach. The first pass would consist of a parsing and tree-building process; the second pass, the data processing proper.

10.3.5   Tree Transformation

This approach to SGML processing is based on the idea that many SGML-processing tasks boil down to a transformation from one data structure to another.[5] Given that SGML provides a powerful framework for the description of data structures (in the form of DTDs), it follows that SGML-processing tasks can be viewed as transformations from one DTD to another. Consider the following simple DTD:

```
<!ELEMENT test - O (a|b|c)+>
<!ELEMENT (a,b,c) - O EMPTY>
```

If we wish to delete all C elements from documents conforming to this DTD, we can think of this task as developing software to transform documents conforming to the preceding DTD into documents conforming to this DTD:

```
<!ELEMENT test1 - O (a|b)+>
<!ELEMENT (a,b) - O EMPTY>
```

If we wish to typeset documents conforming to the test DTD so that we have pages of A elements and pages of B elements, we can consider this task as a transformation to the following DTD:

```
<!ELEMENT test - O (page)+>
<!ELEMENT page - O (a+|b+)>
<!ELEMENT (a,b) - O EMPTY>
```

In order to achieve this sort of transformation, we need to rearrange hierarchies. The general form of the process is shown in Figure 10.8. The SGML parser builds a hierarchical data structure from the original SGML document. This structure is passed into a transformation process that yields another hierarchical data structure. This is then "serialized" to yield another SGML document, which is written back to disk.

This approach of converting one SGML document type to another is especially powerful when publishing SGML to systems that can accept SGML directly. Some require that a specific DTD be used (e.g., World Wide Web or Edgar); others will work with any DTD. In the former case,

---

5. This is not a new idea. See, for example, L. Ingevaldsson, *Software Engineering Fundamentals—The Jackson Approach* (ISBN 0-86238-103-7), for a discussion of the JSP software development method.

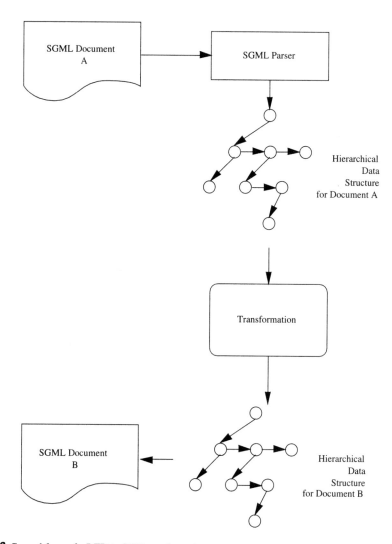

Figure 10.8 General form of a DTD-to-DTD transformation system

clearly there is a strong fit with the DTD->DTD transformation approach. In the latter, there is a partial fit in the sense that we often wish to rearrange/generate content prior to publishing proper, and this can be thought of as a DTD->DTD transformation.[6]

---

6. This idea that *publishing* consists of tree transformation followed by tree formatting is at the heart of the DSSSL standard. See Chapter 16—The DSSSL Standard.

CHAPTER 11

THREE FRAMEWORKS FOR SGML PROCESSING

11.1   Introduction

In this chapter, three simple frameworks for SGML processing are discussed. Each one implements a different SGML-processing paradigm. Using the terminology of the last chapter they are characterized as follows:

- Event sequence processing (C++)

- Event-driven processing (Perl)

- Hierarchical data structure processing (Python)

The three frameworks are presented in overview form in this chapter along with simple examples of applications built with them. In the following chapter, some larger examples of the frameworks in action are presented. The full source code for all three can be found in Appendix C—Source Code for the Frameworks—and on the accompanying CD-ROM.

Caveats

No language is perfect for SGML processing. Even if such a language existed, many developers would still look for ways to use the tools they themselves are most comfortable with. I have chosen C++, Perl,[1] and Python[2] to implement the frameworks for the following reasons:

- They are all freely available on the Internet.

- They are used by large numbers of developers.

- They each have particular strengths for SGML processing.

- They each illustrate a different approach to SGML processing.

- I use all three on a regular basis for SGML processing in "real world" applications.

---

1. The classic introduction to Perl is *Programming Perl*—also known as the *Camel Book*—by Larry Wall and Randal L. Schwartz (ISBN 0-937175-64-1).

2. For an introduction to Python see *Programming Python* by Mark Lutz (ISBN 1-56592-197-6).

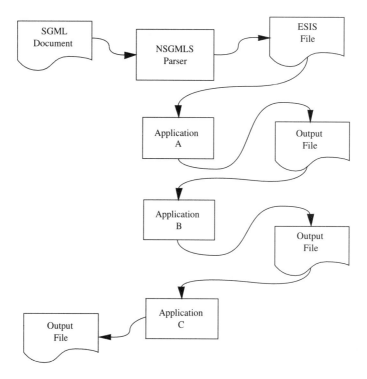

Figure 11.1 A pipeline for processing ESIS

Note that numerous shortcuts have been taken in the code in order to focus on core SGML-processing ideas. The code has been kept as simple as possible, using as few features of the host language as possible. These frameworks are about SGML—not about C++, Perl, or Python.

11.2   Pipelines

A UNIX-style "pipeline" philosophy underlies all three frameworks. Simply put, this philosophy advocates building small applications to perform small, well-defined tasks. These small applications are then combined with other applications via the UNIX pipe mechanism to build bigger applications. Such small applications are commonly referred to as *filters*. Figure 11.1 illustrates a pipeline consisting of three filters that have been "daisy-chained" together to process the ESIS output from the NSGMLS parser.

On architectures that support pipes, this sequence would be invoked using a command like this:

```
NSGMLS foo.sgm | appa | appb | appc > res.out
```

On machines that do not support pipes, the effect can be emulated using intermediate files:

```
NSGMLS foo.sgm >temp0
appa < temp0 >temp1
appb <temp1 >temp2
appc <temp2 >res.out
```

Using a pipeline approach not only allows us to mix standard text-processing utilities with custom programs, but it also allows us to mix and match our SGML-processing frameworks. For example, part of a single processing task might use the C++ framework, another might use the Perl framework. Yet another might be a third-party text-processing utility.

11.3   The C++ Framework

11.3.1   ESIS Events as a Class Hierarchy

In thinking about a C++ framework for SGML processing, it is natural to try to formulate a class hierarchy of ESIS event types. There are many ways to structure a hierarchy of ESIS events. The beginning of one such classification is shown in Figure 11.2.

Such hierarchies lead naturally to the creation of classes in C++. We will use a very simple hierarchy in the C++ framework, as shown in Figure 11.3. Although this is obviously a very simple hierarchy, the intention is to build the ESIS-processing library so that additional layers of hierarchy can be added without "breaking" applications that use this simple one. Moreover, only a subset of

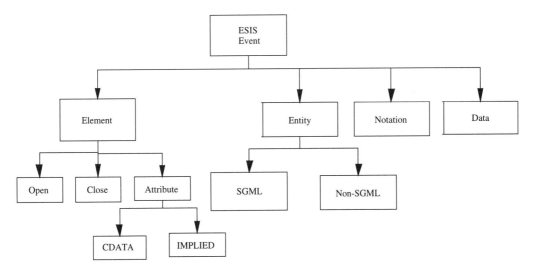

Figure 11.2 Partial hierarchy of ESIS events

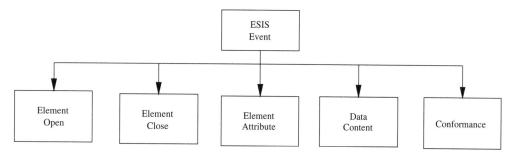

Figure 11.3 Simple ESIS event class hierarchy

the event types produced by NSGMLS are catered for here. Again the intention is to build the framework so as to allow support for other event types in the future without breaking existing code.

11.3.2　Platform Support

This C++ framework was developed using Microsoft Visual C++ 1.5 on a PC running DOS/Windows 3.1. The platform-specific parts of the code are very minor, so it should port easily to other architectures.

11.3.3　A "Do Nothing" Filter

In order to be able to function as a filter in a pipe, it is necessary for all applications to be capable of reproducing their input on their output stream as if nothing has happened. Such a "do nothing" filter is also a useful debugging and timing tool. The code to do this with the C++ framework follows:

```
c>type stet.cpp

#define _DOS              // Tell Visual C++ we are on DOS
#include <afx.h>          // Use the Microsoft Foundation Classes
#include <iostream.h>     // Standard C++ IO
#include "esis.h"         // Header file for the Framework Library

int main()
{
class EsisEvent *e;
        while ((e=GetEvent(stdin))!=NULL) {
                cout << e->GetEsisFormat() << endl;
                delete e;
        }
}
```

On the PC/Windows configuration, this is then compiled as follows to yield stet.exe:

```
cl /AL stet.cpp esis.obj lafxcr.lib;
```

The following sequence of commands shows how the resultant stet.exe can be used in a pipe and also how it can be tested.

Here is a test SGML file:

```
c>type foo.sgm

<!DOCTYPE test [
<!ELEMENT test - O (foo)+>
<!ELEMENT foo - O (#PCDATA)>
<!ATTLIST foo
        att1 CDATA #IMPLIED>
]>
<test>
<foo>
<foo att1 = "Hello">

c>NSGMLS foo.sgm

(TEST
AATT1 IMPLIED
(FOO
)FOO
AATT1 CDATA Hello
(FOO
)FOO
)TEST
C
```

Piping the ESIS through stet produces the following output:

```
c>NSGMLS foo.sgm | stet

(TEST
AATT1 IMPLIED
(FOO
)FOO
AATT1 CDATA Hello
(FOO
)FOO
)TEST
C
```

To prove that both ESIS streams are the same, the fc (file compare) utility can be used as follows:

```
C>NSGMLS foo.sgm > foo.esi
C>NSGMLS foo.sgm | stet > bar.esi
C>fc foo.esi bar.esi
C>fc: no differences encountered
```

We examine the code for stet.cpp in more detail next:

```
#define _DOS
#include <afx.h>
#include <iostream.h>
#include "esis.h"
```

We define the _DOS preprocessor directive to instruct the Microsoft Foundation Classes to generate code for the DOS platform. We then include three header files—one for MFC (afx.h), one for C++ input/output (iostream.h), and one for the ESIS framework library (esis.h).

```
int main()
{
class EsisEvent *e;
```

Here we start the mainline for the application and declare a pointer to an EsisEvent object e. This will serve as the interface between the library and the main program:

```
while ((e=GetEvent(stdin))!=NULL) {
        cout << e->GetEsisFormat() << endl;
        delete e;
}
```

The body of the program consists of a single loop. The variable **e** is set to successive ESIS event objects that are read from the standard input. The GetEsisFormat() method is called for each object to generate the original ESIS line. This is then routed out to standard output. Finally, the memory used by the object is deleted.

11.3.4   An Event Snooping Filter

When running a pipe that is processing ESIS, it is occasionally useful to watch what events are being passed from stage to stage without interfering with the pipe. The following filter achieves this:

```
c>type snoop.cpp

#define _DOS
#include <afx.h>
#include <iostream.h>
#include "esis.h"

int main()
{
class EsisEvent *e;
        while ((e=GetEvent(stdin))!=NULL) {
                cerr << e->GetSummary() << endl;
                cout << e->GetEsisFormat() << endl;
                delete e;
        }
}
```

This is identical to the previous example with the exception of the following line:

```
cerr << e->GetSummary() << endl;
```

Each ESIS object supports the GetSummary() method to produce a descriptive string about itself. This program outputs descriptive strings to standard error and outputs the real ESIS to standard output. A sample usage of snoop follows:

```
C>NSGMLS foo.sgm | snoop >foo.esi

Open Element 'TEST'
Attribute Name='ATT1' Value=IMPLIED Type='UNKNOWN'
Open Element 'FOO'
Close Element 'FOO'
Attribute Name='ATT1' Value='Hello' Type='CDATA'
Open Element 'FOO'
Close Element 'FOO'
Close Element 'TEST'
Conforming
```

The descriptive text output to the display has not interfered with the ESIS format, which has been redirected to foo.esi:

```
C>type foo.esi

(TEST
AATT1 IMPLIED
(FOO
)FOO
AATT1 CDATA Hello
(FOO
)FOO
)TEST
C
```

11.3.5   A Data Removal Filter

The following application removes all data events from an ESIS stream:

```
C>type nodata.cpp

#define _DOS
#include <afx.h>
#include <iostream.h>
#include "esis.h"

int main()
{
class EsisEvent *e;
        while ((e=GetEvent(stdin))!=NULL) {
                if (e->GetEsisEventType()!= DATA_EVENT)
                        cout << e->GetEsisFormat() << endl;
                delete e;
```

```
        } // while
}
```

Each ESIS object provides an implementation of the GetEsisEventType() method. This is used to catch data events that will all have an event type of DATA_EVENT. An example usage of the nodata.exe filter follows:

```
>type foo.sgm

<!DOCTYPE test [
<!ELEMENT test - O (foo)+>
<!ELEMENT foo  - O (#PCDATA)>
<!ATTLIST foo
        att1 CDATA #IMPLIED>
]>
<test>
<foo>I am the first foo element
<foo att1 = "Hello">
I am the second foo element
<foo>I am the third foo element

C>NSGMLS foo.sgm | nodata

(TEST
AATT1 IMPLIED
(FOO
)FOO
AATT1 CDATA Hello
(FOO
)FOO
AATT1 IMPLIED
(FOO
)FOO
)TEST
C
```

Note, that the functionality of this last example can be achieved with the grep program:

```
C>NSGMLS foo.sgm | grep -v "^-"

(TEST
AATT1 IMPLIED
(FOO
)FOO
AATT1 CDATA Hello
(FOO
)FOO
AATT1 IMPLIED
(FOO
)FOO
)TEST
C
```

The grep command says, "Find all lines that start with the - character and output all lines excluding those."

11.3.6   The C++ Framework Interface File

Each ESIS event type has a unique number assigned to it:

```
// ESIS Event Types
#define OPENELEMENT_EVENT       0
#define CLOSEELEMENT_EVENT      1
#define DATA_EVENT              2
#define ATTRIBUTE_EVENT         3
#define CONFORMING_EVENT        4
```

Four attribute types are produced by ESIS, namely, CDATA, ENTITY, NOTATION, and TOKEN. The TOKEN attribute type is used by NSGMLS as a "catch-all" for attributes that are anything other than CDATA, ENTITY, or NOTATION. These are also assigned unique numbers:

```
// Attribute Declared Values
#define ATTR_UNKNOWN        0
#define ATTR_CDATA          1
#define ATTR_ENTITY         2
#define ATTR_NOTATION       3
#define ATTR_TOKEN          4
```

Note the definition of ATTR_UNKNOWN. This is used to handle the situation where an attribute value has been *implied*. In such situations, no declared value information is included in the NSGMLS ESIS. This is illustrated in the following example:

```
c>type test.sgm

<!DOCTYPE test [
<!ELEMENT test - O (foo)+>
<!ELEMENT foo - O (#PCDATA)>
<!ATTLIST foo
        att1 CDATA #IMPLIED>
]>

c>NSGMLS test.sgm
(TEST
AATT1 IMPLIED
(FOO
)FOO
AATT1 CDATA Hello
(FOO
)FOO
)TEST
C
```

The first **foo** element has an implied ATT1 attribute. The fact that it was implied is made known to us in the resultant ESIS, but the fact that the attribute has a declared value of CDATA is not. The second occurrence of **foo** supplies a value for the ATT1 attribute. In this case, the ESIS communicates the extra information that the declared value is CDATA.

The Class Hierarchy

We start with the base class for the simple ESIS event hierarchy used in this framework. We want to ensure that all ESIS event objects will be capable of providing

- a unique integer event type,

- a string corresponding to the ESIS string used to create the object, and

- a summary string to be used for debugging and snooping purposes.

To achieve this, we declare the methods GetEsisFormat(), GetSummary() and GetEsisEvent-Type() as "pure virtual functions" of the base class EsisEvent. In simple English, to use any class derived from EsisEvent, that class must have provided implementations of these three methods.

```
// Esis Event Base Class
class EsisEvent {
public:
    virtual CString GetEsisFormat() = 0;
    virtual CString GetSummary() = 0;
    virtual int GetEsisEventType() = 0;
};
```

The OpenElementEvent class requires storage for the generic identifier string. Methods are also provided to both get and set the generic identifier.

```
class OpenElementEvent : public EsisEvent {
    CString GI;
public:
    void SetGI(CString gi);
    CString GetGI();
    CString GetEsisFormat();
    CString GetSummary();
    int GetEsisEventType();
};
```

The CloseElementEvent is analogous to OpenElementEvent:

```
class CloseElementEvent : public EsisEvent {
    CString GI;
public:
    void SetGI(CString gi);
    CString GetGI();
    CString GetEsisFormat();
    CString GetSummary();
```

```
    int GetEsisEventType();
};
```

Data events have an associated string to store the data and related get/set methods.

```
class DataEvent : public EsisEvent {
    CString Data;
public:
    void SetData(CString d);
    CString GetData();
    CString GetEsisFormat();
    CString GetSummary();
    int GetEsisEventType();
};
```

For attributes, we need to store four pieces of information:

* the name of the attribute,

* the value supplied for the attribute (if any),

* the declared value of the attribute (i.e., CDATA, NOTATION), and

* a boolean to indicate if a value was supplied for the attribute.

```
class AttributeEvent : public EsisEvent {
    CString Name , Value;
    int Type;
    int ValueSupplied;
public:
    AttributeEvent();
    void SetAttrName(CString d);
    void SetAttrType(int t);
    void SetAttrValue(CString t);
    void SetValueSupplied(int n);
    CString GetAttrName();
    int GetValueSupplied();
    CString GetEsisFormat();
    CString GetSummary();
    int GetEsisEventType();
};
```

Finally, we declare a class to represent the conformance event in ESIS. No extra storage or methods are required.

```
class ConformingEvent : public EsisEvent {
public:
    CString GetEsisFormat();
    CString GetSummary();
    int GetEsisEventType();
};
```

The last part of the header file is the declaration of the interface functions for the library. The main interface function is GetEvent(), which takes a file handle and returns a pointer to an EsisEvent derived object or NULL if end of file was encountered.

```
class EsisEvent *GetEvent(FILE *fp);
```

Two utility functions are provided to simplify conversion between integer attribute codes and their string representations.

```
char *AttrTypeToString(int t);
int AttrStringToType(char *s);
```

11.4   The Perl Framework

The Perl[3] framework adopts a similar philosophy to the C++ framework in that applications are intended to be used as filters in a pipe. In the C++ framework, each application has its own driver application responsible for establishing the iteration that will repeatedly fetch and then process ESIS events. For a broad class of applications, this loop will take the following form:

```
while ((e=GetEsisEvent(stdin)!=NULL){
   switch (e->GetEventType()) {
     case OPENELEMENT_EVENT:
         x = e->GetGI();
         CallOpenFunction (x);
     break;
     case CLOSEELEMENT_EVENT:
         x = e->GetGI();
         CallCloseFunction (x);
     break;
     case DATA_EVENT:
         HandleData();
     break;
       ...
   }
}
```

The implementation of CallOpenFunction (x) in the preceding pseudo-code is easy in languages like Perl that support the run-time detection and binding of subroutines. This makes implementing an event dispatcher easy, and we will use this approach in this Perl framework.

---

3. Developed with Perl 4.

11.4.1   A "Do Nothing" Application in Perl

Perl excels at expressing text-processing tasks concisely, and the "do nothing" application in Perl certainly does not disappoint in this regard. It is two lines long and looks like this:

```
c>type stet.pl

require 'esis.pl';
&esis();
```

The first line tells Perl to load the library code from the file esis.pl. The second line calls the entry point to the esis() library. Here is how stet.pl is invoked to produce the same result as the stet.cpp application in the C++ framework:

```
c>type foo.sgm

<!DOCTYPE test [
<!ELEMENT test - O (foo)+>
<!ELEMENT foo - O (#PCDATA)>
<!ATTLIST foo
        att1 CDATA #IMPLIED>
]>
<test>
<foo>I am the first foo element
<foo att1 = "Hello">
I am the second foo element
<foo>I am the third foo element

C>NSGMLS foo.sgm | perl stet.pl

(TEST
AATT1 IMPLIED
(FOO
-I am the first foo element
)FOO
AATT1 CDATA Hello
(FOO
-I am the second foo element
)FOO
AATT1 IMPLIED
(FOO
-I am the third foo element
)FOO
)TEST
C
```

11.4.2   An Event-Snooping Application

The event-snooping application illustrates the general form that Perl applications using the framework conform to. Essentially, including the esis.pl library provides a Perl application with an esis() subroutine. This subroutine reads ESIS events from standard input and dispatches them to various subroutines if they have been defined. If they have not been defined, the library simply outputs the original ESIS. The subroutine names are shown in Table 11.1.

Table 11.1: Event handlers for the PERL framework

Routine Name	Purpose
DATA_HANDLER()	Subroutine for all data content events.
CONFORM_HANDLER()	Subroutine for conformance event.
DEFAULT_OPEN_HANDLER()	Subroutine for the start of any element that does not have its own handler.
DEFAULT_CLOSE_HANDLER()	Subroutine for the end of any element that does not have its own handler.
OPEN_X()	Subroutine for the start of element X.
CLOSE_X()	Subroutine for the end of element X.

The first thing to do is include the ESIS library:

```
require 'esis.pl';
```

The data handler outputs an explanatory message on standard error and recreates the original ESIS for routing through to standard output. The DATA_HANDLER() routine is passed a single parameter consisting of the data content.

```
sub DATA_HANDLER {
    print STDERR "DATA=$_[0]\n";
    print "-$_[0]\n";
}
```

The default open handler routine is called when an element is opened if it does not have its own specific OPEN_ handler. It is passed both the name of the element and any attributes associated with it as parameters.

```
sub DEFAULT_OPEN_HANDLER {
local ($x);
    print STDERR "Open Element $_[0]\n";
    if ($#_ > 0) {
        print STDERR "Attributes are :-\n";
        foreach $x (1 .. $#_) {
            &FormatAttribute($_[$x]);
        }
    }
    foreach $x (1 .. $#_) {
        print "A$_[$x]\n";
    }
    print "($_[0]\n";
}
```

To produce explanatory information about attributes, a utility function—FormatAttribute—is used that breaks an attribute ESIS line into its component parts.

```perl
sub FormatAttribute {
local(@fields) = split(/ /, $_[0], 3);
    print STDERR "\tAttribute Name = $fields[0]";
    if (defined $fields[2]) {
        print STDERR "\tType = '$fields[1]'";
        print STDERR "\tValue = '$fields[2]'\n";
    }
    else {
        print STDERR "\tType = UNKNOWN\n";
    }
}
```

The default element close handler and conforming event handlers are straightforward:

```perl
sub DEFAULT_CLOSE_HANDLER {
    print STDERR "End Element $_[0]\n";
    print ")$_[0]\n";
}

sub CONFORM_HANDLER {
    print STDERR "Conforming\n";
    print "C\n";
}
```

Finally, the esis() entry point to the library is called:

```perl
&esis();
```

An example of the snoop application follows:

```
C>type foo.sgm

<!DOCTYPE test [
<!ELEMENT test - O (foo)+>
<!ELEMENT foo - O (#PCDATA|foo)+>
<!ATTLIST foo
        fooat CDATA #IMPLIED>
]>
<test>
<foo>First foo
<foo fooat = "fred">Second foo
<foo fooat = "">Third foo

C>NSGMLS foo.sgm | perl snoop.pl >nul

Open Element TEST
Open Element FOO
Attributes are :-
        Attribute Name = FOOAT   Type = UNKNOWN
DATA=First foo\n
```

```
Open Element FOO
Attributes are :-
        Attribute Name = FOOAT   Type = CDATA     Value = 'fred'
DATA=Second foo\n
Open Element FOO
Attributes are :-
        Attribute Name = FOOAT   Type = CDATA     Value = ''
DATA=Third foo\n
End Element   FOO
End Element   FOO
End Element   FOO
End Element   TEST
Conforming
```

11.4.3   An Element Recursion Gauge

This application monitors occurrences of the element type **foo** and produces a message on standard error indicating the maximum depth at which a **foo** element occurred within another **foo** element.

First, include the ESIS library and initialize two global variables to track the depth of **foo** elements:

```
require 'esis.pl';

$foocount = 0;
$maxfoo = 0;
```

We define a subroutine with the same name as the element type **foo** but prefixed with OPEN_. This will be called by the ESIS library whenever a **foo** element is opened:

```
sub OPEN_FOO {
local($x);
    $foocount++;
    if ($foocount > $maxfoo) {
        $maxfoo = $foocount;
    }
    # Pass on the original ESIS
    foreach $x (1 .. $#_) {
        print "A$_[$x]\n";
    }
    print "($_[0]\n";
}
```

Similarly for the end **foo** event:

```
sub CLOSE_FOO {
    $foocount--;
# Pass on the original
    print ")$_[0]\n";
}
```

Now the ESIS library entry point is invoked.

```
&esis();
```

Finally, the maximum depth variable is output to standard error:

```
print STDERR "Maximum foo depth = $maxfoo";
```

Here is an example using foo.sgm of the last section:

```
C>NSGMLS foo.sgm | perl depth.pl >nul

Maximum foo depth = 3
```

11.5   The Python Framework

The Python[4] framework takes a very different approach from that of the Perl and C++ frameworks. It uses the ESIS output of NSGMLS to construct a tree structure in memory. This tree structure can then be navigated providing complete access to the document hierarchy at all times, as shown in Figure 11.4.

The SGMLTree class encapsulates all the details of the tree structure and transparently manages all the links between the SGMLNode objects that make up the tree. The "do nothing" application example of this chapter looks like this in Python:

```
C>type stet.py

from sgmltree import *
from loadtree import *
from dumptree import *
import sys

Loader = LoadTree();
Dumper = DumpTree();
T      = SGMLTree();
T = Loader.Execute (sys.argv[1]);
Dumper.Execute(T);

C>NSGMLS test.sgm | python stet.py

(TEST
AFOOAT IMPLIED
(FOO
-First foo\n
AFOOAT CDATA fred
(FOO
```

---

4. Developed with Python version 1.4.

```
-Second foo\n
AFOOAT CDATA
(FOO
-Third foo\n
)FOO
)FOO
)FOO
)TEST
C
```

Most of the work in implementing stet.py is in the implementation of the SGMLTree, LoadTree, and DumpTree classes. We will look at the implementation of DumpTree shortly. First, we will examine the class hierarchy of the Python framework, as shown in Figure 11.5.

The SGMLTree class is the core data structure. It maintains a collection of interlinked SGML-Node objects. Each application that processes SGMLTree objects is derived from the SGMLApplet class from which they inherit basic functionality such as tree walking and event dispatching.

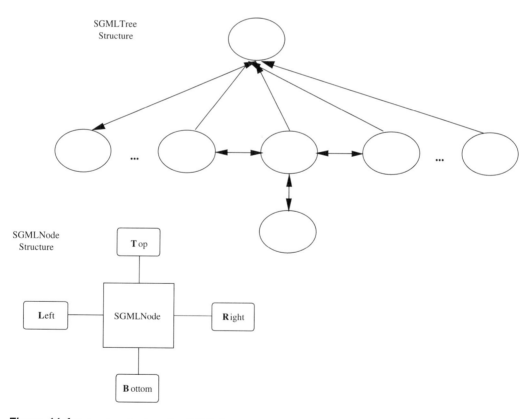

Figure 11.4 Python tree structure of an SGML document

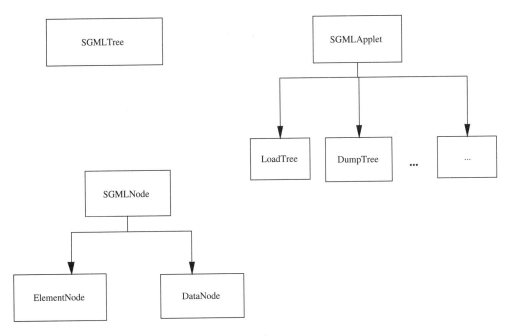

Figure 11.5 Python class hierarchy for the SGML framework

Here we examine the implementation of the DumpTree class.

- Import the SGMLTree class:

```
from sgmltree import *
```

- Define the DumpTree class as a derivative of SGMLApplet:

```
class DumpTree(SGMLApplet):
```

- Constructor calls constructor of superclass:

```
def __init__(self):
        SGMLApplet.__init__(self)
```

The Execute method is the primary entry point for all SGMLApplets. Here a local reference to the SGMLTree structure parameter T is created. The tree is then walked using the Walk method inherited from SGMLApplet.

```
def Execute(self,T):
    self.T = T
    self.Walk()
    print "C"
    return self.T
```

If an SGMLApplet-derived class implements a DATA_HANDLER method, it will be called by the Walk method whenever data content is encountered in the SGMLTree. The handler is actually called twice—once on entry and once on exit from the SGMLDataNode as the tree is walked. The boolean parameter s is TRUE for events generated "on the way down" and false for events generated "on the way up."

```
def DATA_HANDLER(self,s):
    if (s):
        print "-%s" % self.GetData()
```

The SGMLTree structure stores element attributes in a hash table indexed by attribute name. In order to recreate the SGMLTree's ESIS exactly, it is necessary to sort the attributes based on the order in which they were provided in the ESIS stream. To allow for this, each entry in the hash table is a three-tuple: (<order>,<type>,<value>). For example, these lines of ESIS

```
AFOO CDATA Hello
ABAZ CDATA World
(ANELEMENT
```

would lead to the following Python attribute storage:

```
atts["FOO"] = (0,"CDATA","Hello")
atts["BAZ"] = (1,"CDATA","World")
```

The s boolean parameter is TRUE when an element is encountered "on the way down" and FALSE when the element is encountered "on the way up" during a tree walk.

```
def DEFAULT_ELEMENT_HANDLER(self,s):
    if (s):
        atts = self.GetAttributes()
        ordered = []
        for name in atts.keys():
            ordered = ordered + [[atts[name][0],name]]
        ordered.sort()
        for name in ordered:
            if (atts[name[1]][1] == "IMPLIED"):
                print "A%s IMPLIED" % (name[1])
            else:
                print "A%s %s %s" % (name[1],atts[name[1]][1],atts[name[1]][2])
        print "(%s" % self.GetElementName()
    else:
        print ")%s" % self.GetElementName()
```

CHAPTER 12

SOME PROCESSING EXAMPLES

12.1   Synopsis Generation

The intention of this application is to provide a mechanism for generating a summary of an SGML document that shows its hierarchical structure and provides some basic statistics. To keep the report simple, all occurrences of data content are "chopped" to five words or less. An example of the synopsis generator in action follows:

```
c>type memo.sgm

<!DOCTYPE memo SYSTEM "memo.dtd">
<memo>
<from>
<fname>Sean
<sname>Mc Grath
</from>
<to>
<fname>Mark
<sname>Uplang
</to>
<date YEAR = 1965 MONTH = 04 DAY = 27>
<subject>Greeting
<body>
<para>
May you be seven times better a year from tomorrow and if you are
not better may you not be worse.
</body>
</memo>

c>nsgmls memo.sgm | perl hier.pl

Hierarchical Summary Report

<MEMO>
    <FROM>
        <FNAME>
            Sean
        </FNAME>
        <SNAME>
```

```
                    Mc Grath
                </SNAME>
            </FROM>
            <TO>
                <FNAME>
                    Mark
                </FNAME>
                <SNAME>
                    Uplang
                </SNAME>
            </TO>
            <DATE>
            </DATE>
            <SUBJECT>
                Greeting
            </SUBJECT>
            <BODY>
                <PARA>
                    May you be seven times...
                </PARA>
            </BODY>
        </MEMO>
        C
        Total Element Nodes = 11
        Total Data Nodes 6
```

Here is the Perl implementation of this application. The $IndentationLevel variable stores the depth of nesting of elements by incrementing whenever an element open event occurs and decrementing on element close events. The value of $IndentationLevel is used in the various handlers to control the amount of padding on each output line.

```perl
# Synopsis Generator
#
require 'esis.pl';

$IndentationLevel = 0;
$ElementCount    = 0;
$DataNodeCount   = 0;

sub DEFAULT_OPEN_HANDLER {
    print "    " x $IndentationLevel , "<@_[0]>\n";
    $IndentationLevel++;
    $ElementCount++;
}

sub DEFAULT_CLOSE_HANDLER {
    $IndentationLevel--;
    print "    " x $IndentationLevel , "</@_>\n";
}

sub DATA_HANDLER {
    local ($_) = @_;
```

```
      # Match and keep first five words. Replace remainder
      # with ellipsis "..."
      s/^([^ ]* [^ ]* [^ ]* [^ ]* [^ ]*).*$/$1\.\.\./;
      # Deal with ESIS escape codes in data content
         # (See esis.pl for details)
      &unescape_data($_);
      print "    " x $IndentationLevel,"$_\n";
      $DataNodeCount++;
}
print "Hierarchical Summary Report\n\n";
&esis();
printf "Total Element Nodes = %d\nTotal Data Nodes %d\n",
$ElementCount,$DataNodeCount;
```

Here is the same application in the Python framework:

```
#
# Synopsis Generator

from sgmltree import *
from loadtree import *
from dumptree import *

# Define a new SGMLApplet derived class
class Dumper(SGMLApplet):
    def __init__(self):
        SGMLApplet.__init__(self)

    def Execute(self,T):
        # Variable to record indentation level
        self.IndentationLevel = 0;
        self.T = T
        # Do a tree walk
        self.Walk()
        print "C"
        return self.T

    def DATA_HANDLER(self,s):
        if (s):
            temp = splitfields(self.GetData()," ")
            if (len(temp) > 5):
                print "%s%s..." % ("    " * self.IndentationLevel,
        joinfields(temp[0:5]," "))
            else:
                print "%s%s" % ("    " * self.IndentationLevel,self.GetData())

    def DEFAULT_ELEMENT_HANDLER(self,s):
        if (s):
            print "%s<%s>" % ("    " * self.IndentationLevel,
        self.GetElementName())
            self.IndentationLevel = self.IndentationLevel + 1
        else:
```

```
                self.IndentationLevel = self.IndentationLevel - 1
                print "%s</%s>" % ("     " * self.IndentationLevel,
          self.GetElementName())

# Entry point of the application
Loader = LoadTree();
Dumper = Dumper();
T = SGMLTree();

T = Loader.Execute ();
Dumper.Execute(T);
```

12.2   Simple Text Formatting

Here is a simple but very useful application of the Perl framework for generating word-wrapped, paginated text from arbitrary SGML documents.

```
#
# Simple text formatter

require 'esis.pl';

# Format template for running header
format STDOUT_TOP =
@>>>>>>>>>>>>>>>>>>>>>>>>>>>>>>>>>>>>>>>>>>>>>>>>>>>>>>>>>>>>>>>>>>>>>>>
$%
.

# Format template for body text
format STDOUT =
^<<<<<<<<<<<<<<<<<<<<<<<<<<<<<<<<<<<<<<<<<<<<<<<<<<<<<<<<<<<<<<<<<<<~~
$_
.

sub DEFAULT_OPEN_HANDLER {
}

sub DEFAULT_CLOSE_HANDLER {
}

sub CONFORM_HANDLER {
}

sub DATA_HANDLER {
    local ($_) = @_;
    # Handle ESIS escape codes (see esis.pl for details)
    &unescape_data($_);
    # Write data via formatting templates
    write;
}

&esis();
```

An example using the memo.sgm file of the previous example follows. The 1 in the top right-hand corner is the Perl-generated page count.

```
C>nsgmls memo.sgm | perl textform.pl
                                                               1

Sean
Mc Grath
Mark
Uplang
Greeting
May you be seven times better a year from tomorrow and if you are
not better may you not be worse.
```

12.3   Element Context Reporting

It is often useful to know what contexts a particular element occurs in within documents. We will use the Python framework to develop such an application. The following application is used to generate a list of the contexts in which the FNAME element occurs in the memo example:

```
C>nsgmls memo.sgm | python contexts.py FNAME

['MEMO', 'FROM', 'FNAME']
['MEMO', 'TO', 'FNAME']
```

The tree navigation capabilities of the Python framework make this class of problem quite easy to implement because we can navigate the tree structure at will.

```
#
# Element Contexts reporter

from sgmltree import *
from loadtree import *
import sys

# Declare a new SGMLApplet derived class
class ElementContexts(SGMLApplet):
    def __init__(self):
        SGMLApplet.__init__(self)

    def Execute(self,T,ElementName):
        # Store the Element Name supplied
        self.ElementName = ElementName;
        self.T = T
        # Move to root of the tree
        self.T.MoveToRoot();
        # Perform a tree walk
        self.Walk()
        return self.T
```

```
      def DEFAULT_ELEMENT_HANDLER(self,s):
          if (s):
              if (self.GetElementName() == self.ElementName):
                  # Save current position
                  self.T.PushPosition()
                  # Accumulate "path" by walking backwards
                  # up to the root
                  self.Path = [self.ElementName]
                  while (self.T.HasUp()):
                      self.T.MoveUp();
                      self.Path = [self.T.GetElementName()] + self.Path
                  # Pop position
                  self.T.PopPosition()
                  # Print computed path
                  print self.Path;

  # Application entry point

  if (len(sys.argv) != 2):
      print "Usage: contexts <element name>\n";
  else:
      ElementName = sys.argv[1];

      Loader = LoadTree();
      Contexts = ElementContexts();

      T = SGMLTree();
      T = Loader.Execute ();
      Contexts.Execute(T,ElementName);
```

12.4   Publishing to HTML

In this example, the memo SGML document of this chapter is converted into a simple HTML page using the Perl framework:

```
C>nsgmls memo.sgm | perl memo2htm.pl

<!DOCTYPE html PUBLIC "-//IETF//DTD HTML 2.0//EN">
<HTML>
<TITLE>Memo
</TITLE>
<BODY>
<H1>Memo</H1>
<P>FROM:<B>Sean</B> Mc Grath</P>
<P>To:<B>Mark</B> Uplang</P>
<P>DATE:27/04/1965</P>
Greeting<P>
May you be seven times better a year from tomorrow and if you are
not better may you not be worse.</P>
```

```
</BODY>
</HTML>
```

Note that the output is itself a valid SGML document conforming to the HTML 2.0 DTD. The first few lines of ESIS from a parse of this output are shown here:

```
C>nsgmls memo.sgm | perl memo2htm.pl | nsgmls -mcatalog

AVERSION CDATA -//IETF//DTD HTML 2.0//EN
ASDAFORM CDATA Book
(HTML
(HEAD
ASDAFORM CDATA Ti
(TITLE
-Memo
)TITLE
)HEAD
(BODY
ASDAFORM CDATA H1
(H1
-Memo
)H1
-\n
ASDAFORM CDATA Para
(P
```

The -m switch was used to tell NSGMLS to use the file catalog for entity name resolution.

```
c>type catalog

PUBLIC "-//IETF//DTD HTML 2.0//EN" "HTML2.DTD"
```

Note also the automatically generated SDAFORM attributes on the various elements. These are some of the ICADD attributes used to facilitate the production of large print and braille versions of HTML documents for the reading impaired. Note that this is one instantaneous benefit from making sure your HTML documents are valid SGML! Here is the code for the application:

```
#
# Simple memo to HTML down-translation

require 'esis.pl';

sub OPEN_MEMO {
    print "<!DOCTYPE html PUBLIC \"-//IETF//DTD HTML 2.0//EN\">\n";
    print "<HTML>\n<TITLE>Memo\n</TITLE>\n<BODY>\n";
    print "<H1>Memo</H1>\n";
}

sub OPEN_FROM {
    print "<P>FROM:"
}

sub CLOSE_FROM {
```

```perl
    print "</P>\n";
}

sub OPEN_TO {
    print "<P>To:"
}

sub CLOSE_TO {
    print  "</P>\n";
}

sub OPEN_FNAME {
    print "<B>";
}

sub CLOSE_FNAME {
    print "</B> ";
}

sub OPEN_DATE {
    local ($day,$month,$year);
    $day   = &getattrvalue ("DAY",@_);
    $month = &getattrvalue ("MONTH",@_);
    $year  = &getattrvalue ("YEAR",@_);
    print "<P>DATE:" , $day, "/" , $month , "/" , $year , "</P>\n";
}

sub OPEN_PARA {
    print "<P>\n";
}

sub CLOSE_PARA {
    print "</P>\n";
}

sub DATA_HANDLER {
    # Handle ESIS escape codes (see esis.pl for details)
    &unescape_data(@_);
    print @_;
}

sub CLOSE_MEMO{
    print "</BODY>\n</HTML>";
}

sub DEFAULT_OPEN_HANDLER {
}

sub DEFAULT_CLOSE_HANDLER {
}

sub CONFORM_HANDLER {
}

&esis();
```

12.5 Publishing to RTF

The Microsoft Rich Text Format is a popular down-translation for SGML documents because RTF is supported by many DTP/WP tools and is also the base format for electronic publishing formats such as Microsoft Windows Help and Microsoft Multimedia Viewer.

Rich Text Format is a complex format and is a good candidate for encapsulation into a formatting back-end to be cleanly reused across a variety of publishing projects. Here we implement a rudimentary RTF back-end in Python using the class hierarchy shown in Figure 12.1.

In this simple illustration, the RTF back-end keeps track of the RTF formatting state variables for bold and left indent settings. These variables are exposed to derived classes in the form of methods BoldOn(), SetLeftIndent(), and the like. The idea is to a have a single implementation of the complex formatting state logic and a clean segregation between RTF formatting code minutiae and RTF formatting applications.

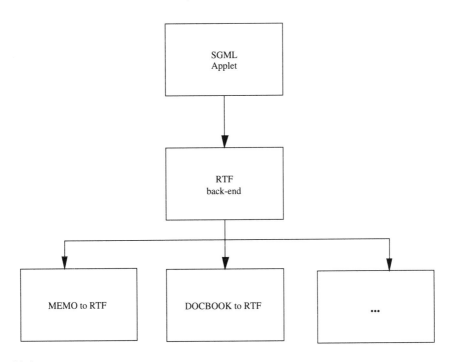

Figure 12.1 RTF back-end inheritance

```
#
# Simple RTF formatting BackEnd and sample memo application

from sgmltree import *
from loadtree import *
from string import *
import sys

class RTFBackEnd(SGMLApplet):
    def __init__(self):
        self.Bold = 0
        self.LeftIndent = 50
        # State variable controlling output of formatting
        # codes
        self.ParaStartRequired = 1
        self.file = None
        SGMLApplet.__init__(self)

    def BoldOn(self):
        self.Bold = 1

    def BoldOff(self):
        self.Bold = 0;

    def GetLeftIndent(self):
        return self.LeftIndent

    def SetLeftIndent(self,l):
        self.LeftIndent = l

    def StartRTF(self,fn):
        self.file = open (fn,"w");
        # RTF Header
        self.file.write ("""{\\rtf1\\ansi{\\fonttbl{\\f0\\fswiss arial;}}
{\\colortbl;\\red0\\green0\\blue0;}""")

    def EndRTF(self):
        self.file.write ("}")
        self.file.close()

    def StartPara(self):
        self.ParaStartRequired = 1;

    def EndPara(self):
        # RTF codes to end paragraph and restore default formats
        self.file.write ("\\par\\pard\n");
        self.ParaStartRequired = 1;

    def FormatText(self,t):
        if (self.ParaStartRequired == 1):
            self.ParaStartRequired = 0;
            # Paragraph level formatting codes
            self.file.write ("\li%d " % self.LeftIndent)
        if (self.Bold == 1):
            # Character level formatting codes
```

```
            self.file.write ("{\\b " + t + "}\n");
        else:
            self.file.write ("{\\b0 " + t + "}\n");
# Sample usage of RTFBackEnd in formatting memos
class Memo2RTF(RTFBackEnd):
    def __init__(self):
        RTFBackEnd.__init__(self)

    def Execute(self,T,fn):
        self.T = T
        self.StartRTF(fn)
        self.Walk()
        self.EndRTF()
        return self.T

    def FROM_HANDLER(self,s):
        if (s):
            self.StartPara()
            self.FormatText ("FROM: ")
        else:
            self.EndPara()

    def TO_HANDLER(self,s):
        if (s):
            self.StartPara()
            self.FormatText ("TO: ")
        else:
            self.EndPara()

    def SNAME_HANDLER(self,s):
        if (s):
            self.FormatText (" ")

    def DATA_HANDLER(self,s):
        if (s):
            d = self.T.GetData()
            d = joinfields (splitfields (d, '\\n'))
            self.FormatText(d)

    def DATE_HANDLER(self,s):
        if (s):
            self.StartPara()
            self.BoldOn()
            day = self.T.GetAttributeValue("DAY")
            month = self.T.GetAttributeValue("MONTH")
            year = self.T.GetAttributeValue("YEAR")
            self.FormatText ("DATE:%s/%s/%s" % (day,month,year))
        else:
            self.BoldOff()
            self.EndPara()

    def SUBJECT_HANDLER(self,s):
```

```
            if (s):
                self.StartPara()
                self.FormatText ("SUBJECT: ")
            else:
                self.EndPara()

        def PARA_HANDLER(self,s):
            if (s):
                self.StartPara()
                self.SetLeftIndent(self.GetLeftIndent() + 720)
            else:
                self.SetLeftIndent(self.GetLeftIndent() - 720)
                self.EndPara()

if (len(sys.argv) != 2):
    print "Usage: memo2rtf <rtf file>\n";
else:
    RTFFile = sys.argv[1];

    Loader = LoadTree();
    RTF = Memo2RTF();

    T = SGMLTree();
    T = Loader.Execute ();
    RTF.Execute(T,RTFFile);
```

The RTF generated from memo.sgm follows:

```
C>nsgmls memo.sgm | python memo2rtf.py memo.rtf
C>type memo.rtf

{\rtf1\ansi{\fonttbl{\f0\fswiss arial;}}
{\colortbl;\red0\green0\blue0;}\li50 {\b0 FROM: }
{\b0 Sean}
{\b0   }
{\b0 mac Grath}
\par\pard
\li50 {\b0 TO: }
{\b0 Mark}
{\b0   }
{\b0 Uplang}
\par\pard
\li50 {\b DATE:27/04/1965}
\par\pard
\li50 {\b0 SUBJECT: }
{\b0 Greeting}
\par\pard
\li770 {\b0 May you be seven times better a year from tomorrow and if you are
        not better may you not be worse.}
\par\pard
}
```

Although the formatting back-end approach has made this example longer that it needed to be, the effort will pay for itself many times over due to the reusability of the RTF back-end component.

12.6 Multifile Processing

More often than not, SGML-processing projects involve processing *collections* of SGML documents. In this section, a technique is presented that uses SGML to manage the processing of document collections. The illustrative problem we will address concerns the batch translation of perhaps thousands of office memoranda into a hyperlinked collection of World Wide Web documents. The overall structure of the resultant document set is shown in Figure 12.2 (using a set of three memos).

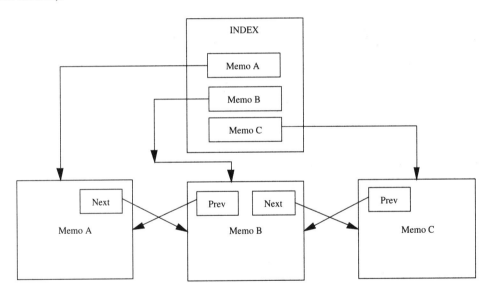

Figure 12.2 A mini-web of memo documents

The following single command is all that will be required to batch convert arbitrary numbers of memos into hyperlinked HTML:

```
C>nsgmls batch.prj | perl -x batch.prj
```

The core idea is to use the SGML file batch.prj to contain not only the memo collection data needed to control the batch process but also the batch processing code itself (in the form of Perl code using the Perl framework).

A sample memo HTML file resulting from such a command follows:

```
C>type memob.htm

<!DOCTYPE html PUBLIC "-//IETF//DTD HTML 2.0//EN">
<HTML>
<TITLE>Memo
</TITLE>
<BODY>
<H1>A collection of memos</H1>
<A href = "memoa.htm">PREV</A><BR>
<A href = "memoc.htm">NEXT</A><BR>
<P>FROM:<B>B</B> Mac Grath</P>
<P>To:<B>Mark</B> Uplang</P>
<P>DATE:27/04/1965</P>
Greeting<P>
May you be seven times better a year from tomorrow and if you are
not better may you not be worse.</P>
</BODY>
</HTML>
```

Note the PREV and NEXT hypertext links that link this memo to the others in the collection. These lines are also generated by the batch-processing code. The first step is to modify the memo to HTML down-translation discussed earlier to allow the provision of next/previous and header text on the command line:

```
#
# Memo to HTML down-translation (Modified to take command line parameters)

require 'esis.pl';
require 'getopt.pl';

sub OPEN_MEMO {
    print "<!DOCTYPE html PUBLIC \"-//IETF//DTD HTML 2.0//EN\">\n";
    print "<HTML>\n<TITLE>Memo\n</TITLE>\n<BODY>\n";
    print "<H1>$HeaderText</H1>\n";
    if ( $PrevFile ne "") {
        print "<A href = \"$PrevFile.htm\">PREV</A><BR>\n";
    }
    if ( $NextFile ne "") {
        print "<A href = \"$NextFile.htm\">NEXT</A><BR>\n";
    }
}

sub OPEN_FROM {
    print "<P>FROM:"
}

sub CLOSE_FROM {
    print "</P>\n";
}

sub OPEN_TO {
    print "<P>To:"
```

```perl
}
sub CLOSE_TO {
    print   "</P>\n";
}

sub OPEN_FNAME {
    print "<B>";
}

sub CLOSE_FNAME {
    print "</B> ";
}

sub OPEN_DATE {
    local ($day,$month,$year);
    $day = &getattrvalue ("DAY",@_);
    $month = &getattrvalue ("MONTH",@_);
    $year = &getattrvalue ("YEAR",@_);
    print "<P>DATE:" , $day, "/" , $month , "/" , $year , "</P>\n";
}

sub OPEN_PARA {
    print "<P>\n";
}

sub CLOSE_PARA {
    print "</P>\n";
}

sub DATA_HANDLER {
    &unescape_data(@_);
    print @_;
}

sub CLOSE_MEMO{
    print "</BODY>\n</HTML>";
}

sub DEFAULT_OPEN_HANDLER {
}

sub DEFAULT_CLOSE_HANDLER {
}

sub CONFORM_HANDLER {
}

&Getopt ('nph');
$NextFile = $opt_n;
$PrevFile = $opt_p;
$HeaderText = $opt_h;

&esis();
```

This new application takes three command-line parameters (-n for next, -p for previous, and -h for header text).

In order to generate the values for these parameters we need a project file to control what memo documents are to be included and in what order. We use an SGML-based project file for this purpose. In this project file we also store the necessary processing codes to create the HTML index page and generate the batch down-translation program "batch.bat":

```
C>type batch.prj

<!DOCTYPE memobatch [
<!ELEMENT memobatch - O (header,memo+)>
<!ELEMENT memo - O EMPTY>
<!ATTLIST memo filename CDATA #REQUIRED>
<!ELEMENT header - O EMPTY>
<!ATTLIST header text CDATA #REQUIRED>
]>
<memobatch>
<header text = "A collection of memos">
<memo filename = "memoa">
<memo filename = "memob">
<memo filename = "memoc">

<![IGNORE CDATA [
#!perl
require 'esis.pl';

@files = ();

sub OPEN_HEADER {
    $HeaderText = &getattrvalue ("TEXT",@_);
}

sub OPEN_MEMO {
    $FileName = &getattrvalue ("FILENAME",@_);
    # Accumulate array of filenames
    $files[++$#files] =  $FileName;
}

sub CLOSE_MEMOBATCH {
    # Generate Index Page
    open (INDEX,">index.htm") || die ("Cannot open index.htm");
    print INDEX "<!DOCTYPE HTML PUBLIC \"-//IETF//DTD HTML 2.0//EN\">\n";
    print INDEX "<TITLE>$HeaderText</TITLE>\n<BODY>\n";
    print INDEX "<H1>$HeaderText</H1>\n";
    for $f (@files) {
        print INDEX "<A href = \"$f.htm\">$f</A><BR>\n";
    }
    print INDEX "</BODY>\n</HTML>";
    close (INDEX);

    # Create Batch File for down-translation
    open (BATCH , ">batch.bat") || die ("Cannot open batch.bat");
```

```
    $f = @files[0];
    # First file has no "PREV" link
    print BATCH "nsgmls $f.sgm | perl memo2htm.pl -h \"$HeaderText\" -n
      @files[1] > $f.htm\n";
    $Count = 1;
    # All others except very last have both "NEXT" and "PREV" links
    for $f (@files[1..$#files-1]) {
        print BATCH "nsgmls $f.sgm | perl memo2htm.pl -h \"$HeaderText\" -p
      @files[$Count-1] -n @files[$Count+1] > $f.htm\n";
    }
    # Last file has no "NEXT" link
    $f = @files[$#files];
    print BATCH "nsgmls $f.sgm | perl memo2htm.pl -h \"$HeaderText\" -p
      @files[$#files-1] >$f.htm\n";
    close (BATCH);
    # Execute the batch file
    system ("batch.bat");
}

sub DEFAULT_OPEN_HANDLER {
}

sub DEFAULT_CLOSE_HANDLER {
}

sub DATA_HANDLER {
}

sub CONFORM_HANDLER {
}

&esis();
__END__
]]>
</memobatch>
```

Note the use of a CDATA marked section (see Section 13.9) to shield the Perl code from the SGML parser. The comment line #!perl is used to tell Perl where to start processing Perl code (the -x command-line parameter tells Perl to skip everything up to the #!perl comment).

The preceding Perl code generates a DOS batch file such as this:

```
nsgmls memoa.sgm | perl memo2htm.pl -h "A collection of memos" -n memob >
      memoa.htm
nsgmls memob.sgm | perl memo2htm.pl -h "A collection of memos" -p memoa -n
      memoc > memob.htm
nsgmls memoc.sgm | perl memo2htm.pl -h "A collection of memos" -p memob
      >memoc.htm
```

As in the Rich Text Format Formatting back-end example, the extra work done here to add complete automation adds complexity in the short term that pays for itself in the long term.

## CHAPTER 13

A CLOSE LOOK AT SOME SUBTLETIES

13.1   Introduction

This chapter focuses attention on some subtle issues—both philosophical and lexical—pertaining to SGML. It also discusses some markup constructs that have not been covered elsewhere in this book. These constructs are covered here either because they are infrequently used in practice or have associated subtleties that demand closer attention than would have been appropriate in Chapters 6 and 7.

13.2   Tight Versus Loose Content Models

Consider the problem of designing an SGML DTD (to be called DECK) that models a deck of playing cards.[1] Conceptually, the combination of a DTD and an SGML declaration allows a validating SGML parser to unambiguously distinguish document instances that conform to the DECK model from those that do not. The DECK model can be thought of as the definition for a *set* of document instances. Moreover, we can think of the DECK model as dividing the universe of SGML document instances into two subsets. This is illustrated in Figure 13.1.

A simple DTD and document instance for DECK follows:

```
<!DOCTYPE deck [
<!ELEMENT deck - O (club|diamond|heart|spade)+>
<!ELEMENT (club,diamond,heart,spade) - O EMPTY>
<!ATTLIST (club,diamond,heart,spade) value NUMBER #REQUIRED>
]>
<deck>
<club value = 3>
<diamond value = 1>
<spade value = 10>
...
</deck>
```

---

1. A 52 card deck, excluding Jokers.

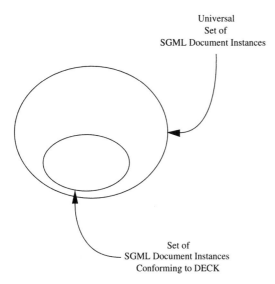

Universal
Set of
SGML Document Instances

Set of
SGML Document Instances
Conforming to DECK

Figure 13.1 DECK documents as a subset of the
SGML document universe

If we add the constraint that DECK documents will consist of cards *sorted* into suits in the order clubs, diamonds, spades, and hearts, this model still works. A validating SGML parser will judge a DECK document sorted in suit order the same way as a document with no suit ordering. However, the model has not captured the extra semantic information about the data. It is "looser" than it needs to be.

Here is a "tighter" model for DECK, called DECK1, that incorporates the extra sorting constraint:

```
<!DOCTYPE deck1 [
<!ELEMENT deck1 - O (club+,diamond+,spade+,heart+)>
<!ELEMENT (club,diamond,spade,heart) - O EMPTY>
<!ATTLIST (club,diamond,spade,heart) value NUMBER #REQUIRED>
]>
<deck1>
<club value = 1>
<club value = 2>
<club value = 3>
...
<diamond value = 1>
<diamond value = 2>
...
<spade value = 1>
...
<heart value = 1>
...
</deck1>
```

The design makes the fact that the data are sorted into suits an explicit part of the model. During data entry using this model, an SGML-aware authoring system would prompt for the clubs first, then the diamonds, and so on. Furthermore, a validating SGML parser using this model would reject documents with mixed suits.

In terms of sets, the DECK1 model can be considered a subset of the DECK model as shown in Figure 13.2. If the intention is that all DECKS should be sorted into suits, then the second model is probably preferable to the first because it allows SGML-aware tools to help in the authoring/data validation process. On the other hand, if being sorted is not a critical requirement, the extra restrictions on authoring and the like might be unnecessarily onerous.

This example illustrates a common tension in DTD design owing to the differing preferences of authors on one hand and software developers on the other. As a general principle, software developers like tight models and authors like loose models. The looser the content model, the more freedom the author enjoys in arranging content. The tighter the model, the easier it is for the software developer to deal with the permutations and combinations of elements that may occur in document instances. Document Type Definitions that allow just about every element type to occur almost everywhere in the document, may be an author's joy but they can be a developer's nightmare.

It can be very tempting to "loosen" a DTD to deal with document structures not foreseen during DTD analysis and design. For example, imagine that having checked thousands of sorted decks of cards, an *unsorted* deck is encountered. Loosening the DTD "solves" the immediate problem at the expense of significantly expanding "the set of valid documents" as illustrated in Figure 13.2.

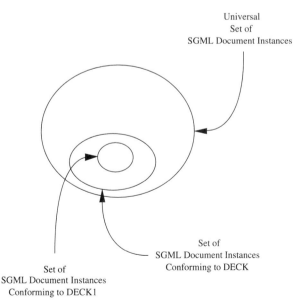

Universal
Set of
SGML Document Instances

Set of
SGML Document Instances
Conforming to DECK

Set of
SGML Document Instances
Conforming to DECK1

Figure 13.2 DECK1 documents as a subset of DECK documents

13.3   Levels of Semantic Checking

There are times when further levels of semantic checking are required over and above the semantic checks directly supported by DTD constructs. In some cases, these could be implemented at the DTD level but at the expense of unwieldy or complex DTDs. In other cases, they simply cannot be enforced at the DTD level without introducing counterintuitive element types into the models.

For example, consider how the semantic constraint "There are 52 cards in a valid deck of cards" would be applied to the DECK model of the previous section. It could be enforced by the parser with a content model like this:

```
<!DOCTYPE deck [
<!ELEMENT deck - O (card,card,card,card...card)> <!-- 52 cards-->
<!ELEMENT card - O EMPTY>
<!ATTLIST card type (club,diamond,spade,heart) #REQUIRED
               value NUMBER #REQUIRED>
]>
<deck>
<card type = club value = 1>
<card type = diamond value = 10>
...
</deck>
```

This will guarantee 52 cards in the deck but will not guarantee that the cards are unique or that the numbering extends from 1 to 13.[2]

Adding the extra semantic constraint that the deck must be sorted into suits and that all 13 cards per suit are present we need a new DTD, perhaps something like this:

```
<!DOCTYPE deck [
<!ELEMENT deck - O (suit,suit,suit,suit)>
<!ELEMENT suit - O (c1,c2,c3,c4,c5,c6,c7,c8,c9,c10,cj,cq,ck)>
<!ATTLIST suit type (club,diamond,spade,heart) #REQUIRED>
<!ELEMENT (c1,c2,c3,c4,c5,c6,c7,c8,c9,c10,cj,cq,ck) - O EMPTY>
]>
<deck>
<suit type = club>
<c1><c2>....
<suit type = diamond>
<c1><c2>....
<suit type = spade>
<c1><c2>....
<suit type = heart>
```

---

2. Note also that <card type = club value = 1> and <card type = club value = 01> are different as far as SGML is concerned (i.e., the NUMBER attribute declared value guarantees that such attributes consist solely of digits without enforcing any numerical interpretation on them).

```
<c1><c2>....
</deck>
```

This DTD guarantees us 52 cards, with each card in each suit accounted for. However, it does not enforce the uniqueness of each suit. To do that we need another change to the DTD:

```
<!DOCTYPE deck [
<!ELEMENT deck - O (clubs,diamonds,spades,hearts)>
<!ELEMENT (clubs,diamonds,spades,hearts) - O
       (c1,c2,c3,c4,c5,c6,c7,c8,c9,c10,cj,cq,ck)>
<!ELEMENT (c1,c2,c3,c4,c5,c6,c7,c8,c9,c10,cj,cq,ck) - O EMPTY>
]>
<deck>
<clubs>
<c1><c2>....
<diamonds>
<c1><c2>....
<spades>
<c1><c2>....
<hearts>
<c1><c2>....
</deck>
```

So far, the DTD is getting bigger with each new semantic constraint but is still manageable. How would the DTD cope with the constraint "If one ace is missing, they must all be missing."?

This is an awkward semantic constraint to enforce at the DTD level. It can be done by adding new element types to differentiate decks with aces from decks without. However the result is an unwieldy and counterintuitive DTD:

```
<!DOCTYPE deck [
<!ELEMENT deck - O (hasaces|noaces)>
<!ELEMENT hasaces - O (hclubs,hdiamonds,hspades,hhearts)>
<!ELEMENT noaces - O (nclubs,ndiamonds,nspades,nhearts)>
<!ELEMENT (hclubs,hdiamonds,hspades,hhearts) - O
(c1,c2,c3,c4,c5,c6,c7,c8,c9,c10,cj,cq,ck)>
<!ELEMENT (nclubs,ndiamonds,nspades,nhearts) - O
(c2,c3,c4,c5,c6,c7,c8,c9,c10,cj,cq,ck)>
<!ELEMENT (c1,c2,c3,c4,c5,c6,c7,c8,c9,c10,cj,cq,ck) - O EMPTY>
]>
```

It is far better to leave this semantic constraint out of the DTD to be implemented downstream. The decision as to where a semantic constraint will be enforced can be difficult, involving human as well as technical issues. Authors typically prefer to leave semantic constraints to the software developers who process the documents. Software developers on the other hand prefer to push as many semantic constraints as possible back out to the authors. The interests of the document owner in preserving the most useful and reusable information content must also be considered.

13.4   Format-Centric Content Models

When creating DTDs, information is often gathered from *rendered* documents (i.e., examining manuals, books, memoranda, and on-line help). As an information resource for creating DTDs, these are a partial but incomplete source.

In the majority of documents, the concept of a paragraph will appear at some level. This concept of *paragraph* will typically appear in the DTD at some level also. However, there may be many items that are *rendered* as paragraphs that have a semantic content that is invisible on the printed page, or monitor screen. There is no way to determine the presence of such semantic content by simply examining the rendered documents. One must talk to the organization that created them for that. Finding out what these semantic components are and incorporating them into the DTD is part of what makes SGML documents so much more useful than their purely format-centric counterparts. Ignoring such semantic components leads to the risk that the SGML will simply capture the format-centric model of the document evident from its rendered form.

Take a simple manual set as an example. Each manual consists of a collection of chapters. A natural model for this is

```
<!ELEMENT manual - O (chap+)>
```

However, what if the first chapter of each manual is *always* concerned with prerequisites and the second chapter is *always* a technical overview. Perhaps something like this would be better:

```
<!ELEMENT manual - O (pre-req,tech-rev,chap+)>
```

Concentrating purely on the format of the rendered manual can obscure such semantic content.

This idea applies to large and small document components alike. Perhaps italic text has been used to render notes, warnings, and emphasis text. Talking to the document creators and discovering that these three element types exist "hidden" behind their rendering as italic text leads to a more information content-centric model.

Note that tables of contents, indices, and the like may have no part in the SGML model of a manual at all. In other words, they may consist completely of *generated* material. In the case of tables of contents, indices, and so on, the fact that the material is derived from other sources is obvious. However, there may be incidents of derivation in the rendered documents that are more subtle. See the example on page 48.

The moral of the story is that there is more to a comprehensive DTD than a collection of element types and content models derived from an analysis of rendered documents. Note, however, that there are times when rendered documents are *unavoidably* the primary source. Tables and mathematical equations are the classic examples of this. Both pose particular challenges for information content-centric modeling as they intertwine information content and format in a deep way.

13.5   Processing Instructions

Processing instructions are an SGML construct that allow application-specific processing codes to be embedded in documents. They are provided to deal with situations where such system-dependent processing is unavoidable. The data in a processing instruction are passed directly on to the processing application without interpretation by the parser.

In the Reference Concrete Syntax, processing instructions start with a <? (PIO) and end with a > (PIC). In the following example, two processing instructions are used to pass Rich Text Formatting codes on to the RTF-aware application that is presumed to be processing the document.

```
C>type test.sgm

<!DOCTYPE test [
<!ELEMENT test - O (#PCDATA)>
]>
<test>
Hello<?{\fs20 > World
<?}>

C>nsgmls test.sgm

(TEST
-Hello
?{\\fs20
- World
?}
-\n
)TEST
C
```

Needless to say, processing instructions should be avoided if possible because they can significantly affect the portability of documents. They are there to provide an escape route to be used in emergencies only.

13.6   Records and Entity End Signals

As far as an SGML parser is concerned, the source SGML document consists of a stream of characters supplied by the system-specific entity manager. In the normal case, this stream of characters will be sprinkled with some sort of "end-of-line" character or character sequence. The mechanism used to achieve this is system-specific. On DOS/Windows, this is typically signaled by the numbers 13 and 10 in that order (carriage return and line feed in ASCII, respectively). On UNIX machines, the number 10 on its own is used (line feed in ASCII).

The notion of end-of-file is as system-specific as the notion of end-of-line. Some operating systems, such as DOS, allow files to be accessed in both text and binary modes. A DOS text file opened in text mode is considered to end with a Control-Z character. This may or may not correspond with the end of the file as far as the lower levels of the operating system are concerned.[3] On UNIX, the Control-D character serves a similar role.

The SGML standard does not concern itself with the specifics of how end-of-line or end-of-file are achieved, leaving these up to the system-specific entity manager. The parser expects the entity manager to convert the source into a collection of one or more records, terminated by an entity end signal. This entity end signal is known by the abstract name EE and is analogous to the use of the EOF constant in the C programming language.

As far as SGML is concerned, each source input line is a record with a RS (Record Start) at the start and a RE (Record End) at the end (with the exception of the very last record, which ends with an EE). It is up to the system-specific entity manager to create this structure, as shown in Figure 13.3.

In the Reference Concrete Syntax, RS is character 10 (ASCII linefeed) and an RE is character 13 (ASCII carriage return). Assuming that the file has been stored in a DOS/Windows text format, the test document will look like this to the entity manager:

```
<!DOCTYPE foo [(13)(10)
<!ELEMENT foo - O (#PCDATA)>(13)(10)
]>(13)(10)
<foo>Control-Z
```

The (13)(10) codes at the ends of the lines are replaced by RE codes and RS codes are added to the start of each record. Finally, the Control-Z is replaced by an EE:

```
RS<!DOCTYPE foo [RE
RS<!ELEMENT foo - O (#PCDATA)>RE
RS]>RE
RS<foo>Ee
```

The RS codes are dealt with early on in the initial parsing process and are ignored by the parser in the most common cases. The RE codes may or may not be considered part of the data content of a document and are therefore preserved for application use. (See Section 13.14—Mixed-Content Models and Section 13.15—Record Boundary Handling.)

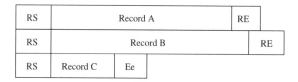

Figure 13.3 Record structure of an SGML document

---

3. A common trick in early versions of DOS was to use an embedded Control-Z character to cut short the operating system's parsing of configuration files such as config.sys and autoexec.bat.

13.7   Delimiter Recognition and Recognition Modes

One of the most fundamental tasks of an SGML parser is to tokenize its input stream, thereby distinguishing data content from markup. Like any markup language—programming languages included—there is a trade-off to be made between human readability on one hand and machine readability on the other. For example, this is a perfectly valid C program:

```
#include <stdio.h>
int main()
{
/* Some different uses of + */
int i=1;
char *s = "i++";
i+=i+++i+++i;
printf ("%d",i);
}
```

In this "document" the plus sign (+) serves a number of different roles:

1. Part of a comment

2. Part of a literal string

3. Part of the += operator

4. Part of the ++ operator

5. The + operator

The C language defines how the parser determines which "role" the plus sign is playing in a variety of ways. For example, the C preprocessor takes care of role 1. The lexical analyzer most likely takes care of the other roles in conjunction with the core grammar of the language and operator precedence rules. These rules allow the compiler to recognize the true meanings of the plus signs in the preceding example, making the document machine readable. However, it is clearly far less readable to humans.

At the other end of the spectrum, the following is easy for a human to read and understand but difficult (actually impossible) for a C compiler:

```
#include <stdio.h>
int main()
{
int i = 1 , j = 1;
i + = j;
j += i
printf ("i = %d
        j = %d",i,j);
}
```

This program has three syntax errors:

1. Newlines are not allowed in constants (such as the string in the printf command).

2. No space is allowed between the + and the = in the assignment to i.

3. The semicolon statement separator cannot be inferred by the C parser.

In this program, the human reader infers a lot of semantics based on how the program has been white-spaced and on the contextual information around each statement.

SGML endeavors to find a compromise between these two extremes by means of a set of recognition modes. Simply put, the idea is that certain delimiters are constrained so as to be recognized as *delimiters* within certain parsing modes and considered *data* in others. Moreover, the standard specifies certain contextual constraints that delimiters must meet in order to be recognized. These contextual constraints typically take the form of a constraint on what character(s) must follow them in order for the parser to conclude that they are indeed delimiters. A delimiter, constrained by some surrounding context information, is known as a delimiter-in-context.

There are ten recognition modes and eight contextual constraints. These are cross-tabulated with the delimiters in the SGML standard (ISO 8879, §9.6.1). An excerpt from the tables is shown in Tables 13.1 through 13.3.

Table 13.1: Examples of delimiters with their recognition modes and contextual constraints

Delimiter Name	String	Modes in which recognized	Contextual Constraint	Description
AND	&	GRP		And Connector
CRO	&#	CON LIT	CREF	Character Reference Open

Table 13.2: Example of a contextual constraint

Contextual Constraint	Meaning
CREF	Must be a character that begins a name or a digit

Table 13.3: Examples of recognition modes

Recognition Mode	Meaning
GRP	Recognized in a group
CON	Recognized in content and marked sections
LIT	Recognized in literals

As can be seen, the character reference open delimiter string &# is only recognized in CON mode with the contextual constraint that it must be followed by a name start character or a digit. The effects of this can be seen in the following document in which only two occurrences of the &# sequence meet the contextual constraint:

```
C>type test.sgm

<!DOCTYPE test [
<!ELEMENT test - O (#PCDATA)>
<!ATTLIST test foo CDATA #REQUIRED>
]>
<test foo = "&#! &#65;">
&#66;
& # 6 6 ;

C>nsgmls test.sgm

AFOO CDATA &#! A
(TEST
-B\n& # 6 6 ;
)TEST
C
```

13.8   Data Content Variations

In Section 6.5.8—Declared Content Variations, element types with RCDATA and CDATA data content were briefly discussed. In this section they are discussed in more detail.

There are times when it is convenient to be able to enter text that *could* be construed as markup in a way that shields it from being recognized as markup by the parser. Perhaps the classic example of this is when we must include examples of SGML markup in an SGML document. However, the problem manifests itself anywhere in which data content *might* contain delimiters likely to attract the attention of the parser. Here is a very simple example taken from an imaginary C programming manual:

```
C>type test.sgm

<!DOCTYPE manual [
<!ELEMENT manual - O (cprog)+>
<!ELEMENT cprog - O (#PCDATA)>
]>
<manual>
<cprog>
#include <stdio.h>
int main()
{
void *s = &s;
}
</cprog>

C>nsgmls test.sgm

test.sgm:7:18:E: element 'STDIO.H' undefined
test.sgm:10:12:E: general entity 's' not defined and no default entity
```

```
(MANUAL
(CPROG
-#include
(STDIO.H
-int main()\n{\nvoid *s = \n}
)STDIO.H
)CPROG
)MANUAL
```

Two things have gone wrong here. First, the angle brackets around stdio.h have caused the parser to consider <stdio.h> as a start-tag. Second, the C syntax for address of variable s combined with the semicolon statement separator is the same as an SGML general entity reference &s;. The CDATA and RCDATA data content types provide ways of dealing with such situations. The RCDATA keyword is used to tell the parser that the data content does not contain any markup other than character entity references, general entity references, and the characters that signal the end of an element. The effect of changing the **cprog** element type to have a declared content of RCDATA follows:

```
C>type test.sgm

<!DOCTYPE manual [
<!ELEMENT manual - O (cprog)+>
<!ELEMENT cprog - O RCDATA>
]>
<manual>
<cprog>
#include <stdio.h>
int main()
{
void *s = &s;
}
</cprog>

C>nsgmls test.sgm

test.sgm:10:12:E: general entity 's' not defined and no default entity
(MANUAL
(CPROG
-#include <stdio.h>\nint main()\n{\nvoid *s = \n}
)CPROG
)MANUAL
```

This has resolved the stdio.h problem because the RCDATA inhibits the parser from checking for start- and end-tags. The entity reference issue, however, remains.

The CDATA declared content type tells the parser that the data content does not include any markup whatsoever apart from a character sequence that would terminate an element.

The effect of replacing the RCDATA with CDATA in the example follows:

```
C>type test.sgm

<!DOCTYPE manual [
<!ELEMENT manual - O (cprog)+>
<!ELEMENT cprog - O CDATA>
]>
<manual>
<cprog>
#include <stdio.h>
int main()
{
void *s = &s;
}
</cprog>

C>nsgmls test.sgm

(MANUAL
(CPROG
-#include <stdio.h>\nint main()\n{\nvoid *s = &s;\n}
)CPROG
)MANUAL
C
```

Note that in both the CDATA and RCDATA cases, the round brackets have disappeared from the element type declaration. This is because CDATA and RCDATA are *declared content* types as opposed to parts of *content models*. The #PCDATA keyword, on the other hand, is part of a content model and thus requires round brackets to delimit it.[4]

The following document illustrates the error that will occur if the brackets are left in:

```
C>type test.sgm

<!DOCTYPE test [
<!ELEMENT test - O (CDATA)>
]>
<test>
Hello World

C>nsgmls test.sgm

test.sgm:5:1:E: element 'CDATA' undefined
(TEST
(CDATA
-Hello World
)CDATA
)TEST
```

The parser has treated **test** as an element type with a model group consisting of one occurrence of the element type CDATA.

---

4. This is also the reason for the leading # character when PCDATA is used in content models. PCDATA without the # in a content model would be interpreted as an element type named PCDATA.

Both CDATA and RCDATA elements need to be treated with caution as a result of the issues surrounding how the parser *terminates* these elements. Conceptually, neither CDATA nor RCDATA elements recognize end-tags, which leads us to question how they recognize *their own* end-tags.

The SGML standard (ISO 8879, §7.6) says that CDATA or RCDATA are terminated by an ETAGO delimiter-in-context. The contextual constraint placed on the recognition of ETAGO is that it must be followed by a name start character.[5] The standard goes on to say that the termination is an error if it would also have been an error had the content been mixed content.

This means that the first occurrence of a character sequence that looks like an end-tag will terminate the CDATA or RCDATA element. Furthermore, this sequence will go on to be judged on its own merits as an end-tag and will generate an error *unless* it is valid markup at that point in the document.

The following example illustrates how ETAGOs that are not followed by a name start character fail to trigger the ending of the CDATA element:

```
C>type test.sgm

<!DOCTYPE test [
<!ELEMENT test - O (foo)+>
<!ELEMENT foo  - O CDATA>
]>
<test>
<foo>
I am a foo element </& </! I am still foo </foo>
</test>

C>nsgmls test.sgm

(TEST
(FOO
-I am a foo element </& </! I am still foo
)FOO
)TEST
C
```

The following example illustrates how, having first triggered the ending of a CDATA element, the (partial) end-tag is then treated on its own merits:

```
C>type test.sgm

<!DOCTYPE test [
<!ELEMENT test - O (foo)+>
<!ELEMENT foo  - O CDATA>
]>
<test>
```

---

5. There are some other constraints when certain optional features of the standard are specified in the SGML declaration. See the SGML standard (ISO 8879, §9.6.2) for details.

```
<foo>
I am a foo element </& </! I am still foo </f
</test>

C>nsgmls test.sgm

test.sgm:8:1:E: end tag for element 'F' which is not open
(TEST
(FOO
-I am a foo element </& </! I am still foo
)FOO
)TEST
```

The following example illustrates a situation in which the end-tag that triggers the end of the CDATA element results in a different form of parsing error:

```
C>type test.sgm

<!DOCTYPE test [
<!ELEMENT test - - (foo)+>
<!ELEMENT foo  - - (#PCDATA|bar)+>
<!ELEMENT bar  - - CDATA>
]>
<test>
<foo>
I am a foo element
<bar>
I am a bar element. </foo>
</test>

C>nsgmls test.sgm

test.sgm:10:26:E: end tag for 'BAR' omitted, but its declaration does not
      permit this
test.sgm:9:1: start tag was here
(TEST
(FOO
-I am a foo element\n
(BAR
-I am a bar element.
)BAR
)FOO
)TEST
```

In this case, the CDATA element is ended via the </foo> end-tag. The parser then concludes from the </foo> end-tag that the </bar> end-tag has been omitted in contravention of its declaration. Making the end-tag of the bar element type omissible fixes this problem:

```
C>type test.sgm

<!DOCTYPE test [
<!ELEMENT test - - (foo)+>
<!ELEMENT foo  - - (#PCDATA|bar)+>
```

```
<!ELEMENT bar  - O CDATA>
]>
<test>
<foo>
I am a foo element
<bar>
I am a bar element. </foo>
</test>

C>nsgmls test.sgm

(TEST
(FOO
-I am a foo element\n
(BAR
-I am a bar element.
)BAR
)FOO
)TEST
C
```

The benefits of CDATA and RCDATA elements have to be weighed against the potential difficulties in protecting their data content against premature termination or inadvertent markup interpretation. Such protection can be achieved in a variety of ways, each with its own advantages and disadvantages. If RCDATA is being used, perhaps the most obvious way is to protect the ETAGO character sequence whenever it occurs. This can be done with a CDATA entity as follows:

```
C>type test.sgm

<!DOCTYPE test [
<!ENTITY etago CDATA "</">
<!ELEMENT test - O RCDATA>
]>
<test>
I am a test element. &etago;test> I am still the test element.
</test>

C>nsgmls test.sgm

(TEST
-I am a test element. </test> I am still the test element.
)TEST
C
```

Of course, going this route may require protecting the & character as well!

```
C>type test.sgm

<!DOCTYPE test [
<!ENTITY amp CDATA "&">
<!ELEMENT test - O RCDATA>
]>
<test>
```

```
In the P&amp;L account...
</test>

C>nsgmls test.sgm

(TEST
-In the P&L account...
)TEST
C
```

Alternative methods include CDATA/RCDATA marked sections (see Section 13.9—Marked Section Variations) and data entities (see Section 13.12—Data Entity Variations).

13.9   Marked Section Variations

In Section 7.8—Marked Sections, we saw how the INCLUDE and EXCLUDE keywords can be used to control whether or not the parser ignores or processes the contents of the marked section. Apart from INCLUDE and EXCLUDE, the standard allows control to be exerted over how the contents of the marked section will be treated by the parser. As with element types, marked sections can be declared to contain CDATA or RCDATA content. An example using CDATA follows:

```
C>type test.sgm

<!DOCTYPE test [
<!ELEMENT test - O (#PCDATA)>
]>
<test>
<![ INCLUDE CDATA [
<!DOCTYPE test - O (#PCDATA)>
]>
<test>
</test>
]]>
</test>

C>nsgmls test.sgm

(TEST
-<!DOCTYPE test - O (#PCDATA)>\n]>\n<test>\n</test>
)TEST
C
```

As can be seen, the marked section contains a significant amount of data that would normally be construed as markup. The CDATA keyword protects it from interpretation.

Note that the first occurrence of the]]> sequence will terminate the marked section. In this respect, it suffers from a drawback similar to that of the CDATA/RCDATA element types discussed in the previous section except that the string is less likely to occur in data. CDATA marked sections are often used to include SGML markup examples in SGML documents as follows:

```
<!DOCTYPE foo [
<!ELEMENT foo - O (#PCDATA)>
]>
<foo>
<![CDATA[
This document starts with the following markup:-
<!DOCTYPE foo [
<!ELEMENT foo - O (#PCDATA)>
]>
<foo>
]]>
```

13.10 Short References

Short references are a very general and powerful way of mapping certain character or character sequences to SGML entities. They are typically used as a markup reduction mechanism. The fact that "white space" characters such as tabs and record start/end codes can be short references makes them particularly powerful for this purpose.

The reference concrete syntax defines a set of characters and character sequences that can be used as short references. By modifying the SGML declaration, others can be added if required. See Table 13.4.

In order to use short references, three things are needed. First, an entity to provide the replacement for the short-reference character sequence. Second, a SHORTREF mapping declaration to map the short-reference character sequence to the desired entity. Third, a USEMAP declaration to indicate when the short-reference map is active.

Table 13.4: Short references in the reference concrete syntax

Short Reference	Interpretation
&#TAB;	Tab character
&#RE;	Record end
&#RS;	Record start
&#RS;B	Record start + tabs or white space (leading blanks)
&#RS;&#RE;	Empty record
B&#RE;	Tabs or white space + RE (trailing blanks)
&#SPACE;	Space
BB	Two or more blanks[*]
"	Quotation mark
=	Equals sign

[*]Note that B means one or more blanks, BB = two or more etc.

The following example uses a short-reference map to cause the parser to treat the "=" character as markup within **stmt** elements. This simplifies markup yet allows the parser to segregate **lvalue** and **rvalue** elements as follows:

```
C>type assigns.sgm

<!DOCTYPE assigns [
<!ENTITY rvalue STARTTAG "rvalue">
<!SHORTREF testmap "=" rvalue>
<!USEMAP testmap assigns>
<!ELEMENT assigns - O (stmnt)+>
<!ELEMENT stmnt - O (lvalue,rvalue)+>
<!ELEMENT (lvalue,rvalue) O O (#PCDATA)>
]>
<assigns>
<stmnt>
var1= 3 * 4/2
<stmnt>
var2 = var1 * 7

C>nsgmls assigns.sgm

(ASSIGNS
(STMNT
(LVALUE
-var1
)LVALUE
(RVALUE
- 3 * 4/2
)RVALUE
)STMNT
(STMNT
(LVALUE
-var2
)LVALUE
(RVALUE
- var1 * 7
)RVALUE
)STMNT
)ASSIGNS
C
```

An application can have multiple short-reference maps each of which can contain multiple short references. Short-reference maps are associated with element types and do not merge with short-reference maps of subelements. In other words, the activation of a short-reference map suspends any other short-reference map that may be active until the end of its element.

USEMAP declarations that appear in DTDs associate short-reference maps with element types. It is also possible to both activate and deactivate short-reference maps from within a document instance as follows:

```
C>type assigns.sgm

<!DOCTYPE assigns [
<!ENTITY rvalue STARTTAG "rvalue"> <!-- See 13.11.3 -->
<!SHORTREF testmap "=" rvalue>
<!ELEMENT assigns - O (stmnt)+>
<!ELEMENT stmnt - O (lvalue,rvalue)+>
<!ELEMENT (lvalue,rvalue) O O (#PCDATA)>
]>
<assigns>
<!USEMAP testmap>
<stmnt>
var1= 3 * 4/2
<stmnt>
<!USEMAP #EMPTY>
var2 = var1 * 7

C>nsgmls assigns.sgm

test.sgm:14:17:E: 'STMNT' not finished but document ended
(ASSIGNS
(STMNT
(LVALUE
-var1
)LVALUE
(RVALUE
- 3 * 4/2
)RVALUE
)STMNT
(STMNT
(LVALUE
-var2 = var1 * 7
)LVALUE
)STMNT
)ASSIGNS
```

Here the USEMAP declaration is in force for the first **stmt** element and turned off for the second. The parser treats the data content of the second **stmt** element as the **lvalue**. Therefore, the parser complains about the unfinished second **stmt** element.

Note that when USEMAP declarations are used within a document instance, only the short-reference map needs to be named. Note also that the #EMPTY keyword causes the deactivation of any active short-reference map. As usual, the USEMAP is effective until the end of the element.

13.11 Text Entity Variations

SGML text entities were discussed in Chapter 7 and mention was made of the fact that certain variations are allowed in order to further specify the purpose/interpretation of the entity. The six variations are discussed in the subsections that follow.

13.11.1 SDATA

An SDATA text entity is one whose replacement text contains characters that are specific to a particular system, device, or application. They are commonly used to make explicit to both the user and the parser that the replacement text may require attention when the hosting document is moved from one system to another. It can, for example, be used for commands that return data as follows:

```
C>type test.sgm

<!DOCTYPE test [
<!ENTITY foo SDATA "date">
<!ELEMENT test - O (#PCDATA)>
]>
<test>
&date;
</test>

C>nsgmls test.sgm

(TEST
-\|date\|
)TEST
C
```

Notice the \| before and after the replacement text; it is used in the ESIS to delineate SDATA entities. In this example, it is intended that processing software will convert the date SDATA entity into a date string such as "16 June 1904."

13.11.2 CDATA

A CDATA text entity is one whose replacement text contains character data. This is text that is not specific to a particular system, device, or application and in which no markup is recognized.

```
C>type test.sgm

<!DOCTYPE test [
<!ENTITY foo CDATA "<bar>">
<!ELEMENT test - O (#PCDATA)>
]>
<test>
&foo;
</test>

C>nsgmls test.sgm

(TEST
-<bar>
)TEST
C
```

Note that the ESIS stream contains no mention of the CDATA entity. The fact that the text <bar> was included in the **test** element via a CDATA entity is not part of the information that structure-controlled applications (i.e., ESIS processors) are allowed to work with.

13.11.3 STARTTAG/ENDTTAG

The STARTTAG/ENDTTAG variations are used when it is desirable to inform the parser unambiguously that the entity is to serve as a start-tag or an end-tag.

```
C>type test.sgm

<!DOCTYPE test [
<!ENTITY foo STARTTAG "bar">
<!ELEMENT test - O (#PCDATA)>
]>
<test>
&foo;
</test>

C>nsgmls test.sgm

test.sgm:6:6:E: element 'BAR' undefined
(TEST
(BAR
)BAR
)TEST
```

Note that the parser has inferred that the foo entity is a start-tag and thus complains that the **bar** element type has not been declared.

Note also that the delimiters for start- and end-tags were automatically generated as part of the entity replacement text and then were parsed to produce the ESIS.

13.11.4 PI

PI is used for entities that are processing instructions.

```
C>type test.sgm

<!DOCTYPE test [
<!ENTITY foo PI "bar">
<!ELEMENT test - O (#PCDATA)>
]>
<test>
&foo;
</test>

C>nsgmls test.sgm

(TEST
```

```
?bar
)TEST
C
```

Note that the delimiters for processing instructions were automatically generated as part of the entity replacement text and then were parsed to produce the ESIS.

13.11.5 MS

MS is used for entities that are marked sections.

```
C>type test.sgm

<!DOCTYPE test [
<!ENTITY foo MS "INCLUDE [bar">
<!ELEMENT test - O (#PCDATA)>
]>
<test>
&foo;
</test>

C>nsgmls test.sgm

(TEST
-bar
)TEST
C

C>type test.sgm

<!DOCTYPE test [
<!ENTITY foo MS "IGNORE [bar">
<!ELEMENT test - O (#PCDATA)>
]>
<test>
&foo;
</test>

C>nsgmls test.sgm

(TEST
)TEST
C
```

13.11.6 MD

MD is used for entities that are markup declarations.

```
C>type test.sgm

<!DOCTYPE test [
```

```
<!ENTITY equals STARTTAG "equals">
<!SHORTREF equals "="   equals>
<!ENTITY MapEQ MD "USEMAP equals">
<!ENTITY MapOff MD "USEMAP #EMPTY">
<!ELEMENT equals - O EMPTY>
<!ELEMENT test - O (#PCDATA|equals)+>
]>
<test>
&MapEQ;
I am an = sign
&MapOff;
I am an = sign

C>nsgmls test.sgm

(TEST
-I am an
(EQUALS
)EQUALS
- sign\nI am an = sign\n
)TEST
C
```

In this example, two MD entities called MapEQ and MapOff are used in the document instance to achieve the same effect in replacement text as USEMAP declarations would have achieved if entered directly.

13.12 Data Entity Variations

In Section 7.7.2—Data Entities, mention was made of the fact that external data entities come in a variety of flavors. There are in fact three of them—CDATA, NDATA, and SDATA—as shown in Table 13.5.

Table 13.5: Data entity types

Data Entity Type	Interpretation
CDATA	The entity contains character data. No markup is recognized in it.
SDATA	The entity contains systems-specific character data (i.e., data that are specific to a system, application, or device).
NDATA	The entity contains non-SGML (i.e., "binary" data).

An example using CDATA follows:

```
C>type test.sgm

<!DOCTYPE test [
```

```
<!NOTATION mydata SYSTEM>
<!ENTITY foo SYSTEM "foo.dat" CDATA mydata>
<!ELEMENT test - O (#PCDATA)>
]>
<test>
&foo;

C>nsgmls test.sgm

(TEST
NMYDATA
sfoo.dat
f<OSFILE FIND>foo.dat
Efoo CDATA MYDATA
&foo
-\n
)TEST
C
```

13.13 Obfuscatory Entity References

In Chapter 7 reference was made to the fact that parameter entities are not exactly analogous to a macro substitution facility such as were provided by the C preprocessor. The difference is that the standard explicitly forbids the use of entities in ways that might obscure the underlying markup structure or appear to be an error to the human eye. This is best illustrated by example. The following document is valid:

```
C>type test.sgm

<!DOCTYPE test [
<!ENTITY % foobar "(foo,bar)*">
<!ELEMENT test - O (%foobar;)>
<!ELEMENT (foo,bar) - O (#PCDATA)>
]>
<test>

C>nsgmls test.sgm

(TEST
)TEST
C
```

Notice that the foobar parameter entity contains a complete, self-contained markup construct—namely a model group with the REP occurrence indicator. The following document is invalid:

```
C>type test.sgm

<!DOCTYPE test [
```

```
<!ENTITY % foobar "(foo,bar)">
<!ELEMENT test - O %foobar;*>
<!ELEMENT (foo,bar) - O (#PCDATA)>
]>
<test>

C>nsgmls test.sgm

test.sgm:3:28:E: character '*' invalid: only delimiter '>', inclusions,
        exclusions and parameter separators allowed
```

Informally, and with some exceptions, the rule is that both the opening and closing delimiters for any given SGML construct must occur within the same entity. See the SGML standard (ISO 8879, §9.4.3) for complete details.

13.14 Mixed-Content Models

SGML elements that can contain a mixture of subordinate elements and/or data are said to have mixed-content models. We have seen that, in general, a record end code (RE) is ignored if it immediately follows a start-tag or immediately precedes an end-tag. In mixed-content models, some records ends could legitimately be part of the data content whereas others could be there purely for reasons of markup. The parsers decision as to which is which may be surprising to the unwary—especially when the validity of PCDATA content is restricted to certain parts of the content model.

The following document illustrates the issue:

```
C>type test.sgm

<!DOCTYPE test [
<!ELEMENT test - O (x , #PCDATA)>
<!ELEMENT x - O (#PCDATA)>
]>
<test>
<x>
Hello World

C>nsgmls test.sgm

test.sgm:5:7:E: start tag for 'X' omitted, but its declaration does not permit
        this
test.sgm:6:3:E: element 'X' not allowed here
```

The problem here is that the **test** element type has a mixed-content model, thus causing the parser to consider record ends as potentially part of the data content. Having consumed the test start-tag, the parser encounters a record end. Because the content model for the **test** element type is mixed content, this record end is perfectly valid PCDATA. By examining the content model, the parser concludes that it is now in the PCDATA part of the content model. It thus tries to *infer* the presence of the **x** element. It concludes that the start-tag for the **x** element was omitted and then complains that the declaration of the **x** element type does not permit this.

By making the start- and end-tags of the **x** element type omissible we get a different error:

```
C>type test.sgm

<!DOCTYPE test [
<!ELEMENT test - O (x , #PCDATA)>
<!ELEMENT x O O (#PCDATA)>
]>
<test>
<x>
Hello World

C>nsgmls test.sgm

test.sgm:6:3:E: element 'X' not allowed here
(TEST
(X
(X
-Hello World\n
)X
)X
)TEST
```

Here, the parser has successfully inferred the presence of an **x** element as a result of encountering the record end after the **test** start-tag. However, it then encounters a second (explicitly provided) **x** element start-tag and complains that **x** is not allowed to occur within **x**!

There are numerous other scenarios in which record ends can yield surprising results in mixed content. As a result, the SGML standard strongly recommends that whenever mixed content is used, PCDATA should be valid *everywhere* in the content model—in other words, that PCDATA always occurs as part of a repeatable OR group:

```
C>type test.sgm

<!DOCTYPE test [
<!ELEMENT test - O (x | #PCDATA)*>
<!ELEMENT x O O (#PCDATA)>
]>
<test>
<x>
Hello World

C>nsgmls test.sgm

(TEST
(X
-Hello World\n
)X
)TEST
C
```

13.15 Record Boundary Handling

In order to make SGML documents legible to humans working with non-SGML-specific tools such as generic text editors and word processors, SGML has to grapple with the thorny issue of how to deal with the notion of a line. The crux of the problem is that there are times when lines— or more specifically end-of-line markers—are significant to the SGML parser and other times when they are not.

For example, many text editors impose a limit on the maximum line length they can handle, thus forcing the use of end-of-line markers purely for compatibility with the text editor. When authoring SGML, it can be natural to insert end-of-line markers to "break up" the text and markup like this:

```
<DOCTYPE foo SYSTEM "foo.dtd">
<foo>
<table>
<row>
<cell>
Line 1
Line 2</cell>
<cell>Cell 2 contains so much text that it will wrap
in this text editor</cell>
</row>
</table>
</foo>
```

Which end-of-line markers are actually part of the content and which are simply segregators between content and markup?

The simple rule that an end-of-line marker (or a *record end* in SGML terminology) in content is insignificant if it immediately follows a start-tag or immediately precedes an end-tag has a number of subtle exceptions. For full details refer to the SGML standard (ISO 8879, §7.6.1). Later in this section we illustrate one of the subtleties that deal with inclusion exceptions. First, we expand the simple rule into a more formal summary.[6]

An RE in data is significant (i.e., is passed to an application) except when it is caused by markup, that is, when it occurs in any of the patterns shown in Table 13.6, where

```
nondata ::=
                comment declaration
            | processing instruction
            | marked section declaration start
            | marked section end
            | included subelement
            | shortref use declaration
            | link set use declaration
```

---

6. Summary created by Charles Goldfarb, James Clark, and Michael Sperberg-McQueen.

Table 13.6: Patterns indicating insignificant RE

Pattern	Examples
element-start nondata* **RE**	<foo>**RE** <foo><!--Hello World-->**RE** <foo><? SetFont(1)>**RE**
RE nondata* element-end	**RE**</foo> **RE**<!--Hello World--></foo> **RE**<? SetFont(1)></foo>
RS nondata+ **RE**	**RS**<!-- Hello World-->**RE** **RS**<? SetFont(1)>**RE**

```
marked section declaration start ::=
        marked section start
      , status keyword specification
      , declaration subset open
```

In applying the rule, a *reference* is transparent; only its replacement is considered:

```
reference ::=
        character reference
      | entity reference
      | short reference
```

Finally, the rule is applied recursively to the data of included subelements.

We now turn to a subtle aspect of record-end handling that deals with inclusion exceptions. In the course of parsing an occurrence of an element, an SGML parser treats the REs relating to subelements differently depending on whether the subelement is native to the content model (i.e., a proper subelement) or an inclusion exception. (In the following examples, bold text is used to indicate the record ends for easy reference. Here is an example of RE-handling relating to element **foo** where **foo** is a proper subelement of **test**.)

```
C>type prop.sgm

<!doctype test [
<!element test - O (#PCDATA|foo)+>
<!element foo - O (#PCDATA)>
]>
<test>Hello**RE**
<foo>I am foo</foo>World</test>

C>nsgmls prop.sgm

(TEST
-Hello**RE**
(FOO
-I am foo
)FOO
```

```
-World
)TEST
C
```

Here is the same document instance but with **foo** as an inclusion exception of **test**:

```
C>type inc.sgm

<!doctype test [
<!element test - O (#PCDATA) +(foo)>
<!element foo - O (#PCDATA)>
]>
<test>HelloRE
<foo>I am foo</foo>World</test>

C>nsgmls inc.sgm

(TEST
-Hello
(FOO
-I am foo
)FOO
-REWorld
)TEST
C
```

Notice that the RE after Hello has *moved* to after the **foo** element. This is a partly a consequence of the second of the three pattern rules listed earlier in this section, namely "RE non-data element-end." At the point where the parser encounters the RE, it does not know what it has yet to encounter before the end of the element. It might conceivably see many megabytes of data before the element end. This would necessitate an unlimited look-ahead by the parser to resolve. To obviate the need for unlimited look-ahead the standard allows such a deferred RE to be deemed to have occurred immediately prior to the next data or proper subelement. In other words, the parser holds on to an included RE until it encounters either (a) a proper subelement or data or (b) the element-end.

In the former case the RE is passed on to the application as if it occurred immediately prior to the subelement or data. In the latter case, the RE is ignored.

13.16 Ambiguous-Content Models

We have already seen a number of areas in which the SGML standard compromises between ease of use on one hand and ease of machine processing on the other. Another such compromise is concerned with limiting the range of permissible content models in order to make it easier to look at an SGML document and understand how the markup is structured.

```
C>type test.sgm

<!DOCTYPE test [
```

```
<!ELEMENT (x,y) - O EMPTY>
<!ELEMENT test - O ((x,y?),y)>
]>
<test><x><y>

C>nsgmls test.sgm

test.sgm:3:30:E: content model is ambiguous: when the current token is the 1st
       occurrence of 'X', both the 1st and 2nd occurrences of 'Y' are possible
```

As can be seen in Figure 13.4, the preceding document could satisfy the content model in two ways. In order to deal with the content model for the **test** element type as constructed in Figure 13.4, the parser would have to be capable of looking ahead to see what is coming next in order to be able to decide which derivation to use.

The situation is not unlike that commonly found in programming languages. For example, consider the following C program:

```
#include <stdio.h>
int x,y,a,b,p,q;
int main()
{
        if (1) x = y; else if (1) a = b; else if (1) p = q;
}
```

It is nonobvious which if goes with which else to the human eye although it is unambiguous to the C compiler thanks to the disambiguating rule that an else is attached to the most recent, else-less if.

It has been argued that the SGML rule forbidding look-ahead is too restrictive. Having said that, it is often a straightforward matter to recast content models to remove the look-ahead requirement and make them unambiguous.

```
C>type test.sgm

<!DOCTYPE test [
<!ELEMENT (x,y) - O EMPTY>
```

Figure 13.4 The two possible interpretations of the document

```
<!ELEMENT test - O (bar,y)>
<!ELEMENT bar - O (x,y?)>
]>
<test>
<bar>
<x>
<y>
<y>

C>nsgmls test.sgm

(TEST
(BAR
(X
)X
(Y
)Y
)BAR
(Y
)Y
)TEST
C
```

The introduction of the intermediate element type **bar** has removed the potential ambiguities about occurrences of the **y** element type. In other words, it can only be parsed one way, as shown in Figure 13.5.

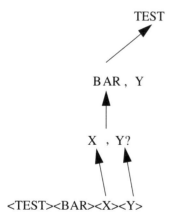

Figure 13.5 The disambiguated document

13.17 Data Attributes

Attributes can be associated with notations as well as element types. The attributes can be provided with values at the point in which they are used in external data entities.

In the example that follows, we have

- a **test** element type that has an image attribute. This image attribute has a declared value of ENTITY.

- a notation declaration declaring bmp to be a notation known on this system. Entities conforming to this notation have a colors attribute that has a declared value of NUMBER.

- an entity named house that is stored in the system file house.bmp. The entity contains non-SGML data (NDATA) with the notation type bmp. The colors attribute of the notation is set to 16.

```
C>type test.sgm

<!DOCTYPE test [
<!NOTATION bmp SYSTEM>
<!ATTLIST #NOTATION bmp colors NUMBER #REQUIRED>
<!ENTITY house SYSTEM "house.bmp" NDATA bmp [colors = 16]>
<!ELEMENT test - O (#PCDATA)>
<!ATTLIST test image ENTITY #REQUIRED>
]>
<test image = house>

C>nsgmls test.sgm

NBMP
shouse.bmp
f<OSFILE NOZAPEOF ASIS>house.bmp
Ehouse NDATA BMP
Dhouse COLORS TOKEN 16
AIMAGE ENTITY house
(TEST
)TEST
C
```

Note the D record type in the ESIS. The D denotes a data attribute. Thereafter, the interpretation of the record is as per normal attributes ('A' records).

13.18 Literal Delimiters

Both single and double quotes can be used as delimiters for literals as long as they are correctly paired as follows:

```
C>type test.sgm

<!DOCTYPE test [
<!ELEMENT test - O (foo)+>
<!ELEMENT foo - O EMPTY>
<!ATTLIST foo  at1 CDATA #REQUIRED
               at2 CDATA #REQUIRED>
```

```
]>
<test>
<foo at1="Hello World" at2 = 'Hello World'>
<foo at1="Sean's" at2 = 'Mark"s'>

C>nsgmls test.sgm

(TEST
AAT1 CDATA Hello World
AAT2 CDATA Hello World
(FOO
)FOO
AAT1 CDATA Sean's
AAT2 CDATA Mark"s
(FOO
)FOO
)TEST
C
```

The abstract names for these delimiters are LIT (a double quote in the reference concrete syntax) and LITA (a single quote in the reference concrete syntax). These can be modified, if required, in the SGML declaration.

13.19 Attribute Value Specifications

In Chapter 6—Elements, Attributes, and Models, we saw how attributes can have one of 15 possible declared attribute values such as CDATA, ENTITY, and ID. It is important to bear in mind that these value keywords refer to the attribute value *after* the parser has (partially) processed it. In SGML terminology, the value assigned to an attribute in a document instance is initially an *attribute value literal*. This value is then subject to further processing to yield an *attribute value*.

The distinction is illustrated in the following document:

```
C>type test.sgm

<!DOCTYPE test [
<!ENTITY hw "Hello World">
<!ELEMENT test - O CDATA>
<!ATTLIST test foo CDATA #REQUIRED>
]>
<test foo = "&hw;">
&hw;

C>nsgmls test.sgm

AFOO CDATA Hello World
(TEST
-&hw;
)TEST
C
```

In the preceding document, the CDATA keyword is used in two different contexts—as a declared content for the **test** element type and as attribute declared value for the foo attribute. The foo attribute is set to the attribute value literal "&hw;". This is then further processed by the parser, which expands the entity reference to yield the attribute value "Hello World." However, the CDATA declared content of the test element type inhibits the interpretation of the "&hw;" within the **test** element.

13.20 Null Declarations

In SGML the string "<!>" is known as the null declaration. It is simply a markup declaration with nothing in it. It can be used to protect against markup interpretation in some cases. For example,

```
C>type test.sgm

<!DOCTYPE test [
<!ELEMENT test - O (#PCDATA)>
]>
<test>
In the P&<!>L account...
</test>

C>nsgmls test.sgm

(TEST
-In the P&L account...
)TEST
C
```

In #PCDATA the & would normally be recognized as an ERO—Entity Reference Open as long as it satisfied its contextual constraint by being followed by a name start character (see Section 13.7). The presence of the null declaration causes the constraint to be broken and thus the & becomes data rather than markup. Finally, the parser consumes the null declaration, which is not passed on to the application.

CHAPTER 14

OPTIONAL SGML FEATURES

14.1 Introduction

A number of features within the SGML standard are optional in the sense that an SGML parser need not implement them in order to be SGML compliant. An individual document can indicate that it requires any combination of these features in its SGML declaration (see Appendix A—The SGML Declaration).

As one would expect with optional features of any standard, tools vary greatly in the level of support for them. This should be born in mind when contemplating their use. Also, some optional features (such as OMITTAG) are more globally supported in SGML tools than others (such as CONCUR).

14.2 Multiple DTDs Per Document

In all the SGML documents we have seen so far, there has been exactly one DTD associated with any given document instance, as shown in Figure 14.1.

A number of the optional features discussed in this chapter involve ways in which a single document can have *multiple* DTDs and multiple instances, as shown in Figure 14.2.

The features that use multiple DTDs in various ways are LINK, CONCUR, and SUBDOC, as described in Table 14.1.

When a single document has multiple DTDs they are gathered together in the prolog of the SGML document.

Table 14.1: Features that utilize multiple DTDs

Feature	Usage
LINK	Simple document transformations from one DTD to another.
SUBDOC	Document instance subcomponents that are themselves self-contained documents with their own DTDs.
CONCUR	Allows multiple document instances to be marked up to multiple DTDs. The instances can have common text.

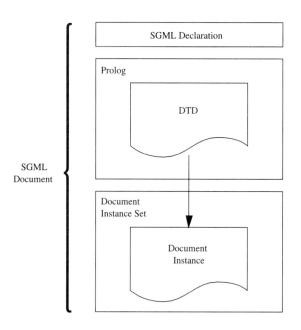

Figure 14.1 Single DTD per document

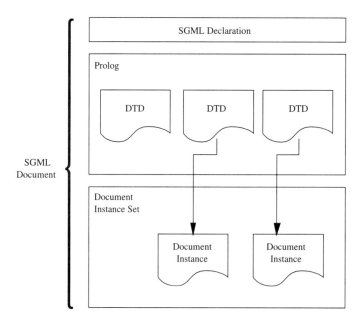

Figure 14.2 Single document – multiple DTDs

14.3   The CONCUR Feature

The following document has two DTDs and an instance of each:

```
<!DOCTYPE doc1 [
<!ELEMENT doc1 - O (foo)+>
<!ELEMENT foo - O (#PCDATA)>
]>
<!DOCTYPE doc2 [
<!ELEMENT doc2 - O (foo)+>
<!ELEMENT foo - O EMPTY>
]>
<(doc1)doc1>
<(doc2)doc2>
<foo>
```

Note that the first DTD encountered in the document is the one considered to be the "base" DTD by the parser. In this example, the parser will expect the first start-tag to be a **doc1** as it is the document element of the base (doc1) DTD. Because doc1 and doc2 are in separate instances, their tags identify (in parentheses) the document types to which they conform. A document can only have multiple DTDs if the EXPLICIT LINK or CONCUR features are being used.

Note also that there is no direct connection between the DTDs and therefore no conflict with the two different **foo** element types in the preceding example. The **foo** element is an instance of both types, which is possible only because it is empty. Otherwise, these would be two **foo** elements, with the document type specified in their tags:

```
<!DOCTYPE doc1 [
<!ELEMENT doc1 - O (foo)+>
<!ELEMENT foo - O (#PCDATA)>
]>
<!DOCTYPE doc2 [
<!ELEMENT doc2 - O (foo)+>
<!ELEMENT foo - O EMPTY>
]>
<(doc1)doc1>
<(doc2)doc2>
<(doc1)foo>
Text of foo
</(doc1)foo>
<(doc2>foo>
```

14.4   The LINK Feature

14.4.1   Introduction

The LINK feature provides a mechanism for specifying simple markup transformations to be executed by the SGML parser. It is typically used to allow the parser to *dynamically* add attributes and attribute values to elements. In other words, the markup information communicated to the application by the SGML parser can include attributes that are not actually *present in* the document at all. The most prevalent use of LINK is for the purposes of specifying presentation information such as font size and paragraph margins.[1]

Both the philosophy and mechanics of LINK are best explained by example. Consider the following simple document:

```
C>type foo.sgm

<!DOCTYPE fruit [
<!ELEMENT fruit - O (apple|orange|pear)+>
<!ELEMENT (apple,orange,pear) - O (#PCDATA)>
]>
<foo>
<apple>
<apple>
<orange>
<pear>
```

Consider the problem of adding formatting information to this document so that **apple** elements appear in red, **orange** elements appear in green, and **pear** elements appear in blue. Naturally, the information required to achieve this is very system- and application-specific. However, a number of SGML-based approaches can be used to solve this problem while controlling the amount of system-specific information required in the document itself. First, processing instructions can be added as follows:

```
C>type foo.sgm

<!DOCTYPE fruit [
<!ELEMENT fruit - O (apple|orange|pear)+>
<!ELEMENT (apple,orange,pear) - O (#PCDATA)>
]>
<foo>
<? .SetColor Red>
<apple>
<apple>
<? .SetColor Green>
<orange>
<? .SetColor Blue>
<pear>
```

In this example, it is assumed that the document-formatting software has a .SetColor command for controlling text color.

Alternatively, a Color attribute can be added:

---

1. Note that LINK here is not a navigational hyperlink but what the hypertext vernacular calls a *processing link*.

```
C>type foo.sgm

<!DOCTYPE fruit [
<!ELEMENT fruit - O (apple|orange|pear)+>
<!ELEMENT (apple,orange,pear) - O (#PCDATA)>
<!ATTLIST (apple,orange,pear) Color (RED,GREEN,BLUE) #REQUIRED>
]>
<foo>
<apple Color = RED>
<apple Color = RED>
<orange Color = GREEN>
<pear Color = BLUE>
```

Given that, in this example, all the apples are red, all oranges are green, and so on, there is a third alternative[2]:

```
C>type foo.sgm

<!DOCTYPE foo [
<!ELEMENT foo - O (apple|orange|pear)+>
<!ELEMENT (apple,orange,pear) - O (#PCDATA)>
<!ATTLIST apple  Color CDATA #FIXED "RED">
<!ATTLIST orange Color CDATA #FIXED "GREEN">
<!ATTLIST pear   Color CDATA #FIXED "BLUE">
]>
<foo>
<apple>
<apple>
<orange>
<pear>
```

Using this approach, the SGML parser does most of the work in adding the attributes:

```
C>nsgmls foo.sgm

(FOO
AColor CDATA RED
(APPLE
)APPLE
AColor CDATA RED
(APPLE
)APPLE
AColor CDATA GREEN
(ORANGE
)ORANGE
AColor CDATA BLUE
(PEAR
```

---

2. An extended version of this approach is used in the ICADD application for the reading impaired. See Section D.6.13—
    ICADD.

```
)PEAR
)FOO
C
```

There are a number of problems with these mechanisms. Methods 1 and 2 involve compromising the device-independent, purpose-independent purity of the document. They also involve manually adding the formatting information—a task that SGML systems strive to eliminate. The third method is more appealing in the sense that there is more automation (the parser—not a human being—is adding the attributes) and less pollution of the document. However, it is limited to simple one-to-one mappings and also suffers from being purpose-specific.

Taking the SGML philosophy of separating formatting from content to its logical conclusion leads to the idea that this sort of formatting-related markup does not *belong* in the DTD or the document instance at all. Also, part and parcel of the SGML philosophy is that where formatting is an automatic by-product of structure (as is the case here) it should be *automatically* added.

Taken together, these two ideas lead to the functionality provided by the LINK feature. Using LINK, the parser can be instructed to add attributes to elements and/or rename the elements themselves prior to passing the markup to the application. The transformations can be made conditional in a variety of ways including limiting transformations to elements that occur within other elements, elements having prior siblings, or elements having particular ID attribute values.

In effect, an SGML parser supporting LINK provides an SGML-to-SGML transformation language capable of adding attributes to elements and renaming elements. The transformation can be done in the context of a single DTD or a "source" and a "result" DTD. Multiple transformations can be specified and selected at parse-time. Moreover, transformations can be chained together.

14.4.2   A Simple Example of LINK

The following document illustrates a simple, so-called Link Process Definition to solve the preceding formatting problem:

```
c>type foo.sgm

<!DOCTYPE foo [
<!ELEMENT foo - O (apple|orange|pear)+>
<!ELEMENT (apple,orange,pear) - O (#PCDATA)>
]>
<!LINKTYPE aprinter foo #IMPLIED [
<!ATTLIST apple  Color CDATA #REQUIRED>
<!ATTLIST orange Color CDATA #REQUIRED>
<!ATTLIST pear   Color CDATA #REQUIRED>
<!LINK #INITIAL
       apple  [ Color=RED ]
       orange [ Color=GREEN ]
       pear   [ Color=BLUE ]
>
]>
```

```
<foo>
<apple>
<apple>
<orange>
<pear>

C>nsgmls -aaprinter foo.sgm

(FOO
aAPRINTER Color CDATA RED
(APPLE
)APPLE
aAPRINTER Color CDATA RED
(APPLE
)APPLE
aAPRINTER Color CDATA GREEN
(ORANGE
)ORANGE
aAPRINTER Color CDATA BLUE
(PEAR
)PEAR
)FOO
C
```

The -a option to the NSGMLS parser tells the parser to activate the Link Process Definition (LPD) known as aprinter at the start of the parsing process.

We look at the details of how the LPD is constructed next:

```
<!LINKTYPE aprinter foo #IMPLIED [
```

Link Process Definitions occur at the same level as Document Type Definitions in the prolog and are similarly constructed in some ways. The preceding Link Type Declaration declares a link-type named aprinter and associates it with the DTD foo. The #IMPLIED parameter announces that the DTD of the document to be produced via this LPD is up to the application itself to decide. It may even be a non-SGML representation. A number of variations are possible in the Link Type Declaration as we will see later on.

```
<!ATTLIST apple  Color CDATA #REQUIRED>
<!ATTLIST orange Color CDATA #REQUIRED>
<!ATTLIST pear   Color CDATA #REQUIRED>
```

Here the link rules for attributes to be added to elements as a result of parsing the document with this LPD active are declared. Such attribute definition declarations are essentially identical to those that occur in DTDs.

```
<!LINK #INITIAL
       apple  [ Color=RED ]
       orange [ Color=GREEN ]
       pear   [ Color=BLUE ]
  >
```

This section is the meat of the LPD. It here consists of a single link set declaration containing three link rules. The #INITIAL parameter indicates that when this LPD is active, this is the link set that is initially active. Again there are a number of variations on this structure, which we encounter later. The link set declares three link rules: **apple** elements are to have their Color attribute set to RED; **orange** elements, to GREEN; and **pear** elements, to BLUE.

```
]>
```

This terminates the link type declaration.

14.4.3   Multiple Link Process Definitions

One of the benefits of using LINK to add formatting-oriented attributes is that multiple Link Process Definitions can be declared in a document. By selecting different LPDs to parse the document, different system-specific results can be achieved, *without* compromising the system independence of the source document. For example, imagine a situation in which the document of this section is to be formatted with different font information as well as different colors on an alternative formatting device. An extra LPD bprinter could be added as follows:

```
<!LINKTYPE bprinter foo #IMPLIED [
<!ATTLIST apple
        fontname CDATA #REQUIRED
        fontsize NUMBER #REQUIRED>
<!ATTLIST
        orange Color CDATA #REQUIRED
        blink (yes|no) #REQUIRED>
<!ATTLIST pear blink (yes|no) #REQUIRED>
<!LINK #INITIAL
        apple [ fontname="Times" fontsize = 12]
        orange [ Color=GREEN blink=yes]
        pear [ blink=no ]
>
]>

C>nsgmls -abprinter foo.sgm

(FOO
aBPRINTER FONTNAME CDATA Times
aBPRINTER FONTSIZE TOKEN 12
(APPLE
)APPLE
aBPRINTER FONTNAME CDATA Times
aBPRINTER FONTSIZE TOKEN 12
(APPLE
)APPLE
aBPRINTER Color CDATA GREEN
aBPRINTER BLINK TOKEN YES
(ORANGE
```

```
)ORANGE
aBPRINTER BLINK TOKEN NO
(PEAR
)PEAR
)FOO
C
```

With this LPD, **apple** elements receive fontname and fontsize attributes, **orange** elements receive color and blink attributes, and **pear** elements receive a blink attribute. All that is required to use this LPD rather than the other LPD is that its name be specfied to the SGML parser.

14.4.4   Context-Sensitive Links

We have seen how the LINK feature allows multiple Link Process Definitions to exist in a document and that a parser can be instructed to activate a particular LPD at parse-time. It is also possible to have multiple link sets in a single LPD. The link set with the #INITIAL parameter is the one that will be automatically active when the LPD itself is activated. Additional LINK sets are given individual names and can be activated in a variety of ways to achieve context sensitivity (i.e., to cause particular link rules to apply in some situations and not in others).

14.4.4.1   Ancestor Element

To illustrate how link rules for an element can be made sensitive to the ancestors of that element, we use a slightly modified form of the sample document:

```
C>type foo.sgm

<!DOCTYPE foo [
<!ELEMENT foo - O (apple|orange|pear)+>
<!ELEMENT (apple,orange,pear) - O (seed)+>
<!ELEMENT seed - O EMPTY>
]>
<foo>
<apple><seed>
<apple><seed>
<orange>
<seed>
<seed>
<pear>
<seed>
```

Suppose that we wish to add an attribute to **seed** elements that is sensitive to the parent element of the seed (i.e., seeds within **apples** will have a type attribute with the value apple and so on). This can be achieved using context-sensitive link rules as follows:

```
<!LINKTYPE aprinter foo #IMPLIED [
<!ATTLIST apple  Color CDATA #REQUIRED>
```

```
<!ATTLIST orange Color CDATA #REQUIRED>
<!ATTLIST pear   Color CDATA #REQUIRED>
<!ATTLIST seed type (APPLE,ORANGE,PEAR) #REQUIRED>
<!LINK #INITIAL
        apple  #USELINK alink [Color = RED]
        orange #USELINK olink [Color = GREEN]
        pear   #USELINK plink [Color = BLUE]
>
<!LINK alink
        seed [type = APPLE]
>
<!LINK olink
        seed [type = ORANGE]
>
<!LINK plink
        seed [type = PEAR]
>
]>
```

Here the initial link set in the aprinter LPD is used to set the Color attribute of **apple**, **orange**, and **pear** elements as before. However, the #USELINK parameter specifies another link set that is to be activated for the duration of the corresponding element as shown in Figure 14.3. Here, ovals represent elements and rectangles represent the activation/deactivation of link sets.

14.4.4.2   Prior Element

It is also possible to trigger the activation of a link set from another link set. In the following example, a **first** attribute is added to **seed** elements to isolate the first seed in any fruit:

```
<!DOCTYPE foo [
<!ELEMENT foo - O (apple|orange|pear)+>
<!ELEMENT (apple,orange,pear) - O (seed)+>
<!ELEMENT seed - O EMPTY>
]>
<!LINKTYPE aprinter foo #IMPLIED [
<!ATTLIST seed
        first (YES,NO) #REQUIRED
>
<!LINK #INITIAL
        apple  #USELINK first
        orange #USELINK first
        pear   #USELINK first
>
<!LINK first
        seed #POSTLINK notfirst [first = YES]
>
<!LINK notfirst
        seed [first = NO]
>
```

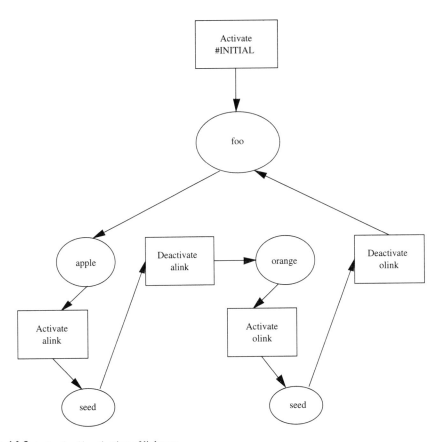

Figure 14.3 Activation/deactivation of link sets

```
]>
<foo>
<apple><seed>
<apple><seed>
<orange>
<seed>
<seed>
<pear>
<seed>

C>NSGMLS -aAPRINTER foo.sgm

(FOO
(APPLE
aAPRINTER FIRST TOKEN YES
(SEED
)SEED
```

```
)APPLE
(APPLE
aAPRINTER FIRST TOKEN YES
(SEED
)SEED
)APPLE
(ORANGE
aAPRINTER FIRST TOKEN YES
(SEED
)SEED
aAPRINTER FIRST TOKEN NO
(SEED
)SEED
)ORANGE
(PEAR
aAPRINTER FIRST TOKEN YES
(SEED
)SEED
)PEAR
)FOO
C
```

At the start of the parsing process, the #INITIAL link set is active. When any one of **apple**, **orange**, or **pear** elements are encountered, the link set given the name "first" is activated. With this link set active, the arrival of a **seed** element causes the "first" attribute to be set to YES. The #POSTLINK parameter tells the parser that the link set known as "notfirst" should be activated after this link rule has been applied. The result is that notfirst will apply to the remainder (i.e., all subsequent **seed** elements) of **apple**, **orange**, or **pear** elements.

Note that #POSTLINK can be used to cycle through a set of link sets by looping back to a previously active link set:

```
<!DOCTYPE foo [
<!ELEMENT foo - O (bar)+>
<!ELEMENT bar - O (#PCDATA)>
]>
<!LINKTYPE PRINTER foo #IMPLIED [
 <!ATTLIST bar Color (RED,GREEN,BLUE) #REQUIRED>
 <!LINK #INITIAL
        bar #POSTLINK second [Color=RED]
 >
 <!LINK second
        bar #POSTLINK third [Color=GREEN]
 >
 <!LINK third
        bar #POSTLINK #INITIAL [Color=BLUE]
 >
]>
<foo>
<bar>one</bar>
```

```
<bar>two</bar>
<bar>three</bar>
<bar>one</bar>
<bar>two</bar>
<bar>three</bar>

C>nsgmls -aprinter foo.sgm

(FOO
aPRINTER Color TOKEN RED
(BAR
-one
)BAR
aPRINTER Color TOKEN GREEN
(BAR
-two
)BAR
aPRINTER Color TOKEN BLUE
(BAR
-three
)BAR
aPRINTER Color TOKEN RED
(BAR
-one
)BAR
aPRINTER Color TOKEN GREEN
(BAR
-two
)BAR
aPRINTER Color TOKEN BLUE
(BAR
-three
)BAR
)FOO
C
```

This example causes the Color attribute of **bar** elements to cycle through the values RED, GREEN, and BLUE continuously.

14.4.4.3   *IDLink*

This form of link set contains link rules specific to an individual element, rather than all elements of a given type. In the following example, we add a link set to be activated when a **seed** element with an ID of sfoo is encountered:

```
c>type foo.sgm

<!DOCTYPE foo [
<!ELEMENT foo - O (apple|orange|pear)+>
<!ELEMENT (apple,orange,pear) - O (seed)+>
<!ELEMENT seed - O EMPTY>
```

```
<!ATTLIST seed id ID #implied>
]>
<!LINKTYPE aprinter foo #IMPLIED [
<!ATTLIST seed
        special (YES,NO) #REQUIRED
>
<!LINK #INITIAL
        seed [special = NO]
>
<!IDLINK sfoo seed
        [special = YES]
>
]>
<foo>
<apple><seed>
<orange><seed id=sfoo>

C>nsgmls foo.sgm

(FOO
(APPLE
aAPRINTER SPECIAL TOKEN NO
AID IMPLIED
(SEED
)SEED
)APPLE
(ORANGE
aAPRINTER SPECIAL TOKEN YES
AID TOKEN SFOO
(SEED
)SEED
)ORANGE
)FOO
C
```

14.4.5 Explicit Links

Although we have not used the term, all the preceding examples are forms of IMPLICIT link, so named as a result of the #IMPLIED parameter in the link type declaration, which indicates that the DTD of the result document is to be implied by the application.

Using so-called EXPLICIT links, the result DTD can be defined as part of the LPD. For example, the following example maps **BAR** elements in the doc1 DTD to **B** elements in the doc2 DTD with A1 attributes:

```
C>type foo.sgm

<!DOCTYPE doc1 [
<!ELEMENT doc1 - O (bar)+>
<!ELEMENT bar - O (#PCDATA)>
```

```
]>
<!DOCTYPE doc2 [
<!ELEMENT doc2 - O (b)+>
<!ELEMENT b - O (#PCDATA)>
<!ATTLIST b a1 CDATA #REQUIRED>
]>
<!LINKTYPE mylink doc1 doc2 [
 <!LINK #INITIAL bar b [a1=v1]>
]>
<doc1>
<bar>
<bar>
```

The version of NSGMLS used in this book only reports explicit link information when generating output in RAST[3] format. RAST output can be generated to a file with the -t option as follows:

```
C>nsgmls -amylink -trast.doc foo.sgm
C>type rast.doc

[DOC1]
[BAR
#LINK-RULE
#RESULT=B
A1=
!v1!
]
[/BAR]
[BAR
#LINK-RULE
#RESULT=B
A1=
!v1!
]
[/BAR]
[/DOC1]
```

Note the #RESULT=B lines, which indicate that the **bar** elements from the doc1 DTD have been transformed into **B** elements in the doc2.DTD.

14.4.6 Simple Links

Simple links are a restricted form of implicit link that consist solely of attributes with fixed values to be associated with the document element type (i.e., the root element type of the DTD).

---

3. Reference Application for SGML Testing. ISO/IEC 13673:1995. The RAST format contains ESIS information but is intended primarily for conformance testing.

```
C>type foo.sgm

<!DOCTYPE foo [
<!ELEMENT foo - O (#PCDATA)>
]>
<!DOCTYPE bar [
<!ELEMENT bar - O (#PCDATA)>
]>
<!LINKTYPE mylink #SIMPLE #IMPLIED [
<!ATTLIST foo a1 CDATA #FIXED avalue>
]>
<foo>

C>nsgmls -amylink foo.sgm

aMYLINK A1 CDATA avalue
(FOO
)FOO
C
```

14.5   The SUBDOC Feature

The SUBDOC feature was mentioned very briefly in Chapter 7—Entities, Notations, and Marked Sections. A SUBDOC entity stores a complete SGML document that just happens to form a component of the document referencing it via a subdocument entity reference. SGML documents that will serve as subdocuments can be complete in all respects *except* that they cannot have their own SGML declaration.

The file bar.sgm contains a complete document instance with its own DTD:

```
C>type bar.sgm

<!DOCTYPE bar [
<!ELEMENT bar - O (#PCDATA)>
]>
<bar>
I am bar

C>nsgmls bar.sgm

(BAR
-I am bar
)BAR
C
```

The file foo.sgm includes the file bar.sgm as a subdocument entity:

```
C>type foo.sgm

<!DOCTYPE foo [
<!ENTITY bar SYSTEM "bar.sgm" SUBDOC>
```

```
<!ELEMENT foo - O (#PCDATA)>
]>
<foo>
Hello &bar; World

C>nsgmls foo.sgm

(FOO
-Hello
sbar.sgm
f<OSFILE FIND>bar.sgm
Sbar
{bar
(BAR
-I am bar
)BAR
}bar
- World
)FOO
C
```

Note that for all intents and purposes, parsing of the containing document is suspended while the subdocument is parsed. In other words, there is no inheritance of markup declarations, ID/ IDREF name spaces, and the like in the subdocument. Subdocuments can use the same DTD as their parent or a completely different DTD. Subdocuments can be nested to a depth controlled by a parameter in the SGML declaration. Parsers typically implement SUBDOC by invoking a child process copy of themselves with the subdocument's name as a parameter.

14.6 Markup Minimization Methods

The only markup minimization mechanisms we have used so far have been tag omission and short references. In this section we discuss the others.

14.6.1 The SHORTTAG Feature

The SHORTTAG feature adds three different markup minimization techniques.

14.6.1.1 *Empty Tags*

The element type name (Generic Identifier) in both start- and end-tags can be omitted. An empty start-tag <> is a repeat tag (i.e., it is inferred to be a start-tag for the most recent element). An empty end-tag </> is inferred to be an end-tag for the most recently opened element that has not yet been closed.

```
C>type foo.sgm

<!DOCTYPE foo [
<!ELEMENT foo - O (bar)+>
<!ELEMENT bar - O (#PCDATA)>
]>
<foo>
<bar>This is the first
<>This is the second
</>

C>nsgmls foo.sgm

(FOO
(BAR
-This is the first
)BAR
(BAR
-This is the second
)BAR
)FOO
C
```

14.6.1.2   Unclosed Tags

Unclosed tags allow tags to omit their closing delimiters when followed by another tag:

```
C>type foo.sgm

<!DOCTYPE foo [
<!ELEMENT foo - O (bar)+>
<!ELEMENT bar - O (#PCDATA)>
]>
<foo<bar>This is the first</bar<bar>This is the second

C>nsgmls foo.sgm

(FOO
(BAR
-This is the first
)BAR
(BAR
-This is the second\n\n
)BAR
)FOO
C
```

14.6.1.3   Null End-Tags

Null end-tags allow a start-tag to specify a single character that will serve to end the element. The character used for this purpose in the reference concrete syntax is / or solidus, but this can be changed if required in the SGML declaration.

```
C>type foo.sgm

<!DOCTYPE foo [
<!ELEMENT foo - O (bar)+>
<!ELEMENT bar - O (#PCDATA)>
]>
<foo<bar/This is the first/<bar>This is the second

C>nsgmls foo.sgm

(FOO
(BAR
-This is the first
)BAR
(BAR
-This is the second\n\n
)BAR
)FOO
C
```

14.6.2   The DATATAG Feature

The DATATAG feature allows a string of characters to function both as data content and as an end-tag for a specified element.

```
<!DOCTYPE foo [
<!ELEMENT foo - O ([bar,","])+>
<!ELEMENT bar O O (#PCDATA)>
]>
<foo><bar>Bar1,Bar2,Bar3
```

Here the "," character acts as an end-tag for the **bar** element.[4] The fact that the start-tag for a bar element can be omitted allows the parser to both end the current and start a new **bar** element at each ",". The document is thus equivalent to this:

```
C>type foo.sgm

<!DOCTYPE foo [
<!ELEMENT foo - O (bar)+>
<!ELEMENT bar - O (#PCDATA)>
]>
<foo><bar>Bar1</bar><bar>Bar2</bar>><bar>Bar3
```

---

4. The DATATAG feature is rarely used in practice. Similar effects can be achieved with short references, which are more widely supported by available tools.

14.6.3 The RANK Feature

The RANK feature is intended to simplify the markup of nested structures that use explicit nesting levels rather than recursive models. For example, a recursive definition of nested lists might look like this:

```
<!DOCTYPE foo [
<!ELEMENT foo  - O (list)+>
<!ELEMENT list - O (item|list)+>
<!ELEMENT item - O (#PCDATA)>
]>
<foo>
<list>
<item>Item level 0
<list>
<item>Item level 1
```

In some situations, it might be desirable to limit and make explicit in the markup, the levels at which items occur. In these situations this form of markup could be used:

```
<!DOCTYPE foo [
<!ELEMENT foo   - O (list)+>
<!ELEMENT list  - O (item|list1)+>
<!ELEMENT list1 - O (item|list2)+>
<!ELEMENT list2 - O (item)+>
<!ELEMENT item  - O (#PCDATA)>
]>
<foo>
<list>
<item>Item level 0
<list1>
<item>Item level 1
```

Using RANK, the numeric part of the **list** element type names can be inferred from the previous tag used:

```
C>type foo.sgm

<!DOCTYPE foo [
<!ELEMENT foo - O (list1)+>
<!ELEMENT list 1 - O (item|list2)+>
<!ELEMENT list 2 - O (item|list3)+>
<!ELEMENT list 3 - O (item)+>
<!ELEMENT item - O (#PCDATA)>
]>
<foo>
<list1>
<item>
<list>
<item>
```

```
C>nsgmls foo.sgm

(FOO
(LIST1
(ITEM
)ITEM
)LIST1
(LIST1
(ITEM
)ITEM
)LIST1
)FOO
C
```

Notice that the second **list** element has been inferred to be a **list1** element.

## CHAPTER 15

THE HYTIME STANDARD

15.1 Introduction

If there is one thing we have learned in the short history of computing it is this: "It is impossible to guess accurately today, what we may wish to do with our data tomorrow." One striking example of the truth of this maxim is the explosive growth in electronic publishing, hypertext, and hypermedia technologies in recent times. These new media were largely unknown in 1986 when the SGML standard was adopted. It is a telling proof of concept of SGML that documents represented in SGML *prior* to the emergence of these new media have been readily adaptable to them. All thanks to the separation of medium and message that is at the heart of the SGML philosophy.

With the addition of purely electronic media, the already nebulous notion of a document becomes even more so. Electronic document content can include sound, video, virtual reality simulations, and so on. Furthermore, such documents can contain *behaviour.*[1] In other words, documents can contain executable code within themselves.[2] Documents can modify their own content and interact with other objects both human and electronic. They can reproduce, destroy themselves, destroy other documents, and change and be changed. They can contain rich links to other document objects, which can themselves be linked to other documents in potentially infinite *webs* of interconnected, heterogeneous information.

Such hyper-document concepts represent a revolution in the concept of a document perhaps as important as the one heralded by Gutenburg's original printing press. However, embracing these new concepts and capabilities can come at a price. Hypertext and hypermedia systems are often *proprietary* requiring the addition of purpose-specific markup to documents. As a consequence, hyper-documents can be tied into particular systems or vendors and can be hard to reuse for other purposes. The inherent structure of the hyper-document can be buried in a sea of proprietary markup codes. Does this sound familiar? All the issues raised as problems with "normal"

---

1. The emergence of Object Orientation as a development paradigm has lead to a convergence of the concepts of document and object. Documents that can contain behavior (i.e., executable code) plus state information as well as data can be thought of as persistent objects in OO terminology.

2. Examples include Java, ActiveX, VBScript, and MID (Metafile for Interactive Documents).

documents (see Section 1.3—The Problems with Documents) are equally applicable in the hyper-document domain.

The question then naturally arises—Can SGML ideas be gainfully applied to hyper-documents? The answer is a very definite yes in the form of the HyTime standard (ISO 10744). This standard provides an SGML-based, open systems mechanism for representing hyper-document concepts.

The development of HyTime has led to the development of an SGML modeling technique known as Architectural Forms. This technique is as generic as it is powerful and can be applied to areas other than hyper-documents. Thus, even if you are not specifically interested in hyper-documents, the Architectural Forms section of this chapter may be of interest.

HyTime is a *big* subject and the coverage here is necessarily brief. For a full treatment of the subject, see *Practical Hypermedia: An Introduction to HyTime* by Eliot Kimber in this series.

15.2   Some HyTime Concepts

One of the principle ideas underpinning hyper-documents is the concept of a hyperlink or simply a "link." Hyper-document systems employ a wide variety of mechanisms for establishing connections between objects, and many schemes have been developed to capture the semantics of such links. The variety of linking mechanisms currently used—or that can be contemplated—is *vast*. However, irrespective of the linkage mechanism, two fundamental concepts are invariably involved:

1. How to address objects.

2. How to capture the semantics of the relationships between the addressed objects.

The SGML standard provides a mechanism for very simple object linking via ID/IDREF(S) attributes. This simple cross-reference facility can be thought of as a very basic hyperlink allowing intradocument, one-to-one and one-to-many links to be encoded, as shown in Figure 15.1.

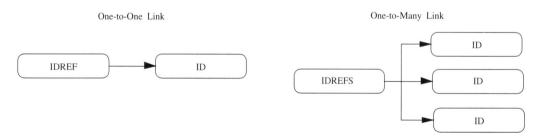

Figure 15.1 Simple one-to-one and one-to-many links

The attribute name can be used to capture the semantics of the relationship among the connected objects, which are called anchors of the link. However, this simple mechanism obviously has limitations in its ability to address the anchors:

- Anchors must be in the same document instance.

- Anchors must have ID attributes.

- Anchors must be elements (i.e., there is no way to address an external entity such as a video clip or a Perl script).

Indeed, many of the more powerful hyper-document link capabilities require addressing beyond SGML's ID/IDREF(s) facility. Consider the following examples:

- "The first occurrence in the history section of a paragraph containing the text 'Napoleon'."

- "The first six words in the third bulleted list of the last contract document."

- "The 1 inch square in the top left hand corner of the video sequence from frame 10 to frame 20."

- "The sound sample of Churchill's speech up to the point where he says, 'The end of the beginning.'"

Before we look at some of HyTime's linking and addressing capabilities in more detail, we need to discuss the powerful concept of Architectural Forms on which HyTime is based.

15.3   Architectural Forms

The power of SGML as a language for the creation of other languages can be brought to bear directly on the problem of representing hyper-document concepts. All that is required is a DTD or DTD fragment that uses element types, content models, and the like to represent the necessary structures. The following two documents are SGML encodings of the same document by two document designers:

Designer A

```
<!DOCTYPE foo [
<!ELEMENT foo       - O (para+,chapter+)>
<!ELEMENT chapter  - O (para+)>
<!ATTLIST chapter id ID #IMPLIED>
<!ELEMENT para      - O (#PCDATA|xref|indexterm)+>
<!ELEMENT xref      - O (#PCDATA)>
<!ATTLIST xref to IDREF #REQUIRED>
<!ELEMENT indexterm - O (#PCDATA)>
]>
<foo>
```

```
<para>For more <indexterm>information</indexterm> see <xref to =
"foo1">principles of foo - a developers perspective</xref>
...
<chapter id = foo1>
<para>Foo means different things to different people...
```

Designer B

```
<!DOCTYPE foo [
<!ENTITY mdash SDATA "mdash">
<!ELEMENT foo       - O (p+,foostuff+)>
<!ELEMENT foostuff - O (p+)>
<!ATTLIST foostuff fooname ID #IMPLIED>
<!ELEMENT p         - O (#PCDATA|foolink)+>
<!ELEMENT foolink  - O (#PCDATA)>
<!ATTLIST foolink
           name IDREF #REQUIRED
           relevance (low,medium,high) #REQUIRED>
]>
<foo>
<p>For more information see <foolink relevance = high name = "foo">
principles of foo&mdash;a developers perspective</foolink>
...
<foostuff fooname = foo>
<p>Foo means different things to different people...
```

Although there are differences in element types and element content models in the DTDs, the approaches used to represent cross references in both DTDs are, intuitively, the same. It is as if the two designers have arrived at differing *syntactic* solutions to the same *semantic* problem.

Looking at it another way, it is as if the concept of cross reference they both employ is a *meta-cross reference*. Both DTDs use the meta-cross-reference model to create concrete cross-reference element types, namely, **xref** and **foolink**. For each variation on a theme in a particular DTD, there might be a meta-theme identifiable at some higher level. This led to the idea of a *meta-DTD*—a DTD that acts as a template for the creation of other DTDs. The idea is illustrated in Figure 15.2.

Formalizing such meta-DTDs has a number of benefits:

- Systems that process SGML documents by operating at a meta-DTD level are immune to differences between the DTDs of individual document instances. As long as the documents conform to the meta-DTD, they are effectively equivalent.

- Designers wishing to make their documents conform to some meta-DTD can do so without having to adopt someone else's DTD or DTD fragment. They are free to use their own naming conventions, content model variations, and so on.

- Enterprises that share documents with others in their industry can do so at the meta-DTD level while enhancing their own DTDs to meet specific requirements of their enterprise.

In the preceding example, Designer A and Designer B have designed DTDs to capture the semantics of a basic hyperlink (cross reference). The DTDs are different, but the abstract type of

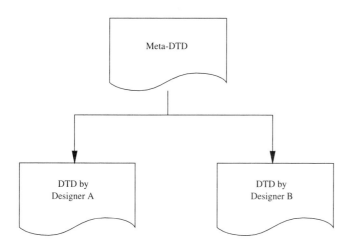

Figure 15.2 The concept of a meta-DTD

hyperlink they seek to capture is the same. From the vantage point of a system processing hypertext links, both these documents could be considered equivalent.

By analogy with object-oriented design, both of the preceding DTDs are derived from the same *base class*. Such classes in HyTime are known as Architectural Forms. To be more exact, Architectural Forms are examples of *abstract base classes*—never intended to be instantiated on their own—rather intended to act as templates for the derivation of other classes. Taking the analogy with object-oriented systems further, systems that rely solely on features of the abstract base class or classes can be considered *polymorphic* (i.e., they can function with any DTD, or object, that conforms to the Architectural Form, or abstract base class).

Figure 15.3 illustrates how the hyperlinking portion of the DTDs from Designers A and B can be considered to be derived from an architectural form MyLink in a meta-DTD known as MyArch.

Informally, the architectural form for MyLink in the MyArch meta-DTD says, "To be a valid instance of MyLink, an element type must have a linkend attribute to hold the anchor address. It must signal the fact that it is a MyLink element in the MyArch architecture by providing an attribute called MyArch set to the value MyLink. If an attribute name other than linkend is to be used to serve as the linkend attribute, a mapping attribute MyNames must be provided."

The attributes that serve to connect a particular element type with a particular architectural form are known as *architecture attributes*. Conceptually, they provide run-time type information[3] to document processors that can use them to deduce the architectural form or forms an element type conforms to. The MyNames attribute maps the architecture attribute name linkend to the attribute name used by the DTD. The following pseudo-code illustrates conceptually how a MyArch processor might use these attributes:

---

3. Analogous to the RTTI capability of C++.

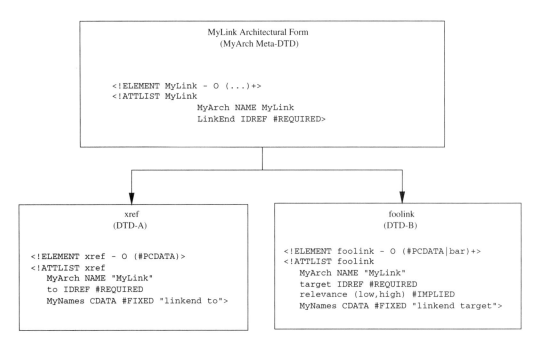

Figure 15.3 Two DTDs derived from the same architectural form

```
if (element has a MyArch Attribute) {
   ArchForm = element's MyArch Attribute
   if (ArchForm == "MyLink") {
      if (element has an attribute whose name is (mapped to) LinkEnd) {
         Process the LinkEnd...
      }
      else
         Error "LinkEnd attribute expected..."
   }
   // Other architectural forms in MyArch architecture....
}
```

15.4   Some HyTime Linking and Addressing Mechanisms

HyTime provides a rich set of mechanisms for specifying the addresses of objects and how those objects are to be linked. A number of the more common mechanisms are discussed in the following sections.

15.4.1   Absolute Addressing

A unique identifier is the most basic form of addressing, occurring everywhere from postal codes to Internet IP Addresses to RAM locations. An example of absolute addressing in C follows:

```
int anchor1
int *link;
link = &anchor1;
```

This form of addressing is illustrated in Figure 15.4.

In the following example, a simple application of the HyTime clink (Contextual Link) architectural form of addressing is used for the **anchor1** element. The linkend attribute is the address of the anchor.

```
<!DOCTYPE htest [
<!ELEMENT htest   - O (anchor1|foolink)+>
<!ELEMENT anchor1 - O (#PCDATA)>
<!ATTLIST anchor1
          id ID #IMPLIED>
<!ELEMENT foolink - O (#PCDATA)>
<!ATTLIST foolink
          HyTime NAME "clink"
          linkend IDREF #REQUIRED>
]>
<htest>
<anchor1 id = foo1>I am Anchor 1</anchor1>
<foolink linkend = foo1>I am a foolink pointing to anchor 1
</foolink>
</htest>
```

Note that a clink has only one anchor address (linkend) because the link element itself is its other anchor. The link established is illustrated in Figure 15.5.

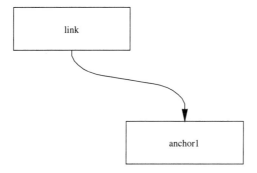

Figure 15.4 Absolute addressing in C

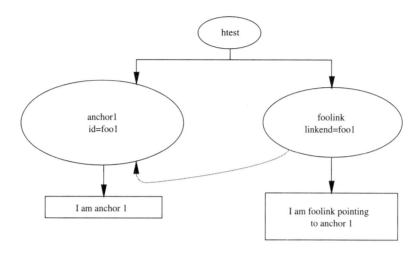

Figure 15.5 The clink architectural form used with an absolute addressing mechanism

15.4.2   Indirect Addressing

Indirect addressing is characterized by the fact that an absolute address is arrived at via some intermediary mechanism or mechanisms. An example from C follows:

```
int anchor0;
int *locator1 = &anchor0;
int **locator2 = &locator1;
```

This is illustrated in Figure 15.6.

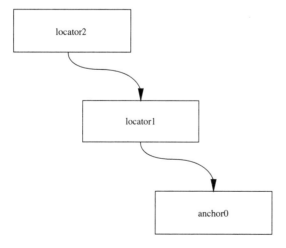

Figure 15.6 Simple indirect addressing in C

HyTime provides many ways to achieve indirect addressing. An example using the nameloc architectural form follows:

```
<!DOCTYPE htest [
<!ELEMENT htest - O (anchor1|fooref|nameloc)+>
<!ELEMENT anchor1 - O (#PCDATA)>
<!ATTLIST anchor1
          id ID #IMPLIED>
<!ELEMENT foolink - O (#PCDATA)>
<!ATTLIST foolink
          HyTime NAME "clink"
          linkend IDREF #REQUIRED>
<!element nameloc - O (nmlist*) >
<!attlist nameloc
          id ID #REQUIRED
          HyTime name "nameloc">
<!element nmlist - O (#PCDATA)>
<!attlist nmlist
          HyTime name "nmlist"
          nametype (entity|element) "element"
          docorsub entity #implied>
]>
<htest>
<anchor1 id = foo1>I am Anchor 1</anchor1>
<foolink linkend = locator>I an foolink indirectly pointing to anchor 1</anchor>
<nameloc id=locator>
<nmlist>
foo1
</nmlist>
</nameloc>
</htest>
```

This is illustrated in Figure 15.7.

15.4.3   Independent Links

The HyTime ilink (Independent Link) architectural form provides a way of linking objects in which the link information can be housed anywhere (i.e., it is *independent* of the linked objects). An example from C follows:

```
struct Person {
int *Height;
char *Name;
};

char *name1 = "Sean Mc Grath";
int *Height1 = 76;
char *name2 = "Mark UpLang";
int *Height2 = 72;
```

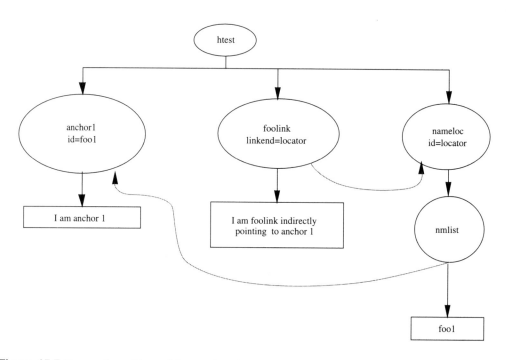

Figure 15.7 The nameloc architectural form used as a indirect addressing mechanism

```
struct Person Personae[2];
Personae[0].Name = name1;
Personae[0].Height = Height2;
Personae[1].Name = name2;
Personae[1].Height = Height1;
```

This is illustrated in Figure 15.8.

In this example, an association between names and height is maintained in the Personae data structure. The name and height data objects are completely unaware of the existence of any external semantic links they may be part of. An analogous construct using the ilink architectural form follows:

```
<!DOCTYPE htest [
<!ELEMENT htest - O (Person|name|height)+>
<!ELEMENT Person - O EMPTY>
<!ATTLIST Person
        HyTime Name "ilink"
        anchrole CDATA #FIXED "Name Height"
        linkends IDREFS #REQUIRED>
<!ELEMENT (name,height) - O (#PCDATA)>
<!ATTLIST (name,height) id ID #IMPLIED>
]>
```

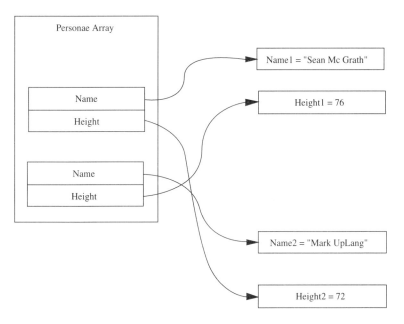

Figure 15.8 An example of independent linking in C

```
<htest>
<name id = n1>Sean Mc Grath
<height id = h1>76
<name id = n2>Mark UpLang
<height id = h2>72
<Person linkends = "n1 h1">
<Person linkends = "n2 h2">
</htest>
```

The linkends attribute of the Person element type is used to hold the related ID reference values. The anchrole attribute establishes the semantics of the link indicating that the first such ID reference is the Name part of the link. The second ID reference is the Height part of the link.

15.4.4   Tree-Based Addressing

HyTime provides a powerful addressing mechanism for hierarchical structures that is particularly powerful for addressing components of SGML documents. The idea is to allow a location in a tree structure to be specified in terms of the navigation steps required to get there from a given starting point. This allows objects to be addressed down to the granularity of the node structure of the tree.

The treeloc architectural form uses a list of integers known as a marklist. Each integer n represents the n-th child of the current location. In the following document, a treeloc is used to address the word *is* in the **anchor1** element.

```
<!doctype htest [
<!ELEMENT htest    - O (anchor1|foolink|treeloc)+ +(emph)>
<!ELEMENT anchor1  - O (#PCDATA)>
<!ATTLIST anchor1
          id ID #IMPLIED>
<!ELEMENT foolink  - O (#PCDATA)>
<!ATTLIST foolink
          HyTime NAME "clink"
          linkend IDREF #REQUIRED>
<!ELEMENT emph     - O (#PCDATA)>
<!element treeloc  - O (marklist*) >
<!attlist treeloc
        id ID #required
        locsrc IDREFS #REQUIRED
        HyTime name "treeloc">
<!element marklist - O (#PCDATA)>
]>
<htest>
<anchor1 id=foo1>This <emph>is</emph> anchor 1</anchor1>
<foolink linkend = locator>I am foolink, pointing to the emphasized word "am"
      in anchor1</foolink>
<treeloc id=locator locsrc=foo1>
<marklist>
1 2 1
</marklist>
</treeloc>
</htest>
```

The tree structure of the **anchor1** element is shown in Figure 15.9. An element conforming to the treeloc architectural form must supply a locsrc attribute, which specifies the starting point in the tree for the marklist. In this example, it specifies the element with id = foo1, which is the **anchor1** element.

The first integer (1) in the marklist refers to the starting point, namely anchor1. The second integer (2) specifies the second child of the current location. The third integer (1) specifies the first child of the **emph** element, thus locating the text "is" within the **emph** element. The tree structures used by addressing mechanisms such as treeloc are common across both the HyTime and DSSSL Standards (See Chapter 16) and are known as groves.

15.4.5 Query-Based Addressing

A particularly interesting class of addressing mechanism in HyTime is based on a query language known as SDQL (Standard Document Query Language). SDQL (defined as part of DSSSL) allows locations within groves to be specified in terms of query expressions. When used to create hypertext for example, these query expressions provide a run-time location mechanism particularly suited to locating anchors that may move over time (i.e., "the first paragraph containing the word 'Napoleon'").

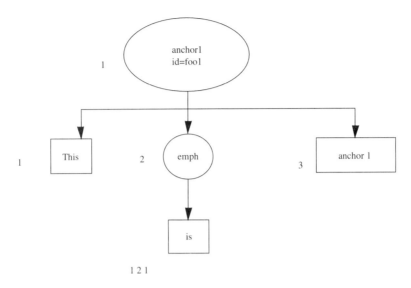

Figure 15.9 Tree structure of the anchor1 element

15.4.6   Chained Addressing

One very powerful feature of HyTime that has no direct analogy with most programming languages is the way in which the addressing/location mechanisms can produce a *chain reaction* effect. When for example, a clink directs a HyTime processor to an element with a particular ID, that ID might be the final destination ID of the anchor. However, it could also be an element with its own HyTime addressing semantics. If so, this triggers *another* level of indirection to another element. This element may in turn have HyTime addressing semantics and so on.

The result is that any of the addressing mechanisms in HyTime—and we have mentioned only a few in this chapter—can be joined together in arbitrarily long chains to produce an infinite variety of addressing mechanisms.

15.5   Using HyTime

The architectural form concepts used in HyTime make the addition of HyTime semantics to existing documents quite straightforward in many cases. This is so because adding fixed attributes to element types in a DTD allows the parser to add the extra attribute information for HyTime at parse time. For example, to allow a HyTime-aware application to process the cross references in the **xref** and **foolink** element types from page 259, the DTDs are modified as follows:

```
<!ELEMENT xref - O (#PCDATA)>
<!ATTLIST xref
            HyTime NAME "clink" #FIXED
            to IDREF #REQUIRED
            HyNames CDATA "linkend to">

<!ELEMENT foolink - O (#PCDATA)>
<!ATTLIST foolink
            HyTime NAME "clink" #FIXED
            target IDREF #REQUIRED
            relevance (low,medium,high) #REQUIRED
            HyNames CDATA "linkend target">
```

Apart from the necessary attributes in the DTD, two other modifications are required. First, the addition of the HyTime token to the AppInfo parameter in the SGML declaration (see Appendix A—The SGML Declaration). Second, a document must declare its compliance with HyTime via the following processing instruction:

```
<?ArcBase HyTime>
```

HyTime consists of a number of modules, and an application can declare which modules it requires using additional processing instructions:

```
<?HyTime MODULE base>
<?HyTime MODULE HyperLink>
```

These two processing instructions indicate to the HyTime processor that this document requires the base and HyperLink modules of HyTime.

## CHAPTER 16

THE DSSSL STANDARD

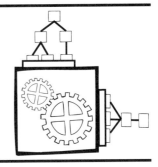

16.1   Introduction

The SGML standard (with the possible exception of the LINK feature) does not standardize mechanisms for transforming and/or formatting SGML documents. This is left up to the individual application such as a typesetter or an on-line document viewer.

Over the years, many diverse and often proprietary approaches have been used to express the semantics of adding presentation information to SGML documents. In general, the process looks similar to that shown in Figure 16.1.

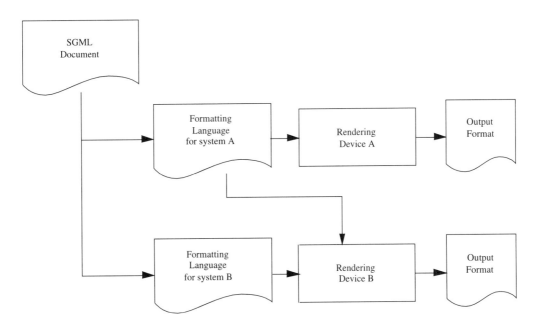

Figure 16.1 Rendering SGML documents

There is typically a one-to-one relationship between formatting languages and systems. For example, the same formatting specification (say for the production of A4 pages for a book) will have to be expressed in Languages A and B in order to allow the same document to be rendered on systems A and B. Moreover, these formatting languages are typically proprietary.

We saw in the last chapter how the growth in hyper-document systems ushered in the need for a standard means of expressing hyper-document concepts. Equally, the growth in diversity and complexity of document-formatting devices has highlighted the need for a standard way of expressing formatting semantics.

This is what DSSSL (Document Style and Semantics Specification Language—ISO/IEC 10179:1996) is concerned with. DSSSL is an open systems standard for expressing the process of transforming and formatting SGML documents. With DSSSL, the process of rendering an SGML document to multiple devices/formats looks similar to that shown in Figure 16.2. When the DSSSL specification is established, it can be used by any DSSSL-compliant rendering system to produce the necessary output format.

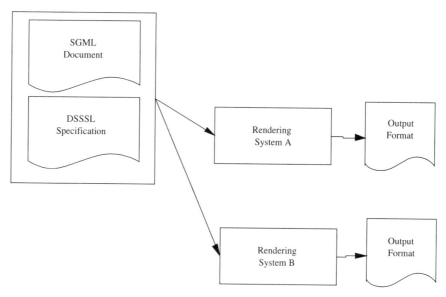

Figure 16.2 Document rendering with DSSSL

16.2   DSSSL Architecture

DSSSL provides mechanisms for expressing two principal forms of the document processing task:

1. How documents should be transformed in preparation for formatting (i.e., rearranging content, addition of new content, etc.).

2. What formatting characteristics to apply to the content (i.e., page geometries, paragraph indents, column layouts, font weight, etc.).

DSSSL-compliant formatting systems can then read these specifications, transform them to their native languages if necessary, and execute them.

Note that DSSSL does not attempt to standardize low level formatting algorithms such as hyphenation and justification. These issues remain the responsibility of the individual implementation. Thus DSSSL compliance does not guarantee that two page layout systems, for example, will render the same document in exactly the same way.

In DSSSL and HyTime, the conceptual model of an SGML document is that of a collection of hierarchical structures corresponding to structures found in the original SGML document known as "grove." *Grove* stands for Graphical Representation Of property ValuEs. A grove is constructed from a grove plan, which defines a set of classes and properties. These grove plans are subsets of Property Sets. When the source data are SGML, the Property Set is the SGML Property Set.

A grove plan that contained the entire SGML Property Set would yield groves that could be converted back to the original SGML without any loss of information (i.e., it could re-create the original SGML document character for character). In many applications not all this information is relevant. Thus a grove plan allows an application to limit the amount of information stored in a grove.[1]

The overall DSSSL architecture is illustrated in Figure 16.3. The overall model is of an SGML document going through a sequence of transformations that derive another SGML document prior to the application of formatting information during the formatting phase. The transformations consist of transforming a grove representation of an SGML document into another grove. This process can be repeated as often as required. The resultant grove can then be transformed back to native SGML. It can also be used as input to the formatting process.

DSSSL has four principal components:

- The Expression Language

- The Transformation Language

- The Style Language

- The Query Language

---

1. The ESIS format can thus be considered an example of an SGML grove plan derived from the SGML Property Set.

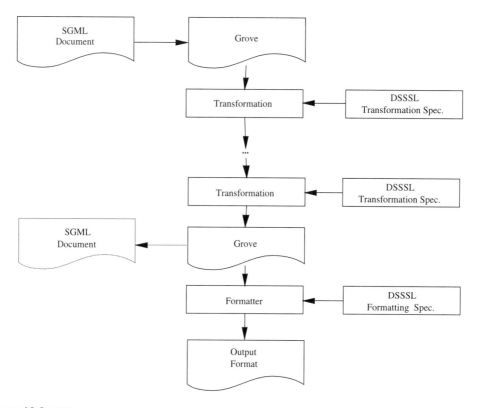

Figure 16.3 DSSSL architecture

16.3   The Expression Language

The DSSSL Expression Language is the base language for all the other component languages. It is a variant of the Scheme[2] programming language. Scheme itself is a dialect of Lisp.

16.4   The Transformation Language

The Transformation Language provides a mechanism for expressing the transformation of
one SGML document into another. The transformation process is controlled by a *transformation*

---

2. IEEE Scheme Standard R4RS.

specification. The transformation specification consists of a set of triples called *associations.* Associations take the following general form:

```
(query expression, transformation, priority)
```

Each triple specifies a query, the transformation to be performed when the query expression is satisfied, and a priority to attach to the transformation. For example, if two transformation specifications are satisfied, then the one with the highest priority is executed.

Note that if the target system accepts SGML (perhaps in a fixed DTD format such as HTML), then the Transformation Language may be sufficient to generate the required output. Note also that the Transformation Language is a completely general SGML-to-SGML transformation mechanism. As such, it has applications beyond document formatting. It can be used to transform from an authoring DTD to an interchange DTD, for example.

16.5   The Style Language

The Style Language provides a mechanism for associating formatting characteristics with document components. The process is controlled by a style specification. This is a sequence of construction rules whereby the input SGML document (grove) is transformed into an intermediate representation known as the *flow object tree.* This flow object tree is then used to generate the final output, which can consist of proprietary typesetting codes or a page description language such as SPDL (ISO/IEC 10180) or PostScript.

16.6   The Query Language

The Query Language is known as SDQL (Standard Document Query Language). It is used in both the transformation and style languages to address objects within groves. SDQL is also used by the HyTime standard.

16.7   DSSSL Specifications

DSSSL uses the idea of a document architecture discussed in Chapter 15—The HyTime Standard. Transformation specifications, style specifications, grove plans, and the like all conform to the DSSSL document architecture.

16.8   DSSSL-O

DSSSL-O (short for DSSS On-line) is a subset of DSSSL's Style Language and is aimed at satisfying the style specification requirements of SGML viewers/browsers. DSSSL-O limits the DSSSL flow object classes to those that are most useful in on-line environments. It also uses a reduced expression language (the Core Expression Language) and a reduced query language (the Core Query Language).

THE SGML DECLARATION

A.1 Overview

The principal purpose of the SGML declaration is to specify (for both human and machine consumption) the lexical environment required by the documents that use the declaration. Collectively referred to as a concrete syntax, the lexical environment includes details such as what character sets to use, what characters to use as delimiters such as STAGO, and limits such as maximum lengths for names and maximum depth of nesting of elements.

A significant portion of the SGML declaration is concerned with issues related to characters and character sets. In order to understand what it says about these things and why they need to be said, it is useful to consider similar issues that often lurk beneath the surface in ordinary programming languages.

Consider the following (not very useful) C program:

```
C>type foo.c

#include <stdio.h>
int main()
{
int n = 65;
  if (n == 'A')
    printf ("n is an A (%d,%c)",n,n);
}
```

Character set issues arise at a number of levels here.

1. The source code itself—the file foo.c—has been keyboarded on a machine that has stored the C program in a particular character set—in this case ASCII.[1]

---

1. ASCII (American Standard Code for Information Interchange) is formally known as ANSI X3.4-1986. ISO has a character set that is nearly identical known as ISO 646. In SGML circles, ISO 646 is the more frequently used name.

2. The C compiler itself will expect source files to be in a particular character set. In the case of a C compiler that reads ASCII files, the lexical analyzer will expect the if keyword to consist of the number 105 followed by the number 102, for example.

3. An ASCII C compiler treats the character constant A as the number 65.

It can be seen that the C program, the C compiler, and the resultant executable program in the preceding example have an inherent reliance on character set details. Moreover, many of these dependencies are left implicit. It is often only through application failures that the dependencies come to light. In keeping with SGML's open systems philosophy, such character set dependencies are made explicit thus enhancing the interoperability both of SGML documents and SGML applications.

Given that the SGML declaration is an intrinsic part of the SGML document itself, there is a clear "chicken and egg" situation with regard to character sets. How can the SGML declaration be in the character set that it itself sets out to describe? Moreover, if the SGML declaration allows the abstract delimiters such as STAGO to be given concrete values, what delimiters are used in the declaration itself? This amounts to the classic "bootstrapping" problem often encountered in operating systems and compiler design. At some level, something must be hard-wired to avoid an endless chain of things defined in terms of other things. Operating systems, for example, typically hard-wire the location of boot code on a storage medium. The boot code must be at that exact storage location because the notion of file does not exist at the point where the boot code is required.

SGML could have been similarly bootstrapped by hard-wiring the character set used in the SGML declaration, say ISO 646. However, doing so would have made the declaration illegible on any non-ISO 646 machine. SGML does not hard-wire the character set to be used in the declaration. It does, however, hard-wire the fact that the characters used in the declaration must have the same meaning they have in ISO 646 (i.e., the SGML declaration starts with a < character). It does not matter what *number* is used to represent this character as long as it exists in the character set. Furthermore, the STAGO delimiter used in the SGML declaration is always <. The full set of these delimiters that are hard-wired to allow the declaration itself to be parsed are part of what is known as the *Reference Concrete Syntax*.

Although ISO 646 is not hard-wired, all SGML systems must know about it. This is done in order to allow ISO 646 to be used as a point of departure for the definition of other character sets in terms of ISO 646 as discussed below.

A.2 Declaring a Character Set

A character set declaration comes in two parts—the base character set is referred to by its name (normally an ISO registered public identifier) and then the particular characters or sequences of characters required from that character set are mapped into slots in the new character set. In the Figure A.1, the ISO 646 characters for A to Z, respectively, are mapped into the same locations in the new character set.

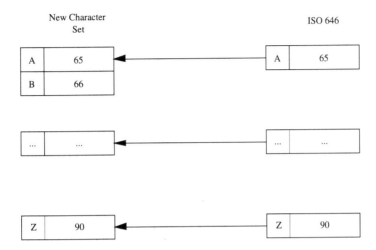

Figure A.1 Character set mapping

The syntax for expressing this mapping in the SGML declaration follows:

```
BASESET   "ISO 646-1983//CHARSET
            International Reference Version (IRV)//ESC 2/5 4/0"
DESCSET
      65 26 65
```

The DESCSET (DESCribed SET) part of the declaration consists of one or more mappings which can take the three forms described in Table A.1.

Table A.1: DESCSET Variations

Format	Interpretation
<to> <count> <from>	Starting at character number <to> in the new character set, map <count> characters from the base character set starting at character number <from>. For example, `32 95 32` makes the 95 characters—from character number 32 to character number 126 in the base character set—map to characters number 32 to 126 in the new character set.
<to> <count> <string>	Starting at character number <to>, map <count> characters (usually 1) to the string <string>. This indicates to the parser that the character numbers are admissable but have no other special meaning attached to them. (The string, however, describes a meaning for humans.)
<to> <count> "UNUSED"	Indicated that <count> characters starting at character number <to> are not used in the document and should generate a parse error if they occur.

Note that multiple pairs of BASESET and DESCSET declarations are allowed, thus making it possible to build a character set by combining parts of more than one base character set. This capability is used frequently to provide access to diacritical mark characters used in many Latin-based languages. For example,

```
BASESET   "ISO 646:1983//CHARSET
           International Reference Version (IRV)//ESC 2/5 4/0"
DESCSET     0    9    UNUSED
            9    2     9
           11    2    UNUSED
           13    1     13
           14   18    UNUSED
           32   95    32
          127    1    UNUSED
BASESET   "ISO Registration Number 100//CHARSET
           ECMA-94 Right Part of Latin Alphabet Nr. 1//ESC 2/13 4/1"
DESCSET   128   32    UNUSED
          160    5    32
          165    1    UNUSED
          166   88    38
          254    1    127
          255    1    UNUSED
```

This is illustrated in Figure A.2.

A.3   Referencing a Character Set

In the examples so far, there have been a number of references to ISO 646 that look like this:

```
"ISO 646:1983//CHARSET
        International Reference Version (IRV)//ESC 2/5 4/0"
```

The naming convention used here is a variation of a Formal Public Identifier (see Section 7.9.8—Formal Public Identifiers). This variation is only used for FPIs that have a Public Text class of CHARSET.

In FPIs that refer to character sets, the fourth part of the identifier (in all other cases, a language code such a //EN for English) is a so-called designating sequence. These designating sequences are detailed in ISO 2022—a standard that describes how to identify character sets.

A.4   Details of the SGML Declaration
A.4.1   Overall Structure

The SGML declarations consist of six component parts, identified by certain keywords. The overall structure is shown here with **bold** text used to identify the major part boundaries:

Result Character
Set

ISO 646

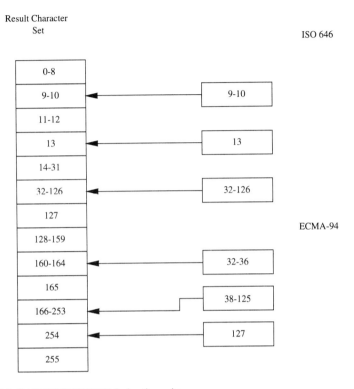

ECMA-94

Figure A.2 Multiple BASESET/DESCSET declaration pairs

```
<!SGML "ISO 8879:1986"
CHARSET
  Details of the character set used by the document
CAPACITY
  Details of various capacities required for successful parsing
SCOPE
  Whether or not the following Concrete Syntax refers to the entire document or
  just the document instance
SYNTAX
  Details of the Concrete Syntax
FEATURES
  The optional features of SGML that may be required by this document
APPINFO
  Application specific information
>
```

The individual sections are discussed (in a slightly different order to that required in the SGML declaration) next.

A.4.2   Document Character Set (CHARSET)

The character set to be used by the document (for all markup) is defined in CHARSET. In the majority of situations, the character set used by the document and the character set supported by the parser are very similar or identical. In this situation, only very simple mapping is required to create the document character set. A common example follows:

```
BASESET  "ISO 646-1983//CHARSET
          International Reference Version (IRV)//ESC 2/5 4/0"
DESCSET    0  9 UNUSED
           9  2  9
          11  2 UNUSED
          13  1 13
          14 18 UNUSED
          32 95 32
         127  1 UNUSED
```

A common example of when such a simple mapping in not sufficient is when EBCDIC and ISO 646 are mixed. For example, to use an ISO 646-aware parser to parse documents encoded in EBCDIC, a mapping can be defined to convert the EBCDIC character numbers to corresponding ISO 646 numbers. For example,

```
BASESET  "ISO 646-1983//CHARSET
          International Reference Version (IRV)//ESC 2/5 4/0"
...
DESCSET   193  1 65
...
```

Here character code 65 in ISO 646 (capital A) is mapped to character code 193 in EBCDIC (capital A).[2]

A.4.3   Concrete Syntax (SYNTAX)

A.4.3.1   Overall Structure

This portion of the SGML declaration serves to define the lexical details of the markup language. Here, the abstract delimiters such as ETAGO are given concrete characters or character strings. Rules are defined for what characters may appear in names such as generic identifier names, whether or not case is significant, what character should be treated as Record End by the parser, and so on.

---

2. In practice, it may be more convenient to use external utility software to achieve these mappings (i.e., convert the document from EBCDIC to ISO 646 prior to parsing it).

The SYNTAX can have seven parts, the overall structure is shown here with **bold** text used to delimit the major parts:

```
SYNTAX
  SHUNCHAR
     Details of what characters are ignored
  BASESET
  DESCSET
    Definition of a character set portion.
    (There can be more than one BASESET/DESCSET pair here.)
  FUNCTION
    Characters with specially assigned functions
  NAMING
    Rules for building valid names
  DELIM
    Characters or character strings to serve as delimiters
  NAMES
    Reserved names
  QUANTITY
    Maximum number of occurrences for various things
```

A.4.3.2   *Shunned Characters (SHUNCHAR)*

Shunned characters are characters that must not be used in any document character set using this SYNTAX clause. The idea is to explicitly state which characters are likely to have special meanings on particular systems and thus cause problems when documents are being transferred from machine to machine.

An embedded Control-Z in a text file, for example, might be construed as end-of-file on some systems. In the following example, ^Z indicates the single character Control-Z (26 in ISO 646):

```
C>copy /b foo.sgm con:

<!DOCTYPE foo [
<!ELEMENT foo - O (#PCDATA)>
]>
<foo>
Hello
^Z
World
```

When typed to the screen, it is as if the line World does not exist:

```
C>type foo.sgm

<!DOCTYPE foo [
<!ELEMENT foo - O (#PCDATA)>
]>
<foo>
Hello
```

In the default SGML declaration used by NSGMLS, character 26 of ISO 646 is a shunned character. This allows the parser to detect the presence of the ^Z and report an error:

```
C>nsgmls foo.sgm

foo.sgm:6:1:E: non SGML character number 26
(FOO
-Hello\n\032\nWorld
)FOO
```

As well as explicitly listing the character numbers of shunned characters, the controls keyword can be specified. This means that any character in the character set that the parser knows to be a control character is also a shunned character.

A.4.3.3   Character Set (BASESET/DESCSET)

The character set part of the syntax declaration defines what is called the *syntax reference character set*. This character set serves to provide a level of indirection between the concrete syntax and the document character set. The idea is that this level of indirection could be used to make the syntax portion of the declaration independent of the document character set and thus reusable with different document character sets.[3]

A.4.3.4   Function Characters (FUNCTION)

In SGML, every character in a character set is assigned to 1 of 18 different classes for SGML syntax purposes.[4] *Function characters* is the collective term for a class of characters that may have an extra SGML meaning over and above potentially being recognized as markup.

Some function characters (RS, RE, and SPACE) are mandatory, and others can be defined if necessary.

A typical function character identification for an ISO 646 based character set follows:

```
FUNCTION
          RE                      13
          RS                      10
          SPACE                   32
          TAB         SEPCHAR     9
```

Note the declaration for the TAB function character. This is an example of a user-defined function character. They take the following general form:

```
<Name> <Function Name> <Character Number>
```

<Function Name> can be one of the function names listed in Table A.2.

---

3. This capability seems to be seldom used in practice (i.e., the syntax reference character set is mapped directly onto the document character set).

4. For example, lowercase letters is the character class consisting of the 26 letters *a* through *z*.

Table A.2: Function Names

Function Name	Interpretation
FUNCHAR	A character that serves as a "do nothing" function character.
MSICHAR	A Markup Scan In CHARacter—it will re-enable the interpretation of markup disabled by a previous MSOCHAR (see below).
MSOCHAR	A Markup Scan Out CHARacter—it will inhibit the interpretation of markup until an Ee signal or an MSICHAR.
MSSCHAR	A Markup Scan Suppress CHARacter—it will suppress the interpretation of markup for the next character in the entity.
SEPCHAR	A character to be added to the separator class. By default RS, RE, and SPACE are members of the separator class.

A.4.3.5   Naming Rules (NAMING)

This section of the syntax declaration is used to specify what characters can appear in names. It is also used to specify the case sensitivity of names in various contexts. The mechanism used is to allow the declaration to specify characters to add to the permanent characters belonging to four character classes namely LCNMSTRT (LowerCase Name Start), UCNMSTRT (UpperCase Name Start), LCNMCHAR (LowerCase Name Character), and UCNMSTRT (UpperCase Name Character). A typical NAMING section follows:

```
NAMING
    LCNMSTRT ""
    UCNMSTRT ""
    LCNMCHAR "-."
    UCNMCHAR "-."
    NAMECASE GENERAL YES
             ENTITY NO
```

Here, the dash (-) and period (.) characters have been added to the characters allowable within the body of a name (i.e., after the initial character).

The NAMECASE section specifies whether or not the parser should perform a lowercase to uppercase translation on names. Names are split into two classes—entity names (ENTITY) and the rest (GENERAL). In this example, lowercase to uppercase translation is performed for all names except entity names.

The potential case insensitivity of names explains the use of four rather than two classes of characters (i.e., when adding characters to the set of valid name characters it is necessary to specify both uppercase and lowercase versions).

A.4.3.6   Delimiters (DELIM)

This is where strings are assigned to the various delimiter roles and any extra short-reference delimiters are defined. The overall format is shown here with **bold** text indicating parts of the syntax:

```
DELIM
     GENERAL SGMLREF
     Details of how delimiter strings differ from
     Reference Concrete Syntax
     SHORTREF
     Details of short reference delimiters
```

All 31 general delimiters used in SGML can be redefined. For example, to specify that round brackets be used to delimit start- and end-tags:

```
DELIM
GENERAL SGMLREF
  STAGO "("
  TAGC  ")"
  STAGC "(/"
```

The short-reference delimiters to be used in the document can be specified in two ways— either by adding to the set specified in the reference concrete syntax or by replacing it:

```
SHORTREF NONE
  "~~"
```

This example, makes "~~" the only valid short-reference delimiter whereas

```
SHORTREF SGML
  "~~"
```

adds the "~~" delimiter to the set defined in the reference concrete syntax.

A.4.3.7   Reserved Names (NAMES)

Unlike the majority of programming languages, SGML does not hard-wire keywords for its own use. The keywords used throughout this book such as DOCTYPE and ELEMENT are simply the set of reserved names specified in the reference concrete syntax, and they can all[5] be changed. For example,

```
NAMES SGMLREF
  EMPTY "VOID"
```

Here the word "VOID" is specified as a replacement for the EMPTY keyword.

A.4.3.8   Quantities (QUANTITY)

QUANTITY allows various maximum values to be specified.

---

5. However, reserved names that occur only in the SGML declaration cannot be changed because it is always in the reference concrete syntax.

Table A.3: Reference Quantity Set

Name	Interpretation
ATTCNT	Maximum number of attributes
ATTSPLEN	Maximum length of attribute specification list
BSEQLEN	Maximum length of blank sequence in short-reference string
DTAGLEN	Maximum length of a data tag
DTEMPLEN	Maximum length of a data tag template
ENTLVL	Maximum nesting level for entities
GRPCNT	Maximum number of tokens in a model group
GRPGTCNT	Maximum grand total of model groups
GRPLVL	Maximum nesting level for model groups
LITLEN	Maximum length of parameter literal or attribute value literal
NAMELEN	Maximum length of a name (i.e., a generic identifier name)
NORMSEP	When calculating the normalized length of a string, a run of separators of length > NORMSEP counts as NORMSEP characters
PILEN	Maximum length of a processing instruction
TAGLEN	Maximum length of a start-tag
TAGLVL	Maximum nesting level for elements

A.4.4   Concrete Syntax Scope (SCOPE)

It is possible to specify that the concrete syntax being defined is to be used only within the document instance(s) that follow the prolog, in which case the reference concrete syntax will be used for the prolog. This is done with the following scope declaration:

```
SCOPE INSTANCE
```

To use the concrete syntax for the entire document, the following scope declaration is used:

```
SCOPE DOCUMENT
```

A.4.5   Capacities Required for Parsing (CAPACITY)

CAPACITY allows values to be specified that can serve as an indication of the processing size capabilities that a parser would require to parse the document successfully. Advances in processing power since the standard was adopted have reduced the usefulness of the CAPACITY section. See ISO 8879, §9.8 for details.

A.4.6   Optional SGML Features Required (FEATURES)

FEATURES allows specification of the optional features required in the form of YES/NO declarations:

```
FEATURES
  MINIMIZE
    DATATAG  NO
    OMITTAG  YES
    RANK     NO
    SHORTTAG NO
  LINK
    SIMPLE   YES 10
    IMPLICIT YES
    EXPLICIT YES 1
  OTHER
    CONCUR   NO
    SUBDOC   YES 10
    FORMAL   YES
```

Here, the only minimization feature enabled is tag omission (OMITTAG). Support for up to ten simultaneously active simple link process declarations is required. Both IMPLICIT and EXPLICIT LINK are enabled with the length of a chain of EXPLICIT links limited to one. Up to ten SUBDOC entities may be open simultaneously. Finally, all public identifiers are to be interpreted as formal public identifiers.

A.4.7   Application Specific Information (APPINFO)

APPINFO is used to allow the specification of application specific information. The contents of the APPINFO parameter is simply passed through to the processing application.

A.5   System Declarations

One of the principal jobs of the SGML declaration is to provide information to the parser about the necessary lexical environment for the parsing process. During processing of the SGML declaration, an individual SGML system may encounter mismatches between the facilities it can provide and the facilities required by the SGML declaration. For example, an SGML application might support a maximum name length of 32 yet find NAMELEN set to 64 in the declaration. As another example, it might find that the declaration specifies the use of an SGML optional feature such as LINK or SUBDOC, which it does not support.

Such system—as opposed to document—limits can be captured by using components of an SGML declaration and used as a succinct piece of documentation about a given SGML system.

When used for this purpose, these SGML declaration components (together with a few other parameters) are known as a *system declaration*.

A.6 The Reference Concrete Syntax

```
SYNTAX
        SHUNCHAR CONTROLS 0 1 2 3 4 5 6 7 8 9 10 11 12 13 14 15 16 17
                          18 19 20 21 22 23 24 25 26 27 28 29 30 31 127 255
        BASESET  "ISO 646-1983//CHARSET International Reference Version
                 (IRV)//ESC 2/5 4/0"
        DESCSET  0 128 0
        FUNCTION RE                      13
                 RS                      10
                 SPACE                   32
                 TAB         SEPCHAR     9
        NAMING   LCNMSTRT    ""
                 UCNMSTRT    ""
                 LCNMCHAR    "-."
                 UCNMCHAR    "-."
                 NAMECASE    GENERAL     YES
                             ENTITY      NO
        DELIM    GENERAL     SGMLREF
                 SHORTREF    SGMLREF
        NAMES    SGMLREF
        QUANTITY SGMLREF
```

A.6.1 Expanded DELIM Parameter

```
DELIM
GENERAL SGMLREF
    AND   "&"    COM   "--"   CRO   "&#"   DSC   "]"
    DSO   "["    DTGC  "]"    DTGO  "["    ERO   "&"
    ETAGO "</"   GRPC  ")"    GRPO  "("    LIT   '"'
    LITA  "'"    MDC   ">"    MDO   "<!"   MINUS "-"
    MSC   "]]"   NET   "/"    OPT   "?"    OR    "|"
    PERO  "%"    PIC   ">"    PIO   "<?"   PLUS  "+"
    REFC  ";"    REP   "*"    RNI   "#"    SEQ   ","
    STAGO "<"    TAGC  ">"    VI    "="

SHORTREF NONE
    "&#TAB;"      "&#RE;"        "&#RS;"         "&#RS;B"
    "&#RS;&#RE;"  "&#RS;B&#RE;"  "B&#RE;"        "&#SPACE;"
    "BB"
    "'"    "#"     "%"     "'"     "("     ")"     "*"
    ","    "-"     ":"     ";"     "="     "@"     "+"
    "["    "]"     "^"     "_"     "{"     "|"     "}"
    "~"    "--"
```

A.6.2   Expanded NAMES Parameter

```
NAMES SGMLREF
ANY                  "ANY"
ATTLIST              "ATTLIST"
CDATA                "CDATA"
CONREF               "CONREF"
CURRENT              "CURRENT"
DEFAULT              "DEFAULT"
DOCTYPE              "DOCTYPE"
ELEMENT              "ELEMENT"
EMPTY                "EMPTY"
ENDTAG               "ENDTAG"
ENTITIES             "ENTITIES"
ENTITY               "ENTITY"
FIXED                "FIXED"
ID                   "ID"
IDLINK               "IDLINK"
IDREF                "IDREF"
IDREFS               "IDREFS"
IGNORE               "IGNORE"
IMPLIED              "IMPLIED"
INCLUDE              "INCLUDE"
INITIAL              "INITIAL"
LINK                 "LINK"
LINKTYPE             "LINKTYPE"
MD                   "MD"
MS                   "MS"
NAME                 "NAME"
NAMES                "NAMES"
NDATA                "NDATA"
NMTOKEN              "NMTOKEN"
NMTOKENS             "NMTOKENS"
NOTATION             "NOTATION"
NUMBER               "NUMBER"
NUMBERS              "NUMBERS"
NUTOKEN              "NUTOKEN"
NUTOKENS             "NUTOKENS"
O                    "O"
PCDATA               "PCDATA"
PI                   "PI"
POSTLINK             "POSTLINK"
PUBLIC               "PUBLIC"
RCDATA               "RCDATA"
RE                   "RE"
REQUIRED             "REQUIRED"
RESTORE              "RESTORE"
RS                   "RS"
SDATA                "SDATA"
SHORTREF             "SHORTREF"
```

```
SIMPLE          "SIMPLE"
SPACE           "SPACE"
STARTTAG        "STARTTAG"
SUBDOC          "SUBDOC"
SYSTEM          "SYSTEM"
TEMP            "TEMP"
USELINK         "USELINK"
USEMAP          "USEMAP"
```

A.6.3   Expanded Quantity Set Parameter

```
QUANTITY SGMLREF
ATTCNT          40
ATTSPLEN       960
BSEQLEN        960
DTAGLEN         16
DTEMPLEN        16
ENTLVL          16
GRPCNT          32
GRPGTCNT        96
GRPLVL          16
LITLEN         240
NAMELEN          8
NORMSEP          2
PILEN          240
TAGLEN         960
TAGLVL          24
```

A.7   The Default SGML Declaration Used by NSGMLS

If an SGML declaration is not supplied to NSGMLS, it will infer the following SGML declaration:

```
                    <!SGML "ISO 8879:1986"
                            CHARSET
        BASESET   "ISO 646-1983//CHARSET
                  International Reference Version (IRV)//ESC 2/5 4/0"
        DESCSET    0  9 UNUSED
                   9  2  9
                  11  2 UNUSED
                  13  1 13
                  14 18 UNUSED
                  32 95 32
                 127  1 UNUSED
        CAPACITY PUBLIC    "ISO 8879:1986//CAPACITY Reference//EN"
        SCOPE    DOCUMENT
```

```
SYNTAX
SHUNCHAR CONTROLS 0 1 2 3 4 5 6 7 8 9 10 11 12 13 14 15 16 17
         18 19 20 21 22 23 24 25 26 27 28 29 30 31 127 255
BASESET  "ISO 646-1983//CHARSET International Reference Version
         (IRV)//ESC 2/5 4/0"
DESCSET  0 128 0
FUNCTION RE                      13
         RS                      10
         SPACE                   32
         TAB       SEPCHAR       9
NAMING   LCNMSTRT  ""
         UCNMSTRT  ""
         LCNMCHAR  "-."
         UCNMCHAR  "-."
         NAMECASE  GENERAL       YES
                   ENTITY        NO
DELIM    GENERAL   SGMLREF
         SHORTREF  SGMLREF
NAMES    SGMLREF
QUANTITY SGMLREF
         ATTCNT    99999999
         ATTSPLEN  99999999
         DTEMPLEN  24000
         ENTLVL    99999999
         GRPCNT    99999999
         GRPGTCNT  99999999
         GRPLVL    99999999
         LITLEN    24000
         NAMELEN   99999999
         PILEN     24000
         TAGLEN    99999999
         TAGLVL    99999999
                             FEATURES
MINIMIZE DATATAG   NO
         OMITTAG   YES
         RANK      YES
         SHORTTAG  YES
LINK     SIMPLE    YES 1000
         IMPLICIT  YES
         EXPLICIT  YES 1
OTHER    CONCUR    NO
         SUBDOC    YES 99999999
         FORMAL    YES
                   APPINFO NONE>
```

NSGMLS OUTPUT FORMAT DETAILS

B.1 The Origins of ESIS

ISO 8879 classifies SGML applications as falling into one of two broad categories:

1. Structure-Controlled Applications—applications that work with SGML data at the element structure level (i.e., applications that are concerned with the structures described by markup rather than the lexical details of the markup itself).

2. Markup-Sensitive Applications—applications that are concerned with the lexical structure of SGML markup.

The set of information that structure-controlled applications are permitted to act upon is known as the Element Structure Information Set and is defined in Attachment 1 of Appendix B of *The SGML Handbook*. This is standardized in ISO/IEC 13673:1995—the SGML conformance testing standard.

Note that in keeping with SGML's philosophy of remaining independent of the applications that may process it, the abstract structures of ESIS are defined rather than the physical format that the ESIS may take. For example, at the start of any element, the ESIS contains (among other things)

- the generic identifier and

- the attribute information.

  Attribute information must conform to these rules (among others):

- Each unspecified impliable attribute must be specified.

- It must not be possible to tell that an attribute value is the default value specified in the DTD.

- The order in which attributes are specified is not significant.

The most common physical form of ESIS is that produced by NSGMLS. The format closely follows that produced by an earlier parser known as SGMLS. SGMLS was also written by James Clark and is derived from the ARCSGML parser written by Dr. Charles F. Goldfarb.

Note that some aspects of the output of NSGMLS having to do with optional features of SGML and multibyte character sets are not discussed here.

The output of NSGMLS is a series of arbitrarily sized lines (records). The first character of each line specifies the type of record. The structure of the rest of the line depends on the type of record.

B.2 Escape Sequences

Within ESIS records that can contain content, the escape sequences shown in Table B.1 can occur.

Table B.1: Escape sequences

Code	Meaning
\\	Denotes a single \ character.
\n	Signals the presence of a record end. Note that this is **two** characters: \ followed by n. Be careful not to confuse it with the common \n encoding of end-of-line character in languages like Perl or C.
\\|	Used to delineate internal SDATA entities.
\nnn	The character whose octal encoding is nnn (i.e., the string "\079" represents the decimal number 65, which is the character A in ISO 646 or ASCII).

B.3 Elements

Element start and end records are shown in Table B.2.

Table B.2: Start and end element records

Record Format	Meaning
"(" <gi>	Denotes the start of an element whose generic identifier is <gi>.
")" <gi>	The end of the an element whose generic identifier is <gi>.

B.4 Attributes

Attribute records are shown in Table B.3.

Table B.3: Attribute records

Record Format	Meaning
"A"<name> <value>	Denotes an attribute for an element. The attribute has the name <name> and value <value>. The <value> field can take the forms detailed in Table B.4.
"D"<name> <value>	Denotes a data attribute (i.e., an attribute for an SGML notation). The attribute has the name <name> and value <value>. The <value> field can take the forms detailed in Table B.4.
"a" <linktype> <name> <value>	Denotes a link attribute (i.e., an attribute added to an element as a result of a link process definition). See Section 14.4—The LINK Feature.

Table B.4: Attribute value formats

Value	Meaning
IMPLIED	The attribute value was not specified in the document and is to be inferred by the processing application. Note that no indication of the type of attribute (i.e., attribute declared value) is supplied.
CDATA <data>	The attribute value is character data. The data itself as supplied is <data>. Note that <data> can be empty.
NOTATION <name>	The attribute is a notation name.
ENTITY <name>...<name>	The attribute is one or more general entity names.
TOKEN <token>...<token>	The attribute is one or more of the following attribute declared values: ID[a] IDREF/IDREFS NAME/NAMES NMTOKEN/NMTOKENS NUMBER/NUMBERS NUTOKEN/NUTOKENS
ID <token>[b]	The attribute has the ID declared value.

[a]As long as -oid option is not specified.
[b]As long as -oid option is specified.

B.5   Data Content

The format of a data record is shown in Table B.5.

Table B.5: Data record format

Record Format	Meaning
"-"<data>	Denotes data content. The <data> will be at least one character long and may be arbitrarily long.

B.6   Notations

The format of a notation record is shown in Table B.6.

Table B.6: Notation record format

Record Format	Meaning
"N" <name>	Denotes a notation with the name <name>.

B.7   Entity Management

The format of entity records is shown in Table B.7.

Table B.7: Entity record formats

Record Format	Meaning
"&" <name>	Denotes a reference to an external data entity <name>.
"{" <name>	Denotes the start of the subdocument entity <name>.
"}"<name>	Denotes the end of the subdocument entity <name>.
"S" <name>	Denotes a subdocument entity with name <name>.
"T" <type> <name>	Denotes an external SGML text entity with name <name> and type <type>. Type can be one of CDATA, NDATA, or SDATA.
"I" <name> <type> <text>	Denotes an internal data entity named <name>. <type> will be one of CDATA or SDATA. The "I" record is only produced for attributes of type ENTITY or ENTITIES unless the -oentity option is being used. When used in conjunction with -oentity, <type> can also be one of PI (processing instruction) or TEXT (SGML text entity).
"E" <name> <type> <notation>	Denotes an external data entity with name <name>. <type> can be one of CDATA , NDATA, or SDATA. <notation> is the name of the governing notation.
"s" <sysid>	Denotes a system identifier. Associated with the next external entity or notation.
"p" <pubid>	Denotes a public identifier. Associated with the next external entity or notation.
"f"<sysid>	Specifies a file name generated by the entity manager.

B.8   Miscellaneous

Some miscellaneous record formats are shown in Table B.8.

Table B.8: Miscellaneous record formats

Record Format	Meaning
"?" <code>	Denotes a processing instruction.
"L" <linenum> <filename>	Specifies the current line number and file name. The file name will be output once when processing of the file begins. Line numbers are enabled with the -l option.
"#"<text>	Specifies the text provided in the APPINFO parameter of the SGML declaration if specified.
"C"	Indicates that the document was conforming.

B.9   Formal System Identifiers

A formal system identifier (FSI) is a system identifier structured to provide a formal interface between the entity manager and the local file system and other physical storage managers of the information.

An FSI consists of one or more storage object specifications. The objects specified by these storage object specifications are concatenated to form the content of the entity.

A storage object specification consists of the storage manager details followed by storage object details. The specification is constructed as SGML markup using the reference concrete syntax.

When FSIs are in use, NSGMLS can infer an FSI from a simple file name. For example,

```
C>type x.sgm

<!DOCTYPE foo [
<!NOTATION acf system "A character Format">
<!ENTITY bar system "bar.dat" CDATA acf>
<!ELEMENT foo - O (#PCDATA)>
]>
<foo>
&bar;

C>NSGMLS x.sgm
(FOO
sA character Format
NACF
sbar.dat
f<OSFILE FIND>bar.dat
Ebar CDATA ACF
```

```
&bar
-\n
)FOO
C
```

The storage manager is specified as OSFILE, indicating that the entity will be located via the host operating system. The FIND attribute specifies that the entity manager will find out for itself how records have been delimited in the entity by looking for a CRLF, CR, or LF code itself.

FIND is the default for CDATA and SDATA entities. Making the entity NDATA causes a different formal system identifier to be inferred as follows:

```
C>type x.sgm

<!DOCTYPE foo [
<!NOTATION abf system "A Binary Format">
<!ENTITY bar system "bar.dat" NDATA abf>
<!ELEMENT foo - O (#PCDATA)>
]>
<foo>
&bar;

C>NSGMLS x.sgm

(FOO
sA Binary Format
NABF
sbar.dat
f<OSFILE NOZAPEOF ASIS>bar.dat
Ebar NDATA ABF
&bar
-\n
)FOO
C
```

Here, the storage manager is again OSFILE. However, no interpretation of record boundaries will be performed (ASIS) and Control-Z will be treated as a data character rather than an end-of-file indicator. These are the default settings for NDATA entities

Formal system identifiers can also be specified explicitly, with storage managers such as URLs. For full details on the storage managers and attributes supported by NSGMLS refer to the documentation with the package, which can be found on the included CD-ROM.

SOURCE CODE FOR THE FRAMEWORKS

C.1   C++ Framework

The C++ header file esis.h follows:

```
//
// Simple ESIS Event Library
//

// ESIS Event Types
#define OPENELEMENT_EVENT          0
#define CLOSEELEMENT_EVENT         1
#define DATA_EVENT                 2
#define ATTRIBUTE_EVENT            3
#define CONFORMING_EVENT           4

//
// Element Attribute Declared Values
//
#define ATTR_UNKNOWN          0
#define ATTR_CDATA            1
#define ATTR_ENTITY           2
#define ATTR_NOTATION         3
#define ATTR_TOKEN            4

//
// Esis Event Base Class
//
class EsisEvent {
public:
    virtual CString GetEsisFormat() = 0;
    virtual CString GetSummary() = 0;
    virtual int GetEsisEventType() = 0;
};

//
// Open Element Event Class
//
class OpenElementEvent : public EsisEvent {
private:
```

```
        CString ElementName;
public:
        void SetElementName(CString e);
        CString GetElementName();
        CString GetEsisFormat();
        CString GetSummary();
        int GetEsisEventType();
};

//
// Close Element Event Class
//
class CloseElementEvent : public EsisEvent {
private:
        CString ElementName;
public:
        void SetElementName(CString e);
        CString GetElementName();
        CString GetEsisFormat();
        CString GetSummary();
        int GetEsisEventType();
};

//
// Data Event Class
//
class DataEvent : public EsisEvent {
        CString Data;
public:
        void SetData(CString d);
        CString GetData();
        CString GetEsisFormat();
        CString GetSummary();
        int GetEsisEventType();
};

//
// Element Attribute Event Class
//
class AttributeEvent : public EsisEvent {
        CString Name , Value;
        int Type;
        int ValueSupplied;
public:
        AttributeEvent();
        void SetAttrName(CString d);
        void SetAttrType(int t);
        void SetAttrValue(CString t);
        void SetValueSupplied(int n);
        CString GetAttrName();
        int GetValueSupplied();
```

```
    CString GetEsisFormat();
    CString GetSummary();
    int GetEsisEventType();
};
//
// Conformance Event
//
class ConformingEvent : public EsisEvent {
public:
    CString GetEsisFormat();
    CString GetSummary();
    int GetEsisEventType();
};

// Main interface function to the library
class EsisEvent *GetEvent(FILE *fp);

// Two utilty conversion functions for Attribute Declared Values
char *AttrTypeToString(int t);
int AttrStringToType(char *s);
```

The C++ implementation file esis.cpp follows:

```
//
// Simple ESIS Event Library
//

#define _DOS
#include <afx.h>
#include <iostream.h>

#include "esis.h"

// Longest ESIS line supported by this simple library
#define MAX_ESIS_LINE 30000

char buffer [ MAX_ESIS_LINE ];

// Main interface function to Library
class EsisEvent *GetEvent(FILE *fp)
{
char *s;
OpenElementEvent *oge;
CloseElementEvent *cge;
AttributeEvent *ate;
ConformingEvent *cone;
DataEvent *dev;
    s = fgets (buffer, MAX_ESIS_LINE , fp);
    if (s == NULL)
        return (EsisEvent *)NULL;
    buffer[strlen(buffer)-1]='\0';
    switch (*s) {
        case '(':
```

```
                // Element Open Event
                oge = new OpenElementEvent;
                oge->SetElementName (++s);
                return oge;
            break;
            case ')':
                // Element Close Event
                cge = new CloseElementEvent;
                cge->SetElementName (++s);
                return cge;
            break;
            case 'A':
                // Element Attribute Event
                ate = new AttributeEvent;
                s = strtok(++s," ");
                ate->SetAttrName (s);
                s = strtok (NULL," ");
                if (strcmp(s,"IMPLIED")==0) {
                    ate->SetValueSupplied(0);
                    ate->SetAttrType(ATTR_UNKNOWN);
                }
                else {
                    ate->SetValueSupplied(1);
                    ate->SetAttrType(AttrStringToType(s));
                    s = strtok (NULL, " ");
                    if (s != NULL)
                        ate->SetAttrValue(s);
                    else
                        ate->SetAttrValue("");
                }
                return ate;
            break;
            case 'C':
                // Conformance Event
                cone = new ConformingEvent;
                return cone;
            break;
            case '-':
                // Data Event
                dev = new DataEvent;
                dev->SetData (++s);
                return dev;
            break;
        }
        return NULL;
    }

    void OpenElementEvent::SetElementName(CString e)
    {
        ElementName = e;
    }
```

```
CString OpenElementEvent::GetElementName()
{
    return ElementName;
}

CString OpenElementEvent::GetEsisFormat()
{
    return "(" + ElementName;
}

CString OpenElementEvent::GetSummary()
{
    return "Open Element '" + ElementName + "'";
}

int OpenElementEvent::GetEsisEventType()
{
    return OPENELEMENT_EVENT;
}

void CloseElementEvent::SetElementName(CString e)
{
    ElementName = e;
}

CString CloseElementEvent::GetElementName()
{
    return ElementName;
}

CString CloseElementEvent::GetEsisFormat()
{
    return ")" + ElementName;
}

CString CloseElementEvent::GetSummary()
{
    return "Close Element '" + ElementName + "'";
}

int CloseElementEvent::GetEsisEventType()
{
    return CLOSEELEMENT_EVENT;
}

void DataEvent::SetData(CString d)
{
    Data = d;
}

CString DataEvent::GetData()
{
    return Data;
}
```

```
CString DataEvent::GetEsisFormat()
{
    return "-" + Data;
}

CString DataEvent::GetSummary()
{
    return "Document Data '" + Data.Left(30) + "...'";
}

int DataEvent::GetEsisEventType()
{
    return DATA_EVENT;
};

AttributeEvent::AttributeEvent()
{
    Type = ATTR_UNKNOWN;
    ValueSupplied = 0;
}

void AttributeEvent::SetAttrName(CString d)
{
    Name = d;
}

void AttributeEvent::SetAttrType(int t)
{
    Type = t;
}

void AttributeEvent::SetAttrValue(CString t)
{
    Value = t;
}

void AttributeEvent::SetValueSupplied(int n)
{
    ValueSupplied = n;
}

CString AttributeEvent::GetAttrName()
{
    return Name;
}

int AttributeEvent::GetValueSupplied()
{
    return ValueSupplied;
}

//
// Create a string representation of an event as per NSGMLS esis
//
```

```
CString AttributeEvent::GetEsisFormat()
{
CString temp;
    temp = "A" + Name + " ";
    if(ValueSupplied>0) {
        temp += AttrTypeToString(Type);
        temp += " ";
        temp += Value;
    }
    else
        temp += "IMPLIED";
    return temp;
}

CString AttributeEvent::GetSummary()
{
CString temp;
    temp = "Attribute Name='" + Name + "'";
    if (ValueSupplied>0)
        temp += " Value='" + Value + "'";
    else
        temp += " Value=IMPLIED";
    temp += " Type='";
    temp += AttrTypeToString(Type);
    temp += "'";

    return temp;
}

int AttributeEvent::GetEsisEventType()
{
    return ATTRIBUTE_EVENT;
}

CString ConformingEvent::GetEsisFormat()
{
    return "C";
}

CString ConformingEvent::GetSummary()
{
    return "Conforming";
}

int ConformingEvent::GetEsisEventType()
{
    return CONFORMING_EVENT;
}

//
// Given a string, return the corresponding attribute declared value
// as an integer
//
```

```
int AttrStringToType(char *s)
{
    if (stricmp(s,"CDATA")==0)
        return ATTR_CDATA;
    if (stricmp(s,"ENTITY")==0)
        return ATTR_ENTITY;
    if (stricmp(s,"NOTATION")==0)
        return ATTR_NOTATION;
    if (stricmp(s,"TOKEN")==0)
        return ATTR_TOKEN;
    return ATTR_UNKNOWN;
}

//
// Given an integer, return the corresponding attribute declared
// value as a string
//
char *AttrTypeToString(int t)
{
    switch (t) {
        case ATTR_CDATA:
            return "CDATA";
        break;
        case ATTR_ENTITY:
            return "ENTITY";
        break;
        case ATTR_NOTATION:
            return "NOTATION";
        break;
        case ATTR_TOKEN:
            return "TOKEN";
        break;
        default:
            return "UNKNOWN";
    }
    return "UNKNOWN";
}
```

C.2 Perl Framework

The Pearl framework ESIS.pl follows:

```
#
# Simple Perl Framework for ESIS processing
#
sub esis {
    while (<STDIN>) {
        chop;
```

```perl
$command = substr($_, 0, 1);
substr($_, 0, 1) = "";
if ($command eq '(') {
    $call = "OPEN_".$_;
    if (defined &$call) {
        &$call($_,@Attributes);
    }
    elsif (defined &DEFAULT_OPEN_HANDLER) {
        &DEFAULT_OPEN_HANDLER($_,@Attributes)
    }
    else {
        foreach $x (@Attributes) {
            print "A",$x,"\n";
        }
        print "(",$_,"\n";
    }
    @Attributes=();
}
elsif ($command eq ')') {
    $call = "CLOSE_".$_;
    if (defined &$call) {
        &$call($_);
    }
    elsif (defined &DEFAULT_CLOSE_HANDLER) {
        &DEFAULT_CLOSE_HANDLER($_)
    }
    else {
        print ")",$_,"\n";
    }
}
elsif ($command eq '-') {
    if (defined &DATA_HANDLER) {
        &DATA_HANDLER($_);
    }
    else {
        print "-",$_,"\n";
    }
}
elsif ($command eq 'A') {
    push (@Attributes , $_);
}
elsif ($command eq 'C') {
    if (defined &CONFORM_HANDLER) {
        &CONFORM_HANDLER($_);
    }
    else {
        print "C\n";
    }
}
else {
```

```perl
                warn "Unknown ESIS Event $command\n";
            }
        }
    }

    sub getattrvalue {
        local( $attrname, @attrlist ) = @_;
        local($i,$l);
        local($aname,$atype,$avalue);

        $l = @attrlist;
        for( $i=0; $i < $l; $i++ ) {
            ($aname,$atype,$avalue) = split (' ',$attrlist[$i],3);
            last if ( $aname eq $attrname )
        }
        $avalue;
    }

    sub hasattribute {
        local( $attrname, @attrlist ) = @_;
        local($i,$l);
        local($aname,$atype,$avalue);

        $l = @attrlist;
        for( $i=0; $i < $l; $i++ ) {
            ($aname,$atype,$avalue) = split (' ',$attrlist[$i],3);
            last if ( $aname eq $attrname )
        }
        if( $aname eq $attrname ) {
            1;
        }
        else {
            0;
        }
    }

    $backslash_in_data = "\\";

    # Code to process NSGMLS escape sequences - (based on James Clark's
    # example code in the sgmls distribution)

    sub unescape_data {
        local($sdata) = 0;
        $_[0] =~ s/\\([0-7][0-7]?[0-7]?|.)/&esc_data($1)/eg;
    }

    sub esc_data {
        local($_) = $_[0];
        if ($_ eq '012' || $_ eq '12') {
    "";                          # ignore RS
        }
        elsif (/^[0-7]/) {
    sprintf("%c", oct);
```

```
    }
    elsif ($_ eq 'n') {
"\n";
    }
    elsif ($_ eq '|') {
$sdata = !$sdata;
"";
    }
    elsif ($_ eq "\\") {
$sdata ? "\\" : $backslash_in_data;
    }
    else {
$_;
    }
}

1;
```

C.3   Python Framework

The implementation of SGMLTree class follows:

```
from string import *

class SGMLNode:
    "SGMLNode class"
    def __init__(self):
        self.T = self.L = self.R = self.B = None
    def __repr__(self):
        return "SGMLNode"

class SGMLDataNode(SGMLNode):
    "SGMLDataNode class"
    def __init__(self,d):
        SGMLNode.__init__(self)# Superclass constructor
        self.data = d
    def __repr__(self):
        return "SGMLDataNode %s" % self.data

class SGMLElementNode(SGMLNode):
    "SGMLElementNode class"
    def __init__(self,en):
        SGMLNode.__init__(self) # Superclass constructor
        self.ElementName = en
        self.attrs = {}# Empty map for attributes
    def __repr__(self):
        return "SGMLElementNode Element = %s Attrs = %s" % \
        (self.ElementName,self.attrs)

class SGMLTree:
```

```
"SGMLTreeNode class"
def __init__(self):
    self.root = SGMLElementNode("!SGML")
    self.Position = self.root
    self.PositionStack = []

def __repr__(self):
    return "SGMLTree"

def MoveToRoot(self):
    self.Position = self.root

def MoveDown(self):
    if (self.Position.B != None):
        self.Position = self.Position.B
    else:
        print "Cannot move B"

def MoveUp(self):
    if (self.Position.T != None):
        self.Position = self.Position.T
    else:
        print "Cannot move T.",self.Position

def MoveRight(self):
    if (self.Position.R != None):
        self.Position = self.Position.R
    else:
        print "Cannot move R"

def MoveLeft(self):
    if (self.Position.L != None):
        self.Position = self.Position.L
    else:
        print "Cannot move L"

def GetSGMLNodeDetails(self):
    return "%s" % self.Position

def AtData(self):
    return (self.Position.__class__.__name__ == "SGMLDataNode")

def AtElement(self,name=""):
    if (self.Position.__class__.__name__ == "SGMLElementNode"):
        if (name == ""):
            return 1
        else:
            return (self.Position.ElementName == name)
    else:
        return 0

def GetData(self):
    if self.Position.__class__.__name__ == "SGMLDataNode":
        return self.Position.data
```

```
        else:
            print "Current Node is not a data node"

    def GetElementName(self):
        if self.Position.__class__.__name__ == "SGMLElementNode":
            return self.Position.ElementName
        else:
            print "Current Node is not an Element node"

    def GetAttributes(self):
        if self.Position.__class__.__name__ == "SGMLElementNode":
            return self.Position.attrs
        else:
            print "Current Node is not an Element node"

    def SetAttributes(self,attrs):
        if self.Position.__class__.__name__ == "SGMLElementNode":
            for key in attrs.keys():
                self.Position.attrs[key] = attrs[key]
        else:
            print "Current Node is not an Element node"

    def GetAttributeValue(self,name):
        if self.Position.__class__.__name__ == "SGMLElementNode":
            return self.Position.attrs[name][2]
        else:
            print "Current Node is not an Element node"

    def InsertBelow(self,l):
        if (hasattr(l,'__class__') and
            (l.__class__.__name__ == "SGMLElementNode" or
             l.__class__.__name__ == "SGMLDataNode")):
            self.Position.B = l
            l.T = self.Position
            l.R = None
            l.L = None
            l.B = None
        else:
            print "Expected SGMLNode Derived Object in InsertBelow. Got %s %s" \
    % (type(l),l)

    def InsertRight(self,l):
        if (self.Position == self.root):
            print "Cannot insert right of root"
            return
        if (hasattr(l,'__class__') and
            (l.__class__.__name__ == "SGMLElementNode" or
             l.__class__.__name__ == "SGMLDataNode")):
            self.Position.R = l
            l.L = self.Position
            l.B = None
            l.R = None
            l.T = self.Position.T
```

```python
        else:
            print "Expected SGMLNode Derived Object in InsertRight. Got %s %s"
        % (type(1),1)

    def HasDown(self):
        return self.Position.B

    def HasRight(self):
        return self.Position.R

    def HasUp(self):
        return self.Position.T

    def HasLeft(self):
        return self.Position.L

    def PushPosition(self):
        self.PositionStack = [self.Position] + self.PositionStack

    def PopPosition(self):
        if not self.PositionStack:
            print "Empty Position Stack"
        else:
            self.Position , self.PositionStack = self.PositionStack[0] ,
        self.PositionStack[1:]

class SGMLApplet:
    def __init__(self):
        self.T = SGMLTree()

    def Walk(self):
        self.T.PushPosition()
        self.T.MoveToRoot()
        self.Walk1()
        self.T.PopPosition()

    def GetData(self):
        return self.T.GetData()

    def GetElementName(self):
        return self.T.GetElementName()

    def GetAttributes(self):
        return self.T.GetAttributes()

    def Walk1(self):
        self.CheckForTrigger(1)
        if (self.T.HasDown()):
            self.T.MoveDown()
            self.T.PushPosition()
            self.Walk1()
            self.T.PopPosition()
            while (self.T.HasRight()):
                self.T.MoveRight()
                self.T.PushPosition()
```

```
                    self.Walk1()
                    self.T.PopPosition()
                self.T.MoveUp()
            self.CheckForTrigger(0)

    def CheckForTrigger(self,s):
        if (self.AtData()):
            # Data node - check for DATA_HANDLER method
            if (hasattr(self,"DATA_HANDLER")):
                getattr(self,"DATA_HANDLER")(s)
        elif (self.AtElement()):
            # Element node - check for handler method
            name = self.T.GetElementName() + "_HANDLER"
            if (hasattr(self,name)):
                getattr(self,name)(s)
            else:
                if (hasattr(self,"DEFAULT_ELEMENT_HANDLER")):
                    getattr(self,"DEFAULT_ELEMENT_HANDLER")(s)
        else:
            print "Unknown Object Type in Tree (%s)" % (type(self.T.Position))

    def AtData(self):
        return self.T.AtData()

    def AtElement(self):
        return self.T.AtElement()
```

The implementation of LoadTree class follows:

```
from sgmltree import *
import sys

class LoadTree(SGMLApplet):
    def __init__(self):
        SGMLApplet.__init__(self)
        self.AttrStore = {}

    def Execute(self):
        self.Loader()
        return self.T

    def Loader(self):
        self.LineCount = 0;
        self.T.MoveToRoot()
        PastePos = "DOWN"
        for self.line in sys.stdin.readlines():
            self.line = self.line[:-1]
            self.LineCount = self.LineCount+1
            if (self.line[0] == "("):
                ElementName = self.line[1:]
                if (PastePos == "DOWN"):
                    self.T.InsertBelow (SGMLElementNode(ElementName))
                    self.T.MoveDown()
```

```
            else:
                self.T.InsertRight(SGMLElementNode(ElementName))
                self.T.MoveRight()
            self.T.SetAttributes(self.AttrStore)
            self.AttrStore = {}
            PastePos = "DOWN";
        elif (self.line[0] == ")"):
            ElementName = self.line[1:]
            while (not self.T.AtElement(ElementName)):
                self.T.MoveUp()
            PastePos = "RIGHT";
        elif (self.line[0] == "A"):
            self.AList = splitfields(self.line[1:],' ')
            if (len(self.AList)==2):
                # Implied
                self.AttrStore[self.AList[0]] =
    [len(self.AttrStore),"IMPLIED",""]
            else:
                self.AttrStore[self.AList[0]] =
    (len(self.AttrStore),self.AList[1],joinfields(self.AList[2:], ' '))
        elif (self.line[0] == "-"):
            if (PastePos == "DOWN"):
                self.T.InsertBelow(SGMLDataNode(self.line[1:]))
                self.T.MoveDown()
                PastePos = "RIGHT"
            else:
                self.T.InsertRight(SGMLDataNode(self.line[1:]))
                self.T.MoveRight()
        elif (self.line[0] == "C"):
            self.T.MoveToRoot()
            break
        else:
            print "Unsupported ESIS event type",self.line[0]
    self.T.MoveToRoot()
    DummyNode = self.T.Position
    self.T.MoveDown()
    DummyNode.T = DummyNode.L = DummyNode.R = DummyNode.B = None
    self.T.Position.T = None
    self.T.root = self.T.Position
```

The implementation of DumpTree class follows:

```
from sgmltree import *

class DumpTree(SGMLApplet):
    def __init__(self):
        SGMLApplet.__init__(self)

    def Execute(self,T):
        self.T = T
        self.Walk()
```

```
        print "C"
        return self.T

    def DATA_HANDLER(self,s):
        if (s):
            print "-%s" % self.GetData()

    def DEFAULT_ELEMENT_HANDLER(self,s):
        if (s):
            atts = self.GetAttributes()
            ordered = []
            for name in atts.keys():
                ordered = ordered + [[atts[name][0],name]]
            ordered.sort()
            for name in ordered:
                if (atts[name[1]][1] == "IMPLIED"):
                    print "A%s IMPLIED" % (name[1])
                else:
                    print "A%s %s %s" %
    (name[1],atts[name[1]][1],atts[name[1]][2])

            print "(%s" % self.GetElementName()
        else:
            print ")%s" % self.GetElementName()
```

SGML Resources for Developers

This appendix contains some pointers to *freely available* tools, documents, and the like that are likely to be of interest to SGML software developers.

D.1 World Wide Web-Based SGML Resource Guides

D.1.1 http://www.falch.no/people/pepper/sgmltool

This site houses a comprehensive guide to SGML tools in all categories from parsers to editors to HyTime engines. The list is maintained by Steve Pepper <pepper@falch.no>.

D.1.2 http://www.sgmlopen.org/

SGML Open is a not-for-profit consortium of SGML vendors. SGML Open aims to promote adoption of SGML especially within the mainstream information technology market. The consortium also addresses SGML tool interoperability issues and has adopted technical resolutions in areas such as entity management and table markup.

D.1.3 http://www.sil.org/sgml/sgml.html

This site is a comprehensive launching pad for SGML-related resources on the Internet. Material is arranged to be easily accessed by subject area. It includes a frequently updated "whats new" section and a comprehensive (>1000 entries) bibliography. The page is maintained by Robin Cover <robin@utafll.uta.edu> or <robin@acadcomp.sil.org>.

D.2 Software Development Tools

D.2.1 SP Parser

James Clark's home page is http://www.jclark.com. This is the site for up-to-the-minute information on SP and SP-based tools. There is a mailing list for developers working with the SP parser. The address for subscriptions is sp-prog-request@jclark.com.

D.2.2   DSSSL Tools

James Clark's home page http://www.jclark.com also contains information about JADE—an implementation of the DSSSL standard also by James Clark (http://www.jclark.com/jade/).

A reference guide to the DSSSL grove plan is available at http://www.comsol.com/sgmlimpl/standards/gguide.sgm.

A DSSSL syntax checker known as DSC has been developed and made available by Henry Thomson (http://www.cogsci.ed.ac.uk/~ht). It embeds a full implementation of R4RS Scheme in James Clark's SP parser. It is available for download at ftp.cogsci.ed.ac.uk/pub/ht/dsc-1.0.tar.gz.

KAWA (http://www.comsol.com/kawa/index.htm) is a DSSSL interpreter written in Java.

D.2.3   Perl Tools

Earl Hood (ehood@convex.com) has developed a collection of Perl programs for processing SGML. They can be found at http://www.oac.uci.edu/indiv/ehood/perlSGML.html.

Norman Walsh has developed a collection of DTD parsing tools in Perl. See http://www.ora.com/homepages/DTDParse/. Also the many Perl archives such as the one at http://www.cis.ufl.edu/perl/ are always worth a visit.

David Megisson has developed sgmls.pm—a Perl 5 toolkit for processing SGMLS and NSGMLS output. See http://www.uottawa.ca/~dmeggins/sgmlspl/.

D.2.4   TCL/TK

Costwish (http://www.venus.co.uk/omf/costwish/costwish/index.html) is an SGML transformation system for UNIX systems. It is based on the TCL/TK toolkit and the SGMLS parser.

D.3   Standards Committees

The URL http://www.ornl.gov/sgml/wg8/wg8home.htm is the home of the ISO/IEC JTC1/SC18/WG8 International Standards committee responsible for the SGML standard.

D.4   FTP Sites

The following sites hold large collections of SGML-related materials including parsers, public domain applications, test suites, and demonstration versions of commercial software:

```
ftp.ifi.uio.no/pub/SGML
```

```
sgml1.ex.ac.uk/pub/SGML
ftp.th-dramstatdt.de/pub/text/sgml
```

The following sites host large collections of publicly available DTDs:

```
actd.saic.com/pub/SGML/misc-dtds
ftp.th-dramstatdt.de/pub/text/sgml/DTD
```

D.5   Usenet

The comp.text.sgml newsgroup is the communications hub of the SGML community. An archive of the newsgroup is available at ftp.ifi.uio.no. See also http://CandL.let.ruu.nl/archive/cts/intro.htm for a shadow archive maintained by Arjan Loeffen.

D.6   Some SGML-Related Industry Standards

D.6.1   AAP—Association of American Publishers

AAP is an SGML Application Standard initiated in 1987. It is now known as the ISO 12083 DTD and is aimed primarily at electronic and paper publication of academic journals.

D.6.2   ATA—Air Transport Association

ATA is a set of DTDs standardized by the airline industry.

D.6.3   CALS—US DOD MIL-M-28001B

CALS stands for Continuous Acquisition and Lifecycle Support. It is an initiative of the U.S. Department of Defense.

D.6.4   IETM

Standing for Interactive Electronic Technical Manual, IETM is a U.S. DOD initiative (MIL-D-87269-IETMDB) to develop interactive manuals that break away from the book model in favor of an interactive, task-oriented model. It makes extensive use of HyTime concepts. See also MID—Metafile for Interactive Documents.

D.6.5   MID

Standing for Metafile for Interactive Documents, MID is also a U.S. DOD initiative. It speci-fies a HyTime-based DTD for capturing control structures used to navigate documents (i.e., a DTD with control structures, conditional expressions, etc.). Code is freely available.

D.6.6   DocBook

DocBook is an initiative of the IT industry aimed primarily at documentation of software products. See http://www.ora.com/davenport/.

D.6.7   EDGAR

Electronic Data Gathering, Analysis and Retrieval System (EDGAR) is an initiative of the Securities and Exchange Commission that uses SGML for filing company returns and the like elec-tronically.

D.6.8   J2008

Technical documentation for the automotive industry is provided by J2008, an initiative of the The Society of Automotive Engineers.

D.6.9   UTF

Universal Text Format (UTF) is an initiative from the International Press Telecommunica-tions Council to use SGML for the transmission and interchange of news items. See http://www.xe.net/iptc.

D.6.10   PCIS

PCIS is an initiative of companies in the electronics industry to standardize documentation of electronic component data.

D.6.11   TEI

Text Encoding Initiative (TEI) uses SGML to encode literature, ancient texts, and the like. See http://CandL.let.ruu.nl/archive/tei/intro.htm.

D.6.12   CML

Chemical Markup Language (CML) is an SGML application for the documentation of chemical compounds. See http://www.venus.co.uk/omf/cml.

D.6.13   ICADD

The International Committee on Accessible Document Design (ICADD) has published guidelines for the design of SGML applications that allows semi-automatic conversion of arbitrary SGML into Braille and other formats. The guidelines specify how to add attributes with fixed values to element types in order to specify how the elements should be treated by the ICADD processing system. The fact that the attributes have fixed values specified in the DTD (i.e., attributes with a default value specified with #FIXED) means that support for ICADD can be achieved without modifications to the SGML document instances. See http://www.ucla.edu/ICADD/.

D.6.14   OFE

Open Financial Exchange (OFE) is an SGML-based standard for the interchange of financial information such as on-line banking transactions. It was jointly developed by Microsoft, Intuit, and Checkfree. The specification is available at http://www.microsoft.com/finserv, http://www.intuit.com, and http://www.checkfree.com.

D.7   Rainbow Makers

Rainbow makers is an initiative from Electronic Book Technologies to provide a collection of free conversion tools to extract information from proprietary systems into low-level SGML. Rainbow makers is a set of programs that translates proprietary word processor/DTP formats into low-level SGML. The DTD they convert to is known as the Rainbow DTD. For more information see http://www.ebt.com and ftp://ftp.ebt.com/pub/nv/dtd/rainbow/.

D.8   Organizations

D.8.1   International SGML Users Group

Numerous regional chapters of the SGML Users Group exist. See the SGML resource guides listed in Section D.1 for details. Alternatively, contact

SGML User's Group
Database Publishing Systems, Ltd.
608 Delta Business Park
Great Western Way
Swindon Wiltshire SN5 7XF
UK
e-mail: plg@dpsl.co.uk, http://www.sil.org/sgml/isug

D.8.2   GCA

The Graphic Communication Association (GCA) has been actively involved with supporting SGML from the early days of the standard. They run training courses and annual major SGML conferences in the United States, Europe, and Asia. Contact them at

100 Daingerfield Rd.
4th floor
Alexandria, VA 22314-2888
USA
http://www.gca.org.

D.8.3   W3C

The World Wide Web Consortium (W3C) was established in 1995 to produce specifications and reference software for use on the World Wide Web. The W3C works on the general application of SGML to the World Wide Web, as well as HTML-specific work. See

```
ftp://sunsite.unc.edu/pub/sun-info/standards/xml/wg/
http://www.w3.org/pub/WWW/Archives/Public/w3c-sgml-wg/
http://www.w3.org/pub/WWW/MarkUp/SGML/Activity
```

D.9   Miscellaneous

D.9.1   DTD for DTDs

Various DTDs have been developed to describe the structures found within DTDs themselves. This concept is not unlike having a YACC grammar for YACC grammars. See ftp://ftp-tei.uic.edu/pub/tei/grammar/dpp/ for an example. These tools by Michael Sperberg-McQueen parse DTDs and produce output similar to the ESIS output from NSGMLS.

D.9.2   DTD Normalizer

NOMDTD is a tool by Richard Light. It processes DTDs, interpreting and expanding parameter entities to yield a normalized version of the DTD. See ftp://ota.ox.ac.uk/pub.ota/TEI/software/normdtd1.exe.

D.9.3   Automated DTD Generation

Fred is a WEB-based service which, given an SGML document instance as input, can produce a DTD as output. See http://www.oclc.com/fred.

D.9.4   SGML Grammars

Extended Backaus Naur Form (EBNF) format productions for the SGML production rules are available at ftp.ifi.uio.no/pub/SGML/productions. Also http://www.tiac.bet/users/bingham hosts a rich hypertext of the syntax productions for both SGML and DSSSL.

Rick Jelliffe has created a set of state transition diagrams to illustrate SGML's recognition modes. See http://allette.com.au/sgml/dfa/index.htm.

D.9.5   DSSSL-O

The DSSSL-O specification can be found at the ftp site sunsite.unc.edu in the directory /pub/suninfo/standards/dsssl/dssslo.

INDEX

Symbols

-
    NSGMLS ESIS record, 295

"
    as attribute value literal delimiter, 232
    in short reference, 216

\#
    NSGMLS ESIS record, 297

#conref, 88

#current, 87

#empty, 218

#fixed, 86

#implied, 86
    in link type declarations, 241

#include, 102

#initial, 241

#pcdata, 18
    minimum size of, 92

#postlink, 244

#required, 85

#result, 249

#uselink, 244

&
    in content model, 73
    in element type declaration, 78
    in general entity reference, 15
    NSGMLS ESIS record, 106, 296

(
    NSGMLS ESIS record, 294
    usage with concur feature, 237

)
    NSGMLS ESIS record, 294
    usage with concur feature, 237

*
    in content model, 73

+
    in content model, 73

+//
    in formal public identifier, 112

,
    in content model, 73
    in element type declaration, 78

/
    in null end tag, 252

//EN
    language code, 280

;
    in entity reference, 15

<!>
    null declaration, 233

</>
    empty tag, 251

<?, 205

<?ArcBase, 270

<?HyTime, 270

=
    in attribute value assignment, 15
    in short reference string, 216

?
    in content model, 73
    in processing instruction declaration, 205
    NSGMLS ESIS record, 297

LICENSE AGREEMENT AND LIMITED WARRANTY

READ THE FOLLOWING TERMS AND CONDITIONS CAREFULLY BEFORE OPENING THIS SOFT-
WARE PACKAGE. THIS LEGAL DOCUMENT IS AN AGREEMENT BETWEEN YOU AND PRENTICE-
HALL, INC. (THE "COMPANY"). BY OPENING THIS SEALED SOFTWARE PACKAGE, YOU ARE
AGREEING TO BE BOUND BY THESE TERMS AND CONDITIONS. IF YOU DO NOT AGREE WITH
THESE TERMS AND CONDITIONS, DO NOT OPEN THE SOFTWARE PACKAGE. PROMPTLY
RETURN THE UNOPENED SOFTWARE PACKAGE AND ALL ACCOMPANYING ITEMS TO THE
PLACE YOU OBTAINED THEM FOR A FULL REFUND OF ANY SUMS YOU HAVE PAID.

1. **GRANT OF LICENSE:** In consideration of your payment of the license fee, which is part of the price
you paid for this product, and your agreement to abide by the terms and conditions of this Agreement, the
Company grants to you a nonexclusive right to use and display the copy of the enclosed software program
(hereinafter the "SOFTWARE") on a single computer (i.e., with a single CPU) at a single location so long as
you comply with the terms of this Agreement. The Company reserves all rights not expressly granted to you
under this Agreement.

2. **OWNERSHIP OF SOFTWARE:** You own only the magnetic or physical media (the enclosed disks) on
which the SOFTWARE is recorded or fixed, but the Company retains all the rights, title, and ownership to
the SOFTWARE recorded on the original disk copy(ies) and all subsequent copies of the SOFTWARE,
regardless of the form or media on which the original or other copies may exist. This license is not a sale of
the original SOFTWARE or any copy to you.

3. **COPY RESTRICTIONS:** This SOFTWARE and the accompanying printed materials and user manual
(the "Documentation") are the subject of copyright. You may not copy the Documentation or the SOFT-
WARE, except that you may make a single copy of the SOFTWARE for backup or archival purposes only.
You may be held legally responsible for any copying or copyright infringement which is caused or encour-
aged by your failure to abide by the terms of this restriction.

4. **USE RESTRICTIONS:** You may not network the SOFTWARE or otherwise use it on more than one
computer or computer terminal at the same time. You may physically transfer the SOFTWARE from one
computer to another provided that the SOFTWARE is used on only one computer at a time. You may not
distribute copies of the SOFTWARE or Documentation to others. You may not reverse engineer, disassem-
ble, decompile, modify, adapt, translate, or create derivative works based on the SOFTWARE or the Documentation without the prior written consent of the Company.

5. **TRANSFER RESTRICTIONS:** The enclosed SOFTWARE is licensed only to you and may not be
transferred to any one else without the prior written consent of the Company. Any unauthorized transfer of
the SOFTWARE shall result in the immediate termination of this Agreement.

6. **TERMINATION:** This license is effective until terminated. This license will terminate automatically
without notice from the Company and become null and void if you fail to comply with any provisions or limitations of this license. Upon termination, you shall destroy the Documentation and all copies of the SOFT-
WARE. All provisions of this Agreement as to warranties, limitation of liability, remedies or damages, and
our ownership rights shall survive termination.

7. **MISCELLANEOUS:** This Agreement shall be construed in accordance with the laws of the United
States of America and the State of New York and shall benefit the Company, its affiliates, and assignees.

8. **LIMITED WARRANTY AND DISCLAIMER OF WARRANTY:** The Company warrants that the SOFTWARE, when properly used in accordance with the Documentation, will operate in substantial conformity with the description of the SOFTWARE set forth in the Documentation. The Company does not warrant that the SOFTWARE will meet your requirements or that the operation of the SOFTWARE will be uninterrupted or error-free. The Company warrants that the media on which the SOFTWARE is delivered shall be free from defects in materials and workmanship under normal use for a period of thirty (30) days from the date of your purchase. Your only remedy and the Company's only obligation under these limited warranties is, at the Company's option, return of the warranted item for a refund of any amounts paid by you or replacement of the item. Any replacement of SOFTWARE or media under the warranties shall not extend the original warranty period. The limited warranty set forth above shall not apply to any SOFTWARE which the Company determines in good faith has been subject to misuse, neglect, improper installation, repair, alteration, or damage by you. EXCEPT FOR THE EXPRESSED WARRANTIES SET FORTH ABOVE, THE COMPANY DISCLAIMS ALL WARRANTIES, EXPRESS OR IMPLIED, INCLUDING WITHOUT LIMITATION, THE IMPLIED WARRANTIES OF MERCHANTABILITY AND FITNESS FOR A PARTICULAR PURPOSE. EXCEPT FOR THE EXPRESS WARRANTY SET FORTH ABOVE, THE COMPANY DOES NOT WARRANT, GUARANTEE, OR MAKE ANY REPRESENTATION REGARDING THE USE OR THE RESULTS OF THE USE OF THE SOFTWARE IN TERMS OF ITS CORRECTNESS, ACCURACY, RELIABILITY, CURRENTNESS, OR OTHERWISE.

IN NO EVENT, SHALL THE COMPANY OR ITS EMPLOYEES, AGENTS, SUPPLIERS, OR CONTRACTORS BE LIABLE FOR ANY INCIDENTAL, INDIRECT, SPECIAL, OR CONSEQUENTIAL DAMAGES ARISING OUT OF OR IN CONNECTION WITH THE LICENSE GRANTED UNDER THIS AGREEMENT, OR FOR LOSS OF USE, LOSS OF DATA, LOSS OF INCOME OR PROFIT, OR OTHER LOSSES, SUSTAINED AS A RESULT OF INJURY TO ANY PERSON, OR LOSS OF OR DAMAGE TO PROPERTY, OR CLAIMS OF THIRD PARTIES, EVEN IF THE COMPANY OR AN AUTHORIZED REPRESENTATIVE OF THE COMPANY HAS BEEN ADVISED OF THE POSSIBILITY OF SUCH DAMAGES. IN NO EVENT SHALL LIABILITY OF THE COMPANY FOR DAMAGES WITH RESPECT TO THE SOFTWARE EXCEED THE AMOUNTS ACTUALLY PAID BY YOU, IF ANY, FOR THE SOFTWARE.

SOME JURISDICTIONS DO NOT ALLOW THE LIMITATION OF IMPLIED WARRANTIES OR LIABILITY FOR INCIDENTAL, INDIRECT, SPECIAL, OR CONSEQUENTIAL DAMAGES, SO THE ABOVE LIMITATIONS MAY NOT ALWAYS APPLY. THE WARRANTIES IN THIS AGREEMENT GIVE YOU SPECIFIC LEGAL RIGHTS AND YOU MAY ALSO HAVE OTHER RIGHTS WHICH VARY IN ACCORDANCE WITH LOCAL LAW.

ACKNOWLEDGMENT

YOU ACKNOWLEDGE THAT YOU HAVE READ THIS AGREEMENT, UNDERSTAND IT, AND AGREE TO BE BOUND BY ITS TERMS AND CONDITIONS. YOU ALSO AGREE THAT THIS AGREEMENT IS THE COMPLETE AND EXCLUSIVE STATEMENT OF THE AGREEMENT BETWEEN YOU AND THE COMPANY AND SUPERSEDES ALL PROPOSALS OR PRIOR AGREEMENTS, ORAL, OR WRITTEN, AND ANY OTHER COMMUNICATIONS BETWEEN YOU AND THE COMPANY OR ANY REPRESENTATIVE OF THE COMPANY RELATING TO THE SUBJECT MATTER OF THIS AGREEMENT.

Should you have any questions concerning this Agreement or if you wish to contact the Company for any reason, please contact in writing at the address below.

Robin Short
Prentice Hall PTR
One Lake Street
Upper Saddle River, New Jersey 07458